> *If these things were so large how come everyone missed it?*
> Queen Elizabeth II - 5th November 2008

THE GLOBAL FINANCIAL CRISIS IS NOT FINANCIAL

'Quality of Information' in Question

SHARAD AWASTHI

Dedicated to all those who lost, even a single dime, because of this crisis

Contents

CONTENTS III

PREFACE VI

ACKNOWLEDGEMENTS XI

INTRODUCTION 13
- IS THE LADDER ON THE RIGHT WALL? 14
- WHAT IS 'FAILURE OF KNOWING'? 15
- NATURE OF THE FINANCIAL CRISIS 16
- THE ROADMAP OF THE BOOK 18
- GLOBAL FINANCIAL CRISIS IS NOT FINANCIAL 19
- THE OPPORTUNITY IN THE FINANCIAL CRISIS 20

CHAPTER 1 22

THE CURRENT CRISIS – SEEMS EVERLASTING 22
- THE MAKING OF THE CRISIS: BEHIND THE SCENES 25
- GLOBAL VIEW: MONEY AS A HUMANKIND CENTRIC INVENTION, GONE OFF-BEAM 26
- THE FINANCIAL SECTOR VIEW: FINANCIAL SYSTEM FAILURE 30
- WORKING VIEW: MALFUNCTIONING NUTS AND BOLTS 48

CHAPTER 2 60

INFORMATION ASYMMETRY 60
- WHAT IS INFORMATION ASYMMETRY? 61
- INFORMATION ASYMMETRY USING THE JOHARI WINDOW 65
- IT IS A CRISIS OF INFORMATION 66
- MITIGATING INFORMATION ASYMMETRY WITH QUALITY OF INFORMATION (QOI) 69

CHAPTER 3 72

QUALITY OF INFORMATION (QOI) 72
- WHAT IS QUALITY OF INFORMATION (QOI)? 74

WHAT WILL QOI ACHIEVE? 76
WHAT IS THE FAILURE OF INFORMATION SYSTEM? 78
SYMMETRIC INFORMATION EXECUTION MODEL – ANALYTICAL FRAMEWORK 79
3 CS OF THE INFORMATION LIFE CYCLE 81

CHAPTER 4 90

INFORMATION CREATION (1ST C) 90

ACCOUNTING: FAR FROM TRUE VALUE 91
ASSET VALUATION: TOO COMPLEX 104
CREDIT RATING: NOT SAME AS CREDIT WORTHINESS 109
MODELLING: IT'S A BLACK BOX 119

CHAPTER 5 134

INFORMATION CORROBORATION (2ND C) 134

AUDIT: RESPONSIBLE, THIS TIME AGAIN ! 135
BASEL FRAMEWORK: RESPONSIBILITY SANS POWER 144
MORAL HAZARD: HAZARD CONTINUES 151
REGULATION: LAGGARD IN THE SYSTEM 158
LEGISLATION AND REGULATION: TWIN REACTIONS 168

CHAPTER 6 172

INFORMATION COMMUNICATION (3RD C) 172

DISCLOSURE: NEED FOR MORE 173
INTERCONNECTEDNESS: INEVITABLE SOURCE OF CONTAGION 177
REPORTING: INFORMATIONAL RISK 184

CHAPTER 7 188

INFORMATION ENABLER 188

FORESIGHT, IS MORE THAN FORECAST 189
REAL-TIME VIEW – JUST IN TIME 194
SYSTEMIC VIEW – THE REAL BIG PICTURE 197

CHAPTER 8 217

QUALITY OF INFORMATION (QOI) 217

Unification 218
  Transparency 222
  Trust 223

CHAPTER 9 227

GLOBAL FINANCIAL ARCHITECTURE 227

  4R High Definition (HD) Infoweaver – Global Financial System Architecture 228
  The Global Financial Architecture 238

CHAPTER 10 262

QOI CHECKLIST FOR C(X)OS 262

REFERENCES 265

Preface

Humankind continuously processes information, when they buy grocery, cross roads, vote in an election, drive vehicle, try a new dress or plan their retirement. In simplistic way, if on one hand, there is a perpetual and rigorous exchange of information in the environment, on the other, the humankind processes information in a peculiar way. They are found to understand differently, the information that makes the environment and their decision making is yet another complex process. In the exchange of information, they interact with a system which in turn interacts with multiple sub-systems. Overall, the quality of information running in the environment is determined by the quality of information processed by humans when extracted by the contributing systems. Some examples of systems are financial, economic, social, political, judicial, eco system etc. Which all factors determine the quality of information, is what this book is about and how global financial crisis is nothing but a case of a very poor quality of information in the financial system.

The reason that provoked me to think about quality of information comes from the question posed by the Queen of Great Britain. In one of the programmes at London School of Economics, the queen asked this fundamental question to the learned academicians of economics and management, "if things were so large, how come everyone missed it?" The answer they gave was not convincing enough to me because it did not touch the root cause of the problem. Subsequently, as the affect of the crisis grew, so did my quest for answer to queen's question. Sadly, till today, I have not heard the experts talk about the root cause of the current crisis. They are still entangled in the financials and economics of the issues.

Nobel laureate Joseph Stiglitz introduced the concept of 'information asymmetry', which has showed direction to that important question and it helped in constructing the complete reasoning for the crisis. According to me, information asymmetry stands out as a cause of the current crisis, which affected the quality of information in the global financial system. It creates blindness to the proceedings in the financial system,

Preface

which is the key factor. It has to be eliminated as part of the solution to the current crisis. If information asymmetry is the vital lacuna in the human transaction, quality of information plugs that gap.

This is what the framework of this book is based on.

Like all great crisis, there is wisdom to be extracted. I thought; why not extrapolate the concept of 'quality of information' to business practice in general and specially, to those who are designing the information systems for the business too.

From retail investors to corporate, from small business holders to multi nationals, from system designers to system integrators, from inventors to technologists, all pursue quality of information. Very often, high quality of information is misunderstood as 'big data' and the purpose gets misled. In fact, it can be reasonable to say that today; information technology is misplaced by the concept of information system. Large investment into information technology is still not creating an effective information system. They may be churning out huge amount of data, but it is still not able to prevent bankruptcies, losses, moral hazard or frauds. So a new thinking and approach is required to pursue high quality of information that can make the financial system, crisis proof.

The readers can find a checklist at the end of the book to verify if your information system is producing high quality of information.

Quality of products and services has been the mainstay of our modern day business world. These are the end result of long drawn processes within an organization. How about measuring the quality of processes? Usually organizations end up defining the quality of processes in its compliance, assuming that resultant quality of information is up to the mark.

It would have been easy to determine the reason of any failure to the underlying technology or the human error, if the systems were water tight. The fact is that systems are interlinked and the effect of one can fail the most robust and well secured system, even though placed in remote and unlikely corner of the world.

I found the consequences of information systems ever more significant to modern society. It puts in perspective, the role of information system something that cannot be taken lightly, as the case has been in the past.

The quality of processes lies less in its compliance and more in delivering the quality of information in the system. This argument is valid for all businesses and not just for financial sector organizations. The readers will find lots of questions in the book typical to the genre of 'Who guards the guardians?' (Quis custodiet ipsos custodes?). It was after the lecture on Long Finance by Prof. Michael Mainelli, founder of think tank Z/Yen, that I got engaged in pursuit for seeking answers to the fundamental question - 'Who regulates the regulators?' There are reverberations of that discussion here in the book, arguing its applicability to auditors and credit rating agencies.

The book has touched on key points related to consequences of information system and it is interesting to see the arguments about the behaviour of the players in the financial system and how system loses sensitivity of the environment. So, when the chapter about the global financial architecture mentions the 4R principle, it puts all the puzzle blocks in their appropriate places, reconstructing a safe financial system for the future.

Similarly, in the book there are concepts like conflict-of-interest, true risk appetite, single-point-of-failure, interconnectedness and others, described with reference to the current crisis, to show how they interplay with information asymmetry and affects the quality of information. These are things which are so obvious when one observes the financial system, yet they perilously exist in our plain sight. The readers will agree with my approach of structured analysis of the financial crisis and there should not be any doubt that there is a very strong argument for reassessing the way the world is viewing the current financial and economic turmoil.

If someone were to ask me, if there is one key take away from this book, I would say that it is the entirety that is meaningful and every moment of reading, will put the readers into thought provoking eddies.

While researching for this book, I was surprised to find how often the authorities and premiere institutes acknowledged the prevailing information asymmetry in the financial system and reasoned the current

Preface

crisis to this inequality. They necessarily did not use this term but in essence, all these authorities and decision making bodies seemed to have struggled with asymmetry and quality of information. This helped my research further in scrutinizing the sources of information asymmetry and poor quality of information in processes like accounting, asset valuation, credit rating, audit and others.

It was interesting to find the volume of analysis that experts have already done about these processes and their failure in contributing to the financial crisis. The only issue with their analysis was the isolated nature of these findings. These analyses did mention the financial and economic implications but failed to connect with each other or derive a common denominator for these failed processes. This leads us back to the objectives of these financial processes. It also raises questions about the quality of information created by them. With all that line of pursuit, it was easy to put a common platform underneath the failed financial processes and conclude that "Global Financial Crisis is not financial" but a crisis of "Quality of Information".

For a first time author, the journey of writing this book was filled with sentiments of all kinds. It was amazing to discover the parallelism of thoughts and approaches by the experts, while astonishing to find that serious problems and challenges still exists in the global financial system. At times, it was frustrating to find that there is no 'Single throat to choke' (STC) in the system and hence it is drifting without accountability.

I consider myself more a proponent of quality of information, than an expert. With this belief, came my argument and thereon, constructing the global financial architecture was straightforward. It just required plugging the areas of information asymmetry in the financial processes and the architecture was complete. Even though, the architecture may look practical but there would be challenges as it requires a complete revamp of the existing financial system.

When I was constructing the global financial architecture, I could empathize with many experts whose papers and articles I had referred. In this new age of globalization and complexities of processes, there is no 'Door to Knock' (DTK). Experts are analysing and media, the world over, is broadcasting but there exists no DTK. So, all the good work of the experts has become a noise. I will not be surprised to find myself adding to that noisy decibel.

The other side of STC and DTK is that there are also many wise people successfully running their businesses. For those wise people, if this book provides a pinch of additional wisdom, in whichever scope of business they dwell into, the author's effort will stand justified.

Sharad Awasthi

London, United Kingdom

www.sharadawasthi.com

contact@sharadawasthi.com

www.facebook.com /Book - Global Financial Crisis is NOT Financial

Acknowledgements

I would like to thank Professor Ian Angell, Professor Emeritus, London School of Economics, for sharing with me the concept of systems thinking and engaging into numerous and lengthy discussions on this topic. Hop, step and jump were once baby steps. Nathalie Mitev, Senior lecturer at London School of Economics had been my mentor and she had helped me take those important steps in conceptualizing this book. My heartfelt appreciation and gratitude goes to her for the guidance and carving out time for me out of her busy schedule.

Even writing on financial crisis takes finances. In this journey of writing as a first time author, I received all the support from my dear wife Anupama, who has, courageously, managed my finances and has backed me wholeheartedly, in my endeavour. I extend my sincere thanks to her for all her love and support.

I extend my thanks to all my friends, in places far and near, who had been following me patiently. Your keen interest in the topic of my book had been motivating me to give some more good thinking.

I also need to acknowledge the thinking and effort of those, whose concepts I have used in the book. Nobel laureate Joseph Stiglitz had conceptualised information asymmetry, a concept that had redefined many problems. I have used the concept extensively and it has set forth direction of my research and analysis. I want to convey my sincere thanks to him.

Last, not least my heart goes out to all those who lost fortunes, homes and jobs in this financial and economic crisis. There are millions who were never responsible for the crisis, yet they suffered the most in this period. Although the pain is unforgettable, it will be wise to be safe in future. The world had been through similar crisis, again and again. It is important to beware of the signals from the system. I am wishing all a speedy recovery.

Introduction

Introduction

What if you woke up to a morning and found that your bank with all your savings has closed down. What if your mortgage could have been cheaper and for years together, you paid much more than what was needed? What if you found that your country's treasury was already empty but they were pretending to be rich? Worst come, your pensions have been blown away by some rogue trader. These scenarios were a fiction some time ago, but are a reality today. All these familiar sounding scenarios have one thing in common. One would not need a Nobel Prize to figure out that it is not the financials or the economics but the lack of information that is the primary cause of these scenarios. Had you knew these troubles are brewing; you would have taken a different action.

Ever since the global crisis broke in 2008, the world is stuck in finding a magic bullet solution in economics and finance. If that was the right way of approaching the crisis, 5 years thence, the global financial crisis would have been overcome. On the contrary, it is even more precariously hanging on the probabilities of bankruptcies and elongated recessions. The ripple effect is still unstoppable.

Is the ladder on the right wall?

There have been truck loads of academic papers, articles and books written about the current financial crisis and its impeding effect on banking, financial market and national economies. Even more, volumes had been written in the analysis of the crisis and umpteen reasons quoted for the trail of bankruptcies that got filed since 2008. The book is NOT analyzing the financial and the economics of the crisis neither is it capturing the chronology of the global financial crisis. Already, there are eminent gurus and pundits doing that.

Unfortunately, none of the experts have looked into the failure of information as key to this crisis. They may talk in piecemeal about the lack of information but certainly not as the 'key' factor for this crisis. Hence, this book is highlighting the relevance and consequence of poor quality of information prevailing in the financial system, even in this technological age of information explosion. The book is finding the root cause to the global financial crisis using the philosophies of information systems and systems thinking.

THE GLOBAL FINANCIAL CRISIS IS NOT FINANCIAL

Earlier the better to clarify the popular misnomer, when the book is discussing the information systems, it is not the information technology that is being discussed. It is the "process of information creation and usage" as a function of a successfully running a system.

What is this book about?

The essence of the book is to draw relationship between failure of trust due to poor quality of Information, termed as 'information asymmetry' and the continued Global Financial Crisis. Many topics in this book would already be known to the readers as a fact about the financial crisis. But the book is putting into context, the big picture as an assortment of those facts threaded through a common outlook of systems thinking.

The central argument of this 3 part book is that the crisis is due to the failure of Information underlying the financial system, which has culminated into blind spots, shadow financial systems and wide-spread information asymmetry.

What is 'failure of knowing'?

The 'failure of knowing' is important to understand because 'knowing' had been the sole reason and natural ingredient for survival of any system. Although, it is limitless to pursue 'knowing' but it is important to understand the limits. 'Knowing' is a process of accumulating information, combined with a factor of time as its natural component. Both time and knowing grows in a normal system. There has to be a natural balance between the processes of 'knowing' with time.

For a running system, the limit of knowing is set by the success of the system at that point in time. Knowing is a

If these things were so large how come everyone missed it?

Queen Elizabeth II ~ 5th November 2008

process which creates products like knowledge, which is fuelled by information. For an intelligent system, knowing has to be more than is required at that time, which helps being proactive to sustain its status. There is a difference between 'knowing' and 'predicting'. Although, there is a fine line dividing these two functions, predicting is a finer and more intelligent part of the 'knowing'. 'Knowing' is about the method applied to the information which was supposed to be known, acquired by either as processed or unprocessed information. If a system is

Introduction

unable to suitably process the information, the system fails and certainly, it is the failure of 'knowing'.

The test of the system is not measured when things go right but when things go wrong. If this is the premise then I have found many experts talking about the information blind-spots in the context of not knowing or knowing late. As a consequence of failure of 'knowing', unabated toxic financial transactions had taken place in the financial system, unabated, which later culminated into the current crisis.

It is that part of the information that should have been compulsorily part of the system, it failed to be. Prediction is an attempt to reconstruct and extrapolate the information as part of the knowing, further into the future to capture the possibilities. Predictions can go right or wrong, it can be forgiven and we don't call it a failure of prediction.

In context to the current crisis, 'knowing' had been significantly ignored as a process that has become a fundamental cause to the development of this crisis. Should 'Knowing' should go wrong, it will only lead to crisis. **What ought to be known, must be known!**

The mechanism of knowing works on an interconnected system of information which is termed as 'information system'. If this mechanism fails, the information system fails, thereby the 'knowing' fails and the system runs into a crisis.

Nature of the Financial Crisis

In our lives, as an individual or as an organization, at every instant, we are seeking information. It could be simple information like seeking directions to an exit door or complex one like deciding on a million dollar investment. Global financial crisis is just one example where the importance of Information has come into the forefront as 'the crucial' success factor.

It is interesting to know that even though this crisis is called '2008 Financial Crisis', it actually began in 2007. This duality of names holds the key for many discussions in the book. The events in 2007 were considered to be just one-off case and not part of the bigger developing crisis. It indicates that either the functionaries were absolutely unaware of the happenings in the financial system or they were in a state of

THE GLOBAL FINANCIAL CRISIS IS NOT FINANCIAL

denial about the consequences of failures in the system. So, it is not wrong to say by that it is the 'failure of knowing' and the solution lies in 'knowing, what ought to be known'.

This is for sure, there is no one reason that can be attributed to the current crisis. So if the experts are looking for one single reason, in all probabilities there is no magic empirical formulae that can resolve the crisis. My argument is that the crisis had been interplay of many parts that had faulty information system which continued to function as additive components leading to this catastrophic crisis. When the banks fail, it is just not the firm that fails but all the participants have losses to suffer too. The shareholders lose the capital they have invested, the creditors lose the receivables, depositors lose the uninsured deposit and taxpayers have to involuntarily risk the bailout money. These losses are sources to wider loses in the financial system and the economy. If many banks fail, the jolt is to the entire system and it will be called catastrophic, if the volumes are gigantic and extent is beyond the local boundaries. This time the financial sector has failed. Not only has the sector failed, it has shown that financial sector had been a single-point-of-failure for all other sectors.

The financial system landscape has changed drastically since last six decades. The assets held by US banks in 1952 were nearly 53% which dropped to, approximately, 26 percent by year 2009. This means that there are other methods of funding, which have come into being, that cater to the funds management and investment cycle. The asset backed mortgage issuers who had pooled the US housing mortgages, had grown to 6% of the total financial sector assets in last twenty years (Council of Economic Advisors, 2010).

What does all this mean? The chain of intermediaries has grown and they use complex methods to arrive at their operations. So this crisis may have seen many commercial and investment banks getting bankrupt. The point is about the changing face of the financial system, which has grown too complex and too large. In most cases, the assets of a single financial institution have out grown the GDP of its country. Imagine such large volume of finances locked up in a state of insolvency if not static illiquidity. It will be very difficult to maneuver the interdependent entities and the underlying economy.

| Introduction

The roadmap of the book

This book is not only relevant to the readers in financial world, but also to all those whose success rests on the strength of Information. I am theorizing the failure and breakdown of information execution cycle as the reason for global financial crisis. This book will take the readers across the landscape of the financial market and reflect on the information mishaps during the period of build-up into financial crisis. Subsequently, the book will arrive at a proposed architecture, addressing the current shortcomings in the information system to arrest the problem of information failures or failure of *'knowing'.* So let us take a journey that would give principle based perspective of the global financial system and its components, analyse where the information symmetry has failed and then create a logical resolution that will *proactively, predict and prevent* another crisis.

The first part dwells on the history of financial crises, since 1900s and it has been part and parcel of the modern civilization. Every time there had been a crisis, the affected parties had reflected on what has gone wrong. Unfortunately, the lessons from the past crisis have not been learnt well and therefore, we continue to tread on paths that had earlier brought crisis too. In this section of the book, we will see the history of the financial markets and banking, to draw a pattern of the crisis repeating itself. This is to prove how mankind had been susceptible, when it comes to handling money matters. There is a consistent pattern found in the history.

The second part consists of a framework for structured analysis of information system. It is based on my newly developed **'Information Lifecycle Execution Model'**. The approach to structured analysis is based on 'Systems Thinking' using the 'rich picture' from soft systems methodology, which is meshed into information execution framework. The information execution model, categorically discusses **12 elements** of financial failures in the areas like accounting, credit rating, risk modeling, regulation and others. As an outcome of the framework based structural analysis, the book identifies gaps in each of the execution phases of the information system. Suggested fixes follow the analysis. Recognizing the scope of failures in the future, a **Principle based Information Architecture** is conceptualized. I am naming the architecture as **'4R HD Infoweaver'.** Few principles that are incorporated include principle of universality, principle of transparency and information symmetry. As mentioned, this book is neutral on technology therefore the architecture developed is based on principles and not technology.

Technology is only an enabler of the principles, which brings efficiency to the effectiveness of these principles.

Global Financial Crisis is NOT Financial

Every time, I have discussed with people about the financial crisis, they are not sure where to start and what all to talk because according to them, it is too complicated and that it is more appropriate for the bankers and the government to understand the complexities, to resolve it. I have a different outlook. Even though, it is the failure of the banks and governments, it is the people who have been affected the most. The severity of the crisis has been felt most by those who did not work in the banks or the governments. So, when I search for reasons I find one principle that needs to be aggressively put forward and it is that 'Banks, like governments are for people and not the other way around'. People are not merely depositors to banks but lenders to the bank. Therefore, the only way these institutions will work for the people is through information sharing which is equal information for all, or information symmetry. It may not seem to be just a financial crisis, if we talk about people, government and equality. That is true and therefore, I am suggesting that *'Global Financial Crisis is NOT financial',* it is more than that.

The solution does not lie in the financial management like interest rates or deficit financing or inflationary controls. It would put the ladder on the wrong wall, if we do so. Those solutions are mere fine tuning the actions of the past, without realizing the new age sentiments of the market. The solution lies in taking control of the known because right now no one seems to know, even the 'known'.

The third part is a logical and step-by-step development of a Principle based information architecture, plugging the gaps and avoiding failures in the financial system, those identified in the various section of the book. The structured analysis of the financial crisis and subsequently the conceptualization of Principle based information architecture will have generic outlook for all the sectors, both financial and non-financial. It will help the C(X)Os revisit their information (system) strategy and that will enhance their **proactive, predictive and preventive** outlook.

| Introduction

The opportunity in the Financial Crisis

If a consorted effort is not put into place to review and repair the faulty parts of the information system, there could be another crisis in waiting. Dodd-Frank legislation, passed by the US lawmakers in 2010, is one such effort. The regulatory committees across the developed economies had made their bit to be more cautious and this is a good opportunity to review the financial system and be critical of its functioning with an attempt to identify the faulty parts and potential weak links. This crisis was never sector specific; it was specific to the conduct of business. By using Principle based information architecture, the players in financial system can convert speculative risks to entrepreneurial risk, information asymmetry to market knowledge and moral hazards to ethical business practices. **There is wisdom to be extracted from these failures and crisis.**

What is the book doing?

I have written this book based on the analysis of the official documents published by global and national financial institutions and authorities. It means to have a look into the failure of **'knowing'** during the years when the crisis was in the making. According to me it is the 'real' failure because it is the failure of those who were supposed to have the foresight to predict and prevent. It is certainly not an attempt to fix responsibilities or blame anyone but to affirm that financial sector needs to act responsibly and those, who have the responsibility of making the financial sector act responsibly, need to act responsibly too.

There is more than reading here. The book attempts to bring learning into practice hence, there is an actionable checklist created for use and reference e.g. As a C(X)O, I have listed 'single-point-of-failure' in my information chain and factored them in my risk assessment?

No endeavor is complete, if it does not show a way forward. In hindsight, there lies wisdom from our century old history of 'modern' financial system and especially from the current financial crisis. With that reference, this book creates a foresight. It will interest those readers who are still worrying, though wiser by now, working to make their business stable, sound and secure.

Many a times, readers' mistake information systems with information technology, hence it is worth mentioning again here, that this book is

THE GLOBAL FINANCIAL CRISIS IS <u>NOT</u> FINANCIAL

neutral on technology, instead it is system specific. Also, it is easy on financial jargons and explanatory in approach, so even readers with no background in finance or technology can make the most from the analytical reading.

Chapter 1

The Current Crisis – seems everlasting

THE GLOBAL FINANCIAL CRISIS IS NOT FINANCIAL

There is no end to the current crisis. What started as a housing mortgage crisis in the US market now seems to be never-ending. No one would have imagined that a default in the housing mortgage market would start threatening the existence of a nation, even after four years of putting the global economy in jeopardy. As the days pass, more adverse economic news from different sectors is hitting the headlines. As governments are doing their best to balance their budgets, their population is struggling to balance their home finances.

If an analyst suggests that this daily news of economic adversity is independent of the triggers in the housing market crisis of 2008, they are in a state of denial.

The consequences of the financial crisis, in varied shapes and forms, go on to appear and reappear even though experts have started to declare that banks are back into the green and market indices have crossed the last five year levels. It is only a small part of the big and damaged picture that is painted rosy. Then one fine day the banks find themselves strained over the credit squeeze. The big picture is much more complicated and different than what appears on the surface.

The financial crises shifted from being financial, and have now turned into an economic crisis engulfing national economies in despair. Nations are struggling with their fiscal and monetary policies to find the solution, and time is running out. Public debt, inflation, growth rate and other social economic parameters are strained, not forgetting the heat in domestic and international politics.

Every time the problem is posed to experts, they immediately jump to dealing with those economic parameters, fiscal and monetary policies such as interest rates, GDP and others, but rarely has anybody tried to deal with the crisis from the 'systems' point of view. One remembers the advertisement for room freshener that masks the foul smell and the residents continue to live happily without removing that smelling trash. In another advertisement, the blindfolded volunteers seem to enjoy the freshness of the environment while standing in dirty public toilets. It is the author's argument throughout the book that a system failure has resulted in this financial failure and fixing the system needs to be the crux of the solution. The sooner it is realized the faster will be the resolution of the crisis. The fact that a crisis is still looming in one form or another suggests that the ladder of fixing the financial crisis is resting on the wrong wall.

The Current Crisis – seems everlasting

The implications of driving long distances on a flat tyre are not just restricted to the tyres; it goes even beyond that, into the mechanics of the vehicle, and most of the time, has proven to be hazardous to other road users too. Also, running on flat tyres includes the responsibility of the driver, and the auto systems, which like the financial system, will break down when its stress limits are reached. Similarly, the financial crisis of 2008 was a result of driving long distances with flat tyres and today, the impact has spilled over to other consequential and interconnected areas, not necessarily in its close vicinity. It is a simplistic example of the current crisis but conveys a lot about the fundamentals that need to be revisited if the financial system and other consequential systems, even though remotely connected, are to operate as **safe, sound and secured.**

Looking at the financial crisis would require a view, one that is farther back in history, more than the last four years with a perspective, wider than only the financial system. It is important to see the 'rich picture', because the fallout of the crisis in the financial system is showing on the monetary, economic, social and political system across continents and countries. History has shown that a financial crisis necessarily does not brew in one day nor are the effects limited to a few days or a few months. All financial crises in the twentieth century have taken at least a decade to recover, be it the Great Depression, the S&L crisis or the collapse of Asian Tigers. As the news media tirelessly reports, the crisis continues and the end is not in sight yet. The imbalances created by the crisis of 2008 in the financial, economic and social system had rocked the global financial giants, firms and countries, all together and societies in general, irrespective of their nationalities. Even after a few years the most powerful of them are still reeling under the fear of defaults and collapse.

> **Doing right things is about finance and economics.**
> **Doing things right is about systems and architecture.**

The chain of crisis continues unabated. The so-called financial crisis started with the collapse of the Too-Big-to-Fail financial institutions, which soon translated into a liquidity crisis that squeezed the economic activities and led to a global economic crisis. The financial crisis has remained since 2007, in one form or another, like the current Eurozone crisis. It will continue to resurface in future also, with varied manifestations if the fundamentals of financial activities are not corrected.

THE GLOBAL FINANCIAL CRISIS IS NOT FINANCIAL

How did we all get here in the first place? With a simplistic view of the chain of events, the governments used their fiscal resources in responding to the global financial meltdown, when it first appeared in 2008. It strengthened the balance sheet of the financial institutions but at the cost of public resources. It plugged the hole and prevented the deep recession but could not revive the prospects of economic growth with certainty. The dark clouds of financial instability still hang, as bailouts (the second one for Greece now) and the slow economic recovery work their way out. So where have things gone wrong? Is the iconic peak of the financial crisis of 2008, an outcome of a crisis of fundamentals? In the system, experts today are confused about the sources of the crisis and their manifestations. Their targets are shifting every day as newer aspects of the crisis unfold. In the same pursuit of analysis, without getting distracted by the manifestations of the original crisis, this book will find answers to the root causes as they became embedded in the financial system.

Even though this is a crisis caused by the top Wall Street bankers yet it has made the survival difficult for the common man. The common man was taken off guard because it was very complex for him to understand the intricate nature of the financial system. Since the failure of 'knowing' has been identified by me as the key cause of crisis, therefore, as a first step to recover from this financial crisis, I have tried to simplify the understanding of causes of the crisis.

So the simplification begins.

The Making of the Crisis: Behind the scenes

How to look at the current crisis

Often, studying the system involves observing the object from far and near, outside and inside, changing the perspective and altering the aspect ratio by distancing oneself from it. All this is done to bring more objectivity to the outlook. Similarly, to prevent any skewed outlook in the analysis of the current financial crisis, let us analyze by zooming into the financial system in three steps.

Step 1

To start with, let us create a basic perspective of our financial system. It may sound strange, but understand what if Martians were to see a place, where the concept of finance is not known. It would then be sensible to relate these modern financial concepts, tools and techniques to the purpose used for humankind here. In the next step, we can zoom into the details of the financial system to understand where things are going wrong.

Seeing the crisis from a Martian's view would be like watching the species of planet earth, called 'humankind' handling a tool called 'money'. Interestingly, humankind, as Adam Smith names them, ran into trouble over and over again in attempting to harness the power of money. A look into time, suggests that in pursuit of this 'money', broadly termed as 'wealth', these species had crossed oceans, conquered land, fought wars, exploited natural resources and undertaken other extraordinary adventures. There seems something curious about this concept of 'money', which make 'humankind' behave in these ways.

Step 2

Then, a closer look would mean understanding the characteristics of the financial sector. This would mean discussion about the set of people involved in managing wealth, the place where the entire crisis actually began, the blind spot in which Too-Big-to-Fail failed and in its failing, failed many others.

Step 3

Finally, we will drill-down to the nuts and bolts of the system, to analyze the squeaky and faulty parts, which had been malfunctioning for a long time without being questioned for its effectiveness.

Global View: Money as a Humankind Centric Invention, gone off-beam

Humankind's most powerful invention, the concept of 'money', has come under question and, like many other inventions; mankind had abused this invention too, with a lasting effect on fellow mankind. Even though mankind has used the concept of money for a long time, still, it seems, he has not learnt the ability to control its effect. Time and again, the world has found itself in a crisis because 'money' created affects that were severely negative to the people, organizations and this time, even nations.

If the twentieth century was a century of wars fought by nations in pursuit of wealth and 'money', then the twenty-first century is a war to manage that accumulated wealth and 'money'. There is no balance sheet to accurately suggest the wealth lost in the current crisis, but certainly the effects have been severe and widespread. Like war, in a pursuit to manage money, the twenty-first century has seen the expansionary powers risk their wealth on the likes of blind bets. Officially, there are financial instruments that allow bets and profits from those, where placing the bet is business-as-usual. Large market players indulge in that practice. If the world wars of the twentieth century had robbed people of their lives across those many nations, the current financial crisis of the twenty-first century has robbed people of their livelihoods in the same landscape. As you are reading this sentence, many more are still losing their livelihoods. Counting from large to small ones, countries are on the edge; many firms have filed for bankruptcy while individuals are trying hard to make ends meet. In 2008 there were 1,117,771 bankruptcy filings in the US courts alone (United States Courts, 2011). The scope of impact, without doubt, is widespread.

One may question the comparison of world wars and the current financial crisis. But the author argues by drawing the comparison with the severity of the threat posed and the extent of damage to the countries, organizations and its people. Twenty-first century weapons of mass destruction, such as CDOs and CDS, are more sophisticated and soundproof than their predecessors. Warren Buffett has been proved right when he shared the fear of destruction from CDO and CDS in Berkshire Hathaway annual report of 2002 (Berkshire Hathaway, 2002). We will learn more about the effects of these weapons of mass destruction, later in the book.

Interestingly, the twentieth-century world wars and twenty-first century financial crisis have mostly the same major players as the US, UK and mainland Europe. In current times, the US has the biggest source of funds and conventional assets under management. It is $36 trillion and accounts for half the global value of assets under management. The US is followed by the UK which has 9% of the global assets under management (Maslakovic, 2010). This is interesting because the centre of gravity for both war and this financial crisis, which had historically

The Current Crisis – seems everlasting

been severe in global consequences, remains the same geographically. It may be coincidental to view the military and the financial centre of gravity in one place, but it is in line with the argument about the ability of handling 'money' by the rich and powerful countries of the world. Even though, the wars have transitioned from being a methodology of political expansion to a status of restricted practice, the financial influence and its expansion needs a fresh look. Looking forward, the responsibility of making finance safe and secure lies with those who indulge in it the most, and the primary objective need not be profit at all times but prevention of another significant addition in the long list of man-made disasters.

Here, in Table 1, there is a list of major financial crises for last hundred years. A quick look at the reasons for the crises seems to have some common factors, such as Moral Hazard, Speculation leading to bubble, Information Asymmetry, Contagion and Loss of Confidence. So what is unique about the current financial crisis? Based on the analysis, as readers will find out, this financial crisis is the mother of all other crises. It encapsulated the troubles of other crises to form a complex situation where one part of the financial system is severely affecting the other parts, such as the economic system, monetary system, political system and, ultimately, the social system. This only proves that lessons are not learnt by previous crises, not only by the participants of the current crisis but also those who have lived through earlier crises. Primarily, if the lessons learnt from the 1973–74 UK housing bubble, Black Monday and Savings & Loans crises, were to be imbibed in their crudest form by the financial system, the author is confident that the current crisis could have been avoided.

THE GLOBAL FINANCIAL CRISIS IS **NOT** FINANCIAL

TABLE I

Year	Name of the Crisis	Reasons
1901	Panic of 1901	"Information Effect" due to corporate takeover struggle of Northern Pacific Railway
1907	Bankers' Panic	Unregulated side bets, financial contagion, lack of financial supervision like central bank, Loss of Confidence
1929	Wall Street Crash	Speculative Boom, Loss of Confidence
1973–1974	Stock Market Crash	Financial System Failure - Collapse of Bretton Woods System, Nixon Shock and Smithsonian Agreement of Dollar Devaluation
1973–1975	Secondary Banking Crisis	UK Housing Bubble, Unregulated lending market, Systemic effect of Bretton Woods System
Early 1980s	Latin American Debt Crisis	High Debt Service, High Credit in Latin American Commercial Banks, US Government Lending Regulation
1983	Israel Bank Stock Crisis	Information Asymmetry, Moral hazard, Unregulated Stock market, Financial System failure, Loss of Confidence
1987	Black Monday	Program Trading, Overvaluation, Contagion
1989–91	Savings & Loan Crisis	Unregulated Real Estate Lending, Deregulation of Thrift Industry, Moral hazard, Increased Speculative Opportunities, Audit Failure, Accounting Failure,
1986–91	Japanese Asset Price Bubble	Financial Deregulation, Speculation,
1990s	Swedish Banking Crisis	Interconnectedness, Systemic Failure
1990s	Finnish Banking Crisis	Speculation, Unregulated Banking Sector
1992	Black Wednesday	European Exchange Rate Mechanism Failure, Systemic Failure
1994	Mexican Peso Crisis	Poor Quality of Credits by Banks, Macro-Economic policies, Unregulated Banking Practices, Moral hazard, Loss of Confidence
1997	Asian Financial Crisis	Financial Contagion, Thai Macro-economic Policies, Real Estate Bubble and Speculation, Asymmetric Information & Herd Mentality
1998	Russian Financial Crisis	Fiscal Deficit, Rubble Exchange Rate, Economic Contagion of Oil and Non-Ferrous Metals
2001	Dot-Com Bubble	Overconfident Market Sentiment on Technological Advancement, Misleading Market Makers, Speculation, Accounting Fraud, Information Asymmetry
2007	Global Financial Crisis	Information Asymmetry, Moral Hazard, Unregulated Mortgage Market, Financial System Failure, Loss of Confidence

Various Sources

Finance is both an art and science of handling money. With the effects of the current crisis making inroads into individuals' balance sheets, the global financial instability still persists. It has a long way to go, before it can be relied upon; 'money' management needs to develop further to control its direction of providing strength and security to mankind, for whom it was primarily intended. In general, finance as a money mechanism forms the core of society's monetary policy and helps create a debt market using secured and unsecured lending, which in a way are engines of growth. Today, finance as an industry is walking a tight rope, balancing the constructive act of bringing growth and development most of the time but frequently gripped by the serious crises that have been hurting much of mankind.

The Financial Sector View: Financial System Failure

A crisis is a culmination of a single or multiple failures of its parts. Similarly, when the financial sector is being analyzed, it is important to figure out the failures of its parts, such as accounting, credit rating, risk modelling, regulation and others. At this early stage of analysis, the author finds that the interdependencies and relationships within these parts did not function, as required. The summation of these individual failures compounded into multiple failures and ultimately, the current global financial crisis. To rephrase, the position of the financial sector is a single point of failure for all other sectors and the effect of any failure of this sector, is systemic in nature.

Purpose: hidden failure

The financial crisis is a combination of process failures. It had lost the purpose of supporting entrepreneurial risk in the pursuit of trading that seemed more like casino betting. Regulators, banks, non-banks and central banks have not been able to restrict their activities to the objectives of a financial community. Even though, at the outset it looks as if all the systems and sub-systems were functioning normally, in compliance with the design, but the financial system as a whole was failing like a termite-infested wooden structure to serve the purpose of providing entrepreneurship in the society. Those pillars supporting the financial structure in question, like the Financial Institutions (FIs), Banks, Central Banks, Regulators, Legislators and Investors, together grouped as market players, are misdirected from their primary purpose,

THE GLOBAL FINANCIAL CRISIS IS NOT FINANCIAL

as they have got entangled in pursuing their modern day micro objectives.

The rise of monolithic firms in the financial services sector had added risk to the financial system as a single point of failure. There are multiple intentions for the rise of these blocks, like 'big was beautiful' and continues to be. They achieved economies of scale and firms were able to manage better, all the services under one umbrella. It also enhanced their bargaining power in the socio-politico environment. The financial services market had grown manifold in the last two decades, due to the consolidation of these services under a single brand and management. But prima facie, this crisis is attributed to this very nature of the cumulative composition of these monolithic blocks, as a single point of failure. With reference to the current crisis, these blocks are also known as Too-Big-to-Fail.

The euphoria of Too-Big-to-Fail made the financial institutions complacent. It was an unwritten law, lived in the spirit, that if any of these institutions would fail, the respective government would rescue them to restore confidence in the banking system. This would be in the larger interest of the retail depositors. On a stability compass, sustaining confidence in the banking system would be directly related to maintaining sovereign credit rating on the economic side and societal peace on the political side. On one hand, this was the underlying sense of bargain which led to the security that made players at ease to take risks and make exposures equivalent to multiple times the global GDP, knowing (at least in theory) that the consequences could be catastrophic.

On the other hand, the central bank and the regulators as powerful authorities had wielded influence with different objectives, though complementing each other. While the regulators looked after the solvency of the firms, the central banks protected the liquidity in the financial system as lenders of last resort, yet both could not stop the Too-Big-to-Fail institutions from failing.

According to research by Oliver & Wyman, since the 1960s and 1970s, the financial sector had tripled every ten years, up until the current crisis. Growth had been through a network of domestic retail banks, regional banks, global banks, insurance groups, reinsurers and investment banks making the financial sector the super sector for all other industry sectors. The more the business was able to leverage the

| The Current Crisis – seems everlasting

availability of the finance, the more prosperous the business became. This in turn translated to profitability of the financial sector.

There had been a downside too. The interconnection of various business and industry sectors with these financial intermediaries moved the financial sector to a position, where it was critical to the survival of all other sectors and therefore, should have been termed more assertively as 'Must not fail' instead of 'Too-big-to-Fail'.

The current financial crisis is a classic case of systemic failure starting from the home mortgage market to financial institutions, and subsequently to national economies. The failure has its roots in the deterioration and defaults in the US sub-prime market which rapidly spread into the credit and fund market via mortgage companies, aggregating to investment banks and ultimately, the banks. The effect was not restricted to the non-prime mortgage market alone but moved to the mortgage-related structured credit market too. When one of the investors in the financial system started to default on these products, the banks wanted to bring Off-Balance Sheet Entities (OBSEs) into the corporate balance sheet using fair value. Since fair value kept on declining with growing defaults, as those products devalued, their schemes failed and ultimately, the holding bank defaulted on liquidity. All grades of credit market were affected. Consequently, the crisis moved from US markets to European and then, emerging markets too. The contagion encapsulated the banking systems, as it snowballed into a classical systemic failure of the global financial system.

It did not stop there.

By definition, systemic failure has its boundaries limited to the financial sector. Later in the book, the author discusses the systemic boundaries beyond the financial sector.

So, which part of the system was responsible for the quality assurance of the financial products in the market? Financial products are the primary mechanisms to channel funds from one sector of the economy to another, and are the building blocks of the economic system's functioning. If the financial products are faulty, then in principle all other parts of the system will be affected where these funds have metamorphosed as securitized products, of course with varying intensity. Considering that the financial products and their activities

THE GLOBAL FINANCIAL CRISIS IS NOT FINANCIAL

have a cyclic influence on the risk, the effects will be visible both in real time and with a time lag.

Nothing was visibly wrong at the outset, as the financial transaction complied with the accounting standards. Still their effects on the economy, as an end result, are in question. Therefore, it is important that the effects are monitored from not only the point of view of financial transaction but also its implication on other participating sectors of the economy.

Does this mean that the current crisis is a failure of rightful feedback and their interpretations?

While pursuing an answer to this question, it is important in the first place to identify the authorities that were accountable for the safety of those financial products even though they were in compliance with the accounting standards.

The Role of Central Banks and Banks: No option choice

Most of the literature speaks of the actions taken by the central banks including the Federal Reserve, European Central Bank, Bank of England and others, after the symptoms of the crisis had begun to appear. Even though, the central banks are also responsible for having an oversight on all banking mechanisms, both deposit and investment, their monetary default detectors failed to trap the alerts from the sub-prime lending market. If there were a report card for the performance of central banks, they all would be in red.

Central banks across the countries, gave a false sense of security by overly securing the market with its role and functions, importantly by playing as a lender of the last resort. They provided or reduced the liquidity with monetary mechanisms, whenever required, and secured deposit insurance to reassure depositors. Central banks played a vital role in the money market and supported the liquidity, which was often at risk due to short-term maturities. In compliance with their charter, central banks across the countries are continuing to play that role and are active in maintaining and supporting the liquidity (Tucker, 2010). But in the US, this crisis has seen a change in the role of the Federal Reserve – a forced change, which is a gross deviation for the role of any central bank. In order to dampen the effects of Too-Big-to-Fail bankruptcy and to avert further crisis, they became counterparty as a last resort, from being a lender of last resort. They had been facilitating financial institutions in buying toxic and distressed assets in order to support the US government-sponsored housing debt (Board of Governors of the Federal Reserve System, 2008), as an example.

As a case, the US Federal Reserve System played a pivotal role during the crisis but was indifferent during the period when the crisis was developing. They failed in two of their four enshrined duties, firstly, in "maintaining the stability of the financial system and containing systemic risk that may arise in financial markets" and secondly, "supervising and regulating banking institutions to ensure the safety and soundness of the nation's banking and financial system and to protect the credit rights of consumers" (Board of Governors of the Federal Reserve System, 2009). This brings us back to the argument that they were misdirected from their primary purpose, as they have got entangled in pursuing their modern day micro objectives.

According to the IMF stability report of October 2010, the central banks were unaware of the implication of the systemic liquidity (IMF, Global Financial Stability Report, October 2010) by the presence of sub-prime credit in the market and the unmitigated systemic risk posed to the overall liquidity in the fund market. The mismatch between the asset and liability in the bank balance sheet was not fully recognized by the central banks. So during the crisis, the central banks had to intervene and supply funds to the money market because the counterparties went dry. As a result, in the last two decades before the crisis, the US market was fuelled by debt. While the US government debt grew and the current account deficit increased more than ten times, China's current account surplus grew by more than 50 times. This is a clear indicator that both the government and the central banks had let the market play with easy credit which was directed towards personal lending. The shift in balance was gradual but skewed the domestic money market while the US central banks took the passenger seat.

Banking is the core of the financial sector as it is the single point of interface with lenders and depositors, and people at large. Any deposit, loan, investment, repatriation, liquidation or other financial activity has to have banks in the chain, even though they may not be participating directly in the primary objective of the participants. Also, needless to say, banks are both residual and active participants in the financial and economic activities; therefore the strength of the banks is the strength of the financial sector. At national level, the banks reflect the dynamism

THE GLOBAL FINANCIAL CRISIS IS <u>NOT</u> FINANCIAL

of the economy and any faltering banking system directly impacts the nation's credit rating and its credibility as an investment destination.

The operational definition classifies banks into three categories based on observed functional diversification and universality. They are classified as traditional banking, insurance and securities. In the first type, banks transform deposits into loans; in the second, financial conglomerates are engaged in at least two of the areas of financial services mentioned and in the third, universal banks are engaged in diversified financial services, holding equity shares in non-financial companies (Pelaez, 2009). It is important that all these types of banks in definition, work to compartmentalize and optimize the risk, mostly entrepreneurial risk, while complementing each other. Although, finance as an industry had been there since mankind began, it is only in the last few centuries that financial instruments and products have been innovated in numerous complexities and variations, and the majority of the population have failed to keep up with the understanding of them. To rephrase, the knowledge of financial products is NOT commonly known. This is the primary risk posed by the financial system. The 'black box' effect is prevalent.

From the system's stability point of view, why were the financial institutions allowed to be too-big-to-fail? Isn't it an important question to be answered?

Whenever the term Too-Big-to-Fail was used for the first time, the role of central banks would have been automatically enhanced to oversee the sustainability of these Too-Big-to-Fail firms. Was Too-Big-to-Fail an amazing feat? The icon brought along with it, the dangers in the financial system; a protective shield, therefore should have been proactively raised with all seriousness. The solvency of these firms should have been the responsibility of national and international financial authorities in the interest of its implications and the systemic risk they posed. The author is sure, things would have been much different today if someone in central banking or the government would have made an **impact analysis** of a scenario where the Too-Big-to-Fail firms filed for bankruptcy in succession.

As a system, the right kind of oversight seems missing in protecting the stability of these important pillars of the financial market.

The Current Crisis – seems everlasting

Sometimes, the priority is misplaced. It becomes focused on the most vulnerable parts of the system, assuming that the probability of failure is least likely on the parts that appear to be the strongest. This is the author's argument for what has happened in the case of Too-Big-to-Fail firms.

The role of regulators: the story of dog- tail in enforcements

The current crisis has its roots in the history of banking regulation and legislations. The financial crisis and legislation have followed each other ever since the history of modern banking has been recorded. Since 1933, when the term 'financial crisis' originated, there had been legislations in response to a crisis but soon a crisis had followed that legislation. As history shows, in reaction to a crisis, the legislations which followed, had created stricter regulations and monitoring mechanisms. In another case, in attempt to proactively modernize the financial market, the legislation had loosened up the regulations, freeing up the players to make riskier investments. In the case of the current crisis, legislation has gone overboard to the levels of deregulations that have resulted in moral hazard. We will discuss later, the effects of regulation in the financial market and their role in the crisis, to understand how they failed to corroborate the financial activities in the system.

In comparison, no other industry sector has a more complex regulatory structure than the financial sector. To regulate the financial market, there were regulatory bodies such as FSA, SEC, Federal Reserve System and others in their respective countries. The BASEL Committee, as an exception, is a pseudo-regulatory body but has a significant influence on the regulation of the financial industry. By the nature of their charter, they tried to ensure that the market was secure from fraud, firms were solvent, investors felt confident of entrepreneurial risks and financial markets were stable. Although the regulators, in following this mission, had contributed to the survival of the national financial market and therefore, had been responsible for the state of the national economies, hence it is natural to point towards an overarching financial authority to seek answers for the crisis and hold them accountable. One important reason that is cited for the failure of regulators is that they themselves had not been able to keep pace (IMF, April, 2008) with the financial innovations and volumes of activities; hence they failed to prevent the current crisis.

THE GLOBAL FINANCIAL CRISIS IS NOT FINANCIAL

The IMF in its report indicates that the current practices for monitoring the funding and liquidity risk need to be improved. There exists an information gap in the collection of data, especially Over-the-counter (OTC) transactions, which is not suitable for liquidity risk analysis. There has been criticism of OTC transactions regarding their opaqueness, which also creates the inability to administer monetary regulation.

The revelation opens up a discussion on the complementary and converging role of the regulatory and monetary authorities. Instead of being discrete in the financial system, the evidence of their being mixed and confused is seen in their current configuration of roles and responsibilities. If it is in fine print, it is not as aggressive as desired. As

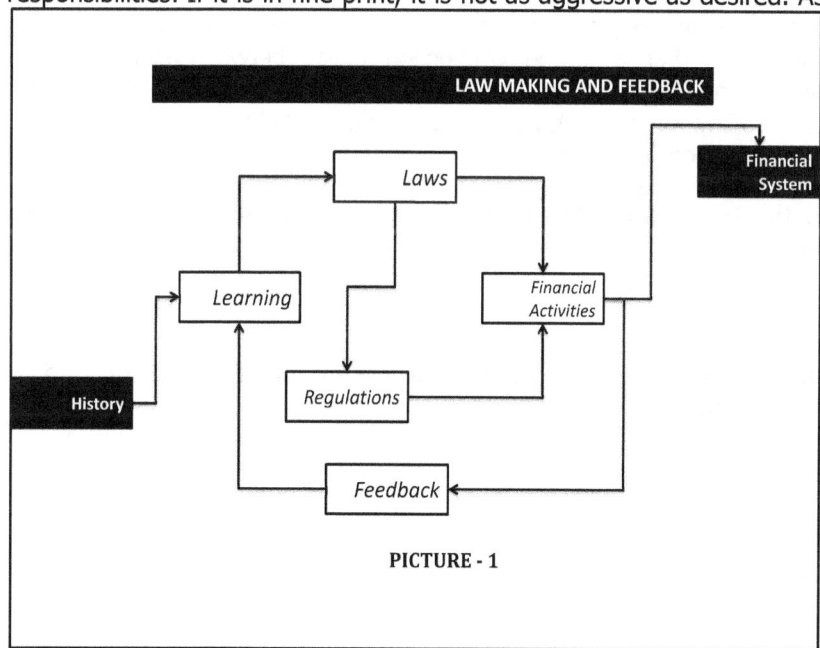

PICTURE - 1

mentioned, the history of modern banking is punctuated by banking regulations, legislations and crises. These three are interdependent processes (a crisis is a process) such that they have constructed the modern banking and financial system. If the financial system has to function, to proactively avert those numbers of crises, then the regulations and legislations have to foresee the future, in rapidly changing times and adapt accordingly.

To highlight the flaw in the regulation and legislation cycle, it is important to have a comprehensive look at the reactive and consequential nature of these processes. It is well understood that these processes for making laws and regulations, are very tedious and therefore spark to fire time, is lengthy and dependent on the perceived seriousness of the crisis. The importance of these laws is in learning from past mistakes, which are corrected by it. ***Seriousness is a function of political fallout and that provokes legislative activities.*** Learning is not only implemented by making corrections in the actions via the compliance to the law but also by preventing the circumstances for which these laws were enacted. Further, the financial system has its own reaction time for these laws and regulations. So there is causality when it comes to crises, legislations and regulations.

History could be a great teacher. Feedback from the financial system does provoke new, or changes to, laws and regulations but the author doubts whether a strong connection exists between learning from history and the enactment of law. If that was the case, the Gramm-Leach-Bliley Act of 1999 (Financial Services Modernization Act) would not have been promulgated.

In the global financial market, the country-specific laws govern the market of that country. But there is a natural alignment of laws and regulations, when countries are participating in the global market. Hence, it brings a contradiction between the constitutional guidance to the national laws for a country and its tendency to shift the laws and regulations towards the countries, where the global financial centre of gravity lies.

THE GLOBAL FINANCIAL CRISIS IS NOT FINANCIAL

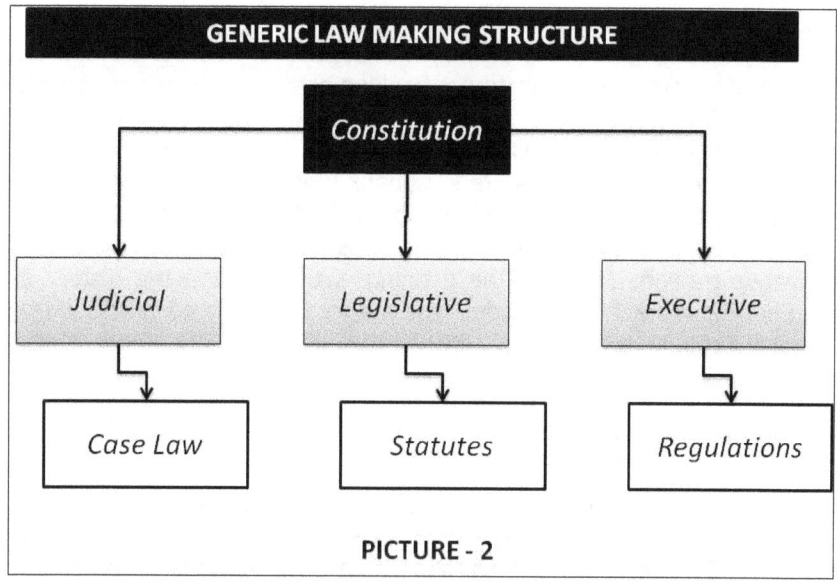

Source - http://firestone.princeton.edu/law/caselaw.php

Following is the basic structure of the law-making followed in different countries. With variations of constitution and legislative ethos in different countries, it is difficult to have unified regulations and legislations to define the interconnected financial market, unless there are commonalities of market type in those countries. As seen earlier, if the centre of gravity of financial activities lies in the US, inherently the global financial market policies will have to follow US legislations and regulations, at least in spirit. There is no harm in following the centre of gravity to maintain the right balance, but the risk of everyone falling together exists in that model, as it did in the current crisis.

Here is the list of iconic laws that the US congress had enacted. We must judge for ourselves how these laws were reactive in those circumstances and subsequently, responsible for another crisis. Also, the readers need to assess how much other countries have inclined their laws towards the centre of gravity.

The Glass-Steagall Act of 1933

In the twentieth century, banking and investment banking were not separate financial functions and this is considered as one of the reasons for the Great Depression of 1929. The US government investigated and

The Current Crisis – seems everlasting

found conflict of interest and related fraudulent practices (moral hazard) in some banking institutions dealing with securities. In order to separate the core depository and investment banking activities, the Glass-Steagall Act of 1933 was promulgated. As a result, the Federal Deposit Insurance Corporation (FDIC) was formed which highlighted the segregation in the banking system by bank types and insured the safety of deposits. The Glass-Steagall Act prohibited depository banks from engaging in investment banking functions such as underwriting and derivative trading. This was the defining law enacted in the history of the financial market. As of today, the author is convinced that this law not only brought long-lasting order to the financial market, but it also brought guiding wisdom to subsequent legislations.

The Financial System Reform Act of 1989

A major market change came with the Financial System Reform Act of 1989. It was a result of the Garn–St. Germain Depository Institutions Act of 1982, which brought changes to the market due to emergent market requirements and demands to arrest stagflation in the US economy. It was a deregulation of Savings & Loan thrifts and the rise of thrifts, insuring troubled assets. Holding companies and depository institutions started to work as 'discount brokers' for securities. The act formally removed the barrier between depository and investment banking and gave flexibility to the thrift firms to decide on the interest for home loans. The thrift firms were further allowed to securitize the loans and use the originate-to-distribute model to transfer risk. The implication of the reform resulted in the infamous Savings and Loans crisis.

The Act brought stricter oversight institutions and regulations to the thrift savings and loan industry, such as the Office of Thrift Supervision (OTS). While one of the legislation deregulated the thrift industry, which led to the S&L crisis, a follow-up legislation plugged the crisis with stricter regulation. The cycle of crisis, legislation and regulation is seen to persist in the history of financial markets and this was the second time it had happened in the last 30 years.

There have been similarities to the S&L crisis of 1989 with the sub-prime crisis of 2008 and the role of the government in making bailouts. It is astounding to find history repeating itself in a short span of 25 to 30 years.

THE GLOBAL FINANCIAL CRISIS IS NOT FINANCIAL

The Financial Modernization Act of 1999 or Gramm–Leach–Bliley Act

The Financial Modernization Act of 1999 appears to revoke the Glass-Steagall Act of 1933. The Act permitted banks, insurance companies, securities firms and other financial institutions to affiliate under common ownership and offer their customers a complete range of financial services. The Act established two new corporate vehicles for the conduct of financial service activities, namely, the financial holding company and the financial subsidiary (Schwakopf, 1999). It also allowed the appointment of any employee, in whatever capacity, of a securities firm as an employee of any other member bank. It was like an official allowance for conflict of interest.

As seen, the Financial Modernization Act of 1999 changed the structure of the regulated financial market which left more room for systemic risk. The market started to relive the period prior to the Glass-Steagall Act of 1933. Depository banking and investment banking merged to define market capitalization. New financial products were created which were funded from the depository pool and traded as securities in the derivative market. Moreover, the trading used Credit Default Swaps (CDS) to hedge their risks, which itself raised the risk in the market.

Then with increased globalization, it added more risk to the system. As a new age method of expanding business, it was also responsible for extending the boundaries of these merged banking activities. With internationalization, came the unrestricted operations of underwriting, distribution and brokerage of securities by these banking firms, especially in countries where financial markets were comparatively more deregulated. This gave profits from the practice of regulatory arbitrage. The firms started to find a spread in the regulation, not only in the various business sectors but also across the countries. Not only was the financial system running a financial supermarket, but the decade also saw a creation of a multinational financial supermarket. No wonder that the impact of the crisis is felt in all corners of the world, much beyond the systemic boundaries of the financial sector.

Many economists have called this legislation the source of the current crisis even though it is counter-argued that European markets had always survived without the Glass-Steagall Act. In fact, those unified banking firms in Europe survived better than their counterparts in the US (Gramm, 2009).

The Current Crisis – seems everlasting

The Dodd–Frank Wall Street Reform and Consumer Protection Act of 2010

After the peak of financial crisis, when the 'too-big-to-fail' firms had shockingly failed and painfully bailed out with tax payer's money, the US government enacted a law to reform the Wall Street and the financial markets. In essence, the act is a modern version of the Glass-Steagall Act of 1933 to plug the conflict of interest and moral hazard due to the 'financial supermarket' nature of the large firms. The results of the act will be seen in years to come, as the regulatory authorities are still in the process of implementing it. As a cycle of stricter regulations reforms the financial market, one finds nothing new being done differently from the previous instances of fixing market failures. It is yet another case of reactive legislation.

But something happened in addition to legislation this time. An inquiry commission was set up by the US House Committee on Oversight and Reform to investigate the financial crisis called the Financial Crisis Inquiry Commission (FCIC). While the concept of oversight committees is helpful in revealing the finer points, the chronology of the FCIC indicates that its findings were published by December 2010, much after the Dodd-Frank Wall Street Reform and Consumer Protection Act was already promulgated. One can argue about the usefulness of the findings of the oversight committee. Since the publication dates for the final report of the FCIC and the promulgation of the Dodd-Frank Act do not match, all that weaknesses investigated and lessons learnt in the FCIC may not have found its place as a correction into the legislation. The legislation is just half-baked. Only the future holds the key to test the promulgation.

The financial sector is different

Strangely, the financial sector is one that has undergone many crises, not seen in any other industry sector. Imagine aviation or the pharmaceutical industry, which share the same attribute of risk, undergoing a crisis of the same magnitude and frequency. By now people would have stopped flying altogether or the medical sciences would have come to a jolting halt. It is this pattern of high frequency and the magnitude of financial crisis that provokes the search for answers to the question; why does the financial sector behave differently?

THE GLOBAL FINANCIAL CRISIS IS NOT FINANCIAL

The author sums up the reasons for this differentiation due to factors such as People, Product and Profit. In short, the 3Ps of financial sector differentiation.

1st P: *People – Skill-set as investors*

Investors are important constituents of the market and it will be inappropriate to ignore the role of home mortgage borrowers, retail investors or institutional investors in making this crisis. If the market responded in a particular way, it is the investor's behaviour that is reflected in it. Of course, there is a difference in the approach to investment by each of these categories of investor, but ultimately they all are in the market to maximize their gains and minimize their losses. Throughout the process of investment, this objective acts as a single point of pursuit. Thus it is the investment as a financial, behavioural and social process that requires a revisit with reference to this crisis. Although, it is convenient to point the finger towards the bankers and their speculative practices for the failure of the market and the subsequent financial crisis, it was also during the boom times that most of the investors received good returns. Whether they are earning profits or not, the investors do have a shared responsibility in the successful running of the market.

The financial sector is the only sector in business which officially allows speculation to earn profits. The financial system being complex, hence those working in the sector require special qualifications and talents to carry on speculation and calculated risk taking. To meet the objectives the firms deploy the best brains to innovate methodologies of risk-returns. Therefore in spirit, the crux of the business in finance is not just limited to finance but has shifted primarily into risk taking. Not going into the specifics of the financial skill-set required for people working in this sector, who can match the spirit of the business, the demand-supply imbalance of this special aptitude has made employment in this sector

> The Question that spirals out from the role of investors in the making of the crisis is all about the approach and behaviour towards risk taking. If the market sentiment airs excessive risk taking, then for an investor it becomes very difficult to hold back and avoid indulging in the contemporary risk. It may be termed as 'herd mentality' in normal parlance.

very lucrative for individuals. The lure to this sector is also driven by the incentives based on the risk-return curve of the firm, which at times translates to be 20 times the average wage in other sectors. It is an intriguing interplay of innovation and incentives in risk taking that makes these people behave differently in this sector. The incentives and the bonuses can compound to seven figures, which at times, as shown in history, had driven ambitions to over risk their limits into losses running into billions. This is the profile of players in the market who can be termed in the category of official investors because their job is to be an investor.

Home mortgage borrowers

Home mortgage borrowers are long-term investors in the market who expect their home value to grow over a period of time, even if they may prefer to live in that property and not sell it at all, to get the profit. In the build-up to the crisis, home loan borrowers were assessed leniently on their credit score. Even knowing the shortfall in their fragile domestic balance sheet and future income capabilities, they did manage to secure mortgages. Sub-prime borrowers are to be considered more accountable and responsible for their behaviour because they over-borrowed intentionally knowing that in the future there will be an income and credit mismatch. Being a party to the toxic transactions in the first place, it is not justified for home borrowers to complain about the new credit squeeze, home foreclosures, bank failures and ultimately, the crisis.

The crisis has revealed another differentiation.

Currently, over one-third of residential foreclosures are believed to be 'strategic' in the sense that borrowers were current on their loan payments but walked away because the value of their property was worth less than its debt. This is one behavior that was not seen in the past by the herd of investors. It is an emergent behavior and the authorities are yet to react to this practice.

Financial market investors

Seldom had the investors played a part as highly informed players in the market. They would have prevented the crisis, if they had sought in-depth information; more information than what was made available to them through official financial disclosures. It hardly was possible to

THE GLOBAL FINANCIAL CRISIS IS NOT FINANCIAL

track and know how their investment was being utilized nor did anyone want to question the risks involved in the 'originate–to-distribute model' quoting the S&L crisis. It was an unquestionable practice for all the investors until the returns were high. With the originate-to-distribute mechanism, once the risk left the aisle of the originator, subsequent distributors had little knowledge of the risk inherited from down the chain. It functioned like a black box when it came to the risk in the up-chain. So losing track of the risk was the method of securitization and re-securitization which probably helped those who had invented this methodology and managed its risk-return.

If numerous investors are following a set behaviour, it neither reduces the market risk nor is the market safe at any time. Market behavior fails to distinguish between mortgage securities business and betting on housing prices. All that an investor can introspect now, is whether the risk taken as 'informed risk' was based on equality of information between trading parties or was it a 'mortgage rush'? They would have realized that there is no such thing as a 'safe risk'.

2nd P: *Product – Generative side of the spectrum*

Financial products are complex and if we were to compare financial products with products from other sectors of economy, such as a car or a mobile phone, the difference is in their genesis. Financial products exist in virtual reality and have no physical appearance. They are conceptual and only provide financial returns based on activities, paradoxically over which, investors has no control. Once an investment has been made, the boundaries of influence and control cross over to someone else, leaving the investor merely as a spectator. Since the financial product is a virtual entity and has no physical significance, it is more of an objective rather than an object. In comparison with products from other industry sectors, even the most complicated products provide some degree of control to users who are equivalent to financial investors in this discussion. Also, the risk is known and well established. Rarely does owning a mobile phone or a car pose a risk to the user. Therefore, in a true sense the difference between the financial product and others, is in the degree of control, the inherent risk and its virtual existence.

Although, there are strict guidelines for the functioning of the financial system, for newer innovations coming into the market it takes time to show its pros and cons. This is the time that is required by the components of that economy to absorb the effects of these financial innovations. It is slow and sometimes the results are visible only after many years of its introduction. Are the financial products also tested like any other products that are being introduced in the market? Are the financial products being monitored continuously for their potential risk during its life cycle? The answers to both these important question, surprisingly, is a blatant 'No'.

Financial innovations and products do not have a defined incubation period like any other products have in their development cycle nor is there any authority with a clear role and responsibility to monitor their financial sustainability. It is 'Every Man for Himself' as it is entirely up to investors to test the water in their own way. Certainly, this becomes a recipe for complicated dynamics in risk taking with perils for economic, social and political dimensions. In order to address this lacuna in the system, there are suggestions for having Financial Stability and Product Safety Administration, although the idea has not taken off yet (Epstein & Crotty, 2009).

Financial products as services are generative in nature. This means that they are intended to grow over time, while all other products are consumables whose value decreases over the period of usage with the exception of real estate. Gold and other precious metals are somewhat financial products too, but they have both consumable and generative characteristics and therefore, have dualities in existence. In the product spectrum, it is financial products in one extreme and consumables on the other side and that defines the uniqueness of these financial products.

Handling financial products: Information black box

As a general behaviour the investors are found to make decisions based on a cursory look into the disclosures and credit rating of that innovated product in cognizance with the market sentiments. Financial innovations are complex to understand not only for ordinary investors but also for many others in the same sector. The devil lies in the details. Financial products have intense mathematical calculations in their construction; hence it is very time-consuming to get into the fine print of disclosures. Credit ratings which critically analyze them, itself are built upon a secret and private methodology. Therefore, it tends to inherit an abundance of informational blind spots and disconnections, leading to misinformation about the product.

THE GLOBAL FINANCIAL CRISIS IS NOT FINANCIAL

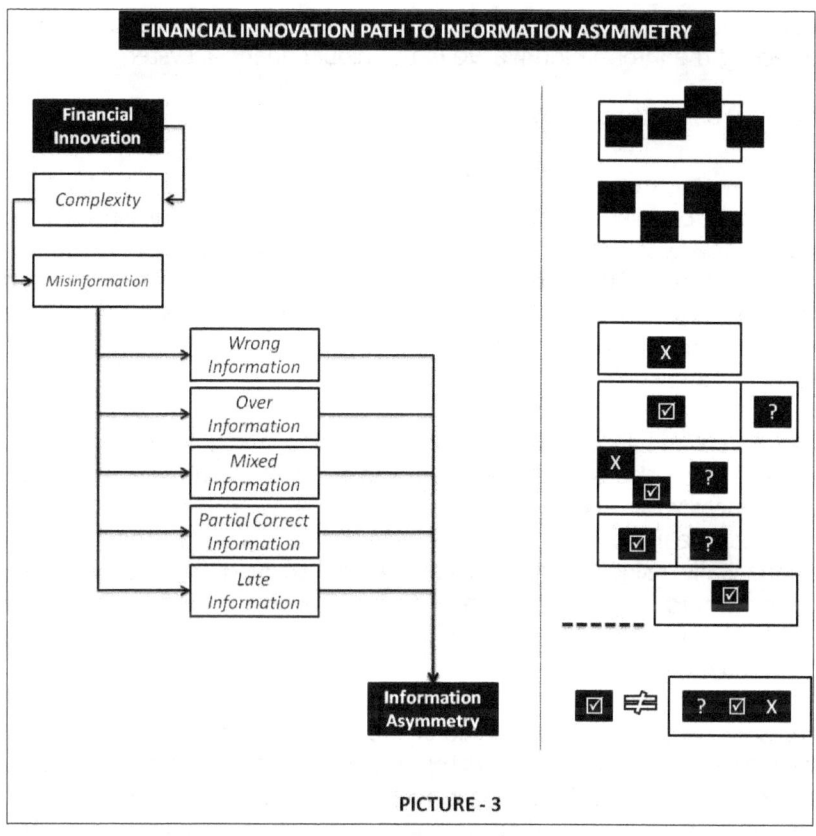

PICTURE - 3

Misinformation comes in many shapes and forms, not necessarily as wrong information; it could be half-information, over-information and mix-information, late information or even partially correct information; together classified as information asymmetry. The effects of information asymmetry make one party know more than the other. It is known that the effects of asymmetry lie in the riskier decisions because of the misinformation variants (information asymmetry) associated with the complexity in products. It is to draw a conclusion here that the dependency between the complex financial innovation and the information asymmetry is direct and proportional. That is the way the financial market runs with asymmetry which forms the weave of the financial operation. Readers will find more details in subsequent chapters.

If the financial system has to be fixed in order to prevent any crisis in the future, that is why primarily the information weaves of the system need to be fixed. The last chapter of the book deals with the solution by correcting the information weave in the global financial system.

3rd P: *Profit: Systemically connected*

The current crisis is a case of a financial market driven by financial innovation, creating blind spots aggravated by the spirit of speculation and recklessness. Banking crises have been occurring very frequently. There have been 30 banking crises since 1985 in both industrialized and emerging markets. In simplistic terms, a banking crisis has a reoccurring probability of 4–5% per year, which is much more than an average driving accident rate (Walter, 2010).

The players are in the business of risk taking and a many times this amount to reckless risk because those who profit are rewarded handsomely with incentives. These incentives could be 20 times more than those earned in other industry sectors. Therefore, the scope of exponentially rising individual incentives linked to a firm's profit, fuels the risk-return aggression. This is one important and fundamental reason why these crises occur so frequently in the financial system, as discussed earlier.

Profits earned in the financial sector are dependent on profits earned in other sectors. The financial sector has an interdependent relationship with non-financial sectors. The transaction cycle starts with lending to other sectors and depending on them to share the gains to close the cycle. If one of the entities (both in a lender's and a borrower's money supply chain) defaults, the entire cycle fails. As in the case of the US home mortgage crisis, in simplistic terms, the banks lent to the home loan borrowers but when the borrowers defaulted and the entire housing sector failed, the financial sector, which was on the lending side of the money supply, failed too. Had the home borrowers' behaviour remained cautious, the banks would have continued with normal business and the crisis would have been averted.

These are the key differentiation found in the financial sector.

Working View: Malfunctioning nuts and bolts

This view describes the financial processes and instruments involved in the making of the financial crisis. It gives a glimpse of how the large financial institutions failed all along as they used financial instruments

THE GLOBAL FINANCIAL CRISIS IS NOT FINANCIAL

and innovations (financial engineering) that were too risky which they were not able to manage in its entirety. Along with the innovations that were risky, the financial volumes at risk and their swaps in some of the mechanisms were much more than the entire global GDP, making the system bulky and intrinsically vulnerable.

It is said that the best brains from the technical institutes of the US and Europe were roped in, to design these financial instruments. So what went wrong with these financially engineered products and innovations that were intended to enhance the shareholders' wealth? Was financial engineering deployed to grow the returns because they managed the risk or grow risks to manage the returns?

In this section, the author discusses the role of important financial processes used to manage large volumes of funds and how they failed the system.

Before that, here is the chronology of events that are typically classified as events in the crisis. This is to put into perspective, all that happened when the crisis was officially accepted by the financial institutions, government, regulators and other market players.

Chronology – January 2007 to December 2008

Year 2007:

- Major losses expected by HSBC
- Significant losses posted by large hedge funds in the US
- Losses due to real estate overvaluation
- Northern Rock faces bank run in the UK
- Panic in financial markets especially with non-banking institutions with respect to credit quality and credit capacity
- Quarterly data reflects losses by major banks and monoliners (companies whose sole line of business is to provide bond insurance services to one industry are called monoline insurers)
- US capital market and investment banks gripped in severe credit deficit

Year 2008:

- Year-end results in the US highlight the losses in investment banking, monoline credit, venture capital and mortgage sectors

The Current Crisis – seems everlasting

- Bear Stearns goes bust and is saved by Federal Reserve as a public-private partnership
- First quarter results in the US indicate continued crisis with increased devaluations
- Middle-East and Asian sovereign funds support the large financial institutions:
    - Credit Suisse – Olayan family of Saudi Arabia
    - Standard Chartered and Merrill Lynch – Temasek Investment
    - Barclays – Qatar government fund
    - Citigroup – CIC investments, China
- Second quarter results lower the credit ratings of credit insurance and merchant banks
- Lowered credit rating shoots up the funding cost
- Credit Default Swaps (CDS) panic as an after-effect of lowered credit ratings
- Reported losses and panic create selling pressures and devalued share prices
- Lehman Brothers, Freddie Mac and Fannie Mae turn red
- US treasury bails out Freddie Mac and Fannie Mae with public-private partnership
- Lehman Brothers fail to get government support and file for bankruptcy under Chapter 11
- Too-Big-to-Failfails and the US central bank avoids being lender of last resort
- Crisis expands to European and Asian markets
- Government, public and private interventions create guarantee plans
- Banks open up their share capital
- Third quarter results and macro-economic data reveal economic slowdown due in other industry sectors as credit dries up
- US government takes recapitalization of banks with $58 billion package
- $20 billion goes to Citigroup and $38 billion to other 20 banks
- December, National Bureau of Economic Research declares 'Recession' in the US economy
- Twenty-five US banks become insolvent and are taken over by FDIC
- US government declares a bailout package for all sectors of the economy, especially $17 billion for the auto sector
- In other affected economies, central banks intervene to lower the credit cost

THE GLOBAL FINANCIAL CRISIS IS NOT FINANCIAL

Year 2009:

- At the end of the third quarter the number of troubled banks was 552
- By the year end 140 banks became insolvent

Various Sources

Events thereafter can be classified more as economic crises and social crises because of the systemic effect of these financial events.

The Current Crisis – seems everlasting

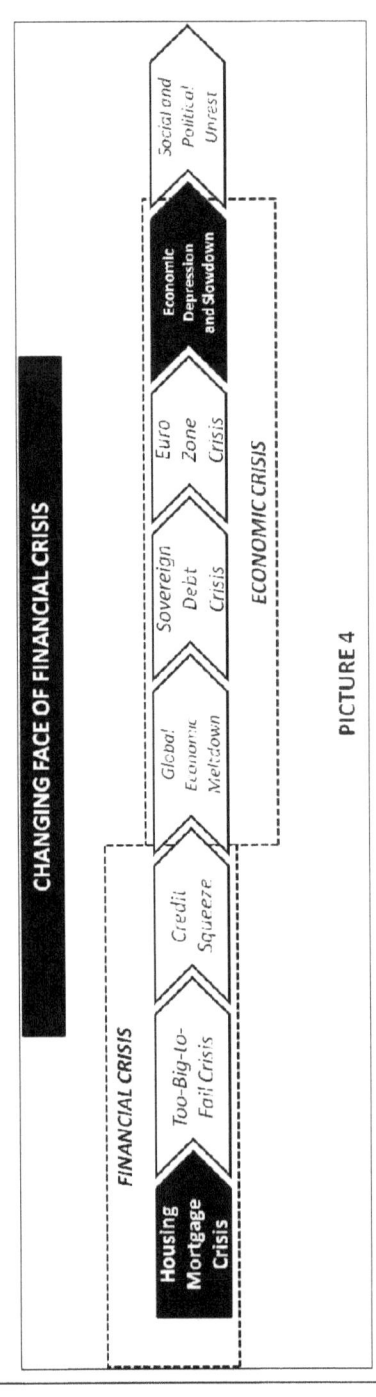

PICTURE 4

THE GLOBAL FINANCIAL CRISIS IS NOT FINANCIAL

Role of hedge funds

Size matters: Hedge fund, in their intention and concept, makes sense in supporting the investor's view for long-term investment and gains. These funds have brought large volumes of investment into the market and would continue to do so, but there are few ills that they carry into the market as a concept of hedge funds. Hedge funds are usually offshore and therefore, regulators do not have a view of their functioning. This makes them a suitable candidate for contributing to information asymmetry in the system. This had been detrimental to the financial system. Since the volumes are large, which is nearly 50% of the volumes on the London Stock Exchange, the sheer size of the fund makes, they can be perilous as any volatile movement can be detrimental to the entrepreneurial intentions of investors.

Technology vs. Humans: Hedge funds have used technology to their benefit. Those funds which have used directional strategy for market response deploy software and robotic programs for managing trading. This would mean that it is not human decision-making that interplays with the reaction of the market but an algorithm that assesses the market situation to respond to selling or buying decisions. The Black Monday crash of 1987 is attributed to this cause. For the purpose of definition, program trading is defined by the New York Stock Exchange as any trading which involves 15 or more stocks with an aggregate value of more than $1 million.

One would argue that there is nothing wrong in using the technology which participates in high-frequency trading, as it promptly and efficiently responds to changing market risks, while keeping all its transactions on record and legal.

The author's argument is directed towards the human sense-making involved in the assimilation of information, as a necessary step in the decision-making process. If trading is robotic, then the market tends to be robotic too, because the steps involved in decision-making are also robotic. Therefore the risk of oversight, if not outright failure, is high. As experts caution about the hazards in high-frequency trading, citing an instance when it took robotic trading 0.36 seconds to make a firm bankrupt, while it took another 45 minutes for the traders (humans) to figure out where things had gone wrong. According to the New York Stock Exchange weekly historic statistics in 2006, before the crisis, automated program trading accounted for about 30% of trading volumes which could go as high as 46% of the trading volume every day. No intelligence is required to deduce that any system that is out of human control, which relies on high computational capabilities of technology, makes trading riskier. There have been other instances of overuse of technology-based high-frequency trading (HFT) which without the use of fundamental sense-making, made large-scale losses in the Flash Crash of 2010.

Risk and Incentives: Although there had been discussions about incentives and performance fees, hedge funds continue to be designed such that the losses are those of the investors and the gains are shared between the fund, managers and the investor. A unidirectional approach to profit incentives and losses brings unwarranted risk taking into the investment practice, especially when methodologies of investments are not shared to the public by the funds.

In a financial system where visibility is only about profit, enclosing the methodology of profit-making into a 'black box' is nothing but a practice promoting information asymmetry that has been attributed to the financial system's overall poor accountability.

Role of OBSEs

OBSEs and Information Asymmetry

Over the last 20 years there had been a dramatic increase in the number of off-balance sheet instruments in the market including swaps, options, forwards and futures. Because of this increase in default risk instruments, over the period of time, in 1992 the Bank of International Settlements (BIS) tried to mitigate the capital ratio to also include the risk of default for this Off-Balance Sheet Entities (OBSE). Although, the imposition of the OBSE requirements draws a parallel with the conventional loan default risk coverage, the two work very differently in the market. The OBSEs have a peculiar status in the financial world. It is a large sum of the fund that is not accounted for in the books of the bank or the firm that is managing that fund. The investor, as the firm's client, gives funds to be managed for profit. Since the funds do not appear in the financial firm's balance sheet it does not fall in the scope of auditors and regulators. The OBSEs, also called Special Purpose Vehicles (SPVs), are used to cater to various factors depending on the requirements to boost the credit rating or tax-related issue or to make a desired effect on the bank's balance sheet. National and multinational

THE GLOBAL FINANCIAL CRISIS IS NOT FINANCIAL

firms used this method extensively for their wealth management and investment strategies (Na'im, 2006). OBSEs are one practice that takes the driver's seat in the current financial crisis, not because these entities failed, but because they were neither audited nor regulated. For the financial system as a whole, this part was completely in the shadow. Even though, the financial institutions were in compliance with the accounting standards and regulatory guidelines, yet the market had witnessed a catastrophic case of information asymmetry with the OBSEs.

The financial institutions may have OBSEs up to 6–8% of the US GDP and that would be in a range of a trillion dollars. This is not a small sum (equivalent to the GDP of some of the G20 countries) to be left unregulated, unlike the normal accounts on a firm's balance sheet. The world has already witnessed the effects of equivalent economies, such as Italy and Spain, running amok.

Accounting standards allow provision for OBSEs in special cases. OBSEs were used extensively to fund long-term illiquid asset requirements by short-term maturity deposits. Since all the holding banks and their subsidiaries were involved in transactions using this method, it became a system-wide acceptable practice and, for reasons unknown, surprisingly it still missed the scanner of the regulators.

Before the crisis, there were two financial practices prevalent in the market which added fuel to the unknowns in the system and which still continue to prevail in this time of current crisis. One, OBSE vehicles were used to issue asset-backed commercial papers for securitizing home loans, credit card receivables and auto loans (may be sub-prime). This had an extended effect on information asymmetry since OBSEs, left unregulated, operated in the space of asymmetric information. The other practice of using the 'repo' market without strict due diligence led to poor collateral and high counterparty risks. Both these practices, being interconnected without a transparent clearing-house, still continue and are a tender spot in the financial system. Little is known about the safety of these transactions. Adding to the hazard is the size of this transaction, again which is equivalent to the GDP of some of the G20 nations. At the time of crisis in 2008, the repo market was valued at nearly $2.8 trillion. This was backed by 37% of the collateral from housing mortgages. So, when the market started to slip and confidence dipped; large non-banking institutions that were too-big-to-fail, took flight from investors (Tett, 2010). Although it was not the process and transactions in 'repo' that slipped in trust deficit but the dark shadow, in which the collaterals were sitting, could not prevent the exodus.

Even today, too much is being controlled by too few.

As mentioned, for now the 'repo' market is not a threat but it is a high potential for the next crisis. Moreover, the Dodd-Frank Act does not mention methods to correct the transparency in the 'repo' market.

Role of CDS: The protection that failed to protect

The volumes were perilous....

The volume of investment business had grown to astronomical levels by 2007. There were more than 20,000 companies in the US, providing debt capital worth nearly $50 trillion to more than 100 million investors. It is not an intelligent guess to estimate that a few billion shares are traded each day. Since large trading volumes were accompanied by risks due to the varied scope of business, market makers protect themselves against defaults using Credit Default Swaps (CDS). Credit default swaps grew from $1 trillion in 2004 to $45 trillion by 2007 since the growth in sub-prime lending was also supported by CDS (IMF, April, 2008).

The financial market was mature and the portfolio had a wide range of debt products which included both primary credit products and securitized credit products. The primary products included credit card debts and auto loans that were approximately $2 trillion. The securitized loans were more than $1 trillion. Consumer debt grew at a healthy rate of 5% up to 2006, but the risk of market decline was elevated when the top 10% of market makers held 90% of the market share. Comparing the size of risk in CDS, held by these market makers, it was nearly three and half times the GDP of the US (Turner, 2000).

The market saw its first decline by March 2008, when insurance companies experienced the decline in the market, which was an outcome of the primary market condition. The downgrades of the credit rating affected the market by a loss of value and the loss was due to the lowering of the expected rate of return from the high-grade product with an AAA, AA or A rating. During the same year, when the sub-prime mortgage market started to default, the burden of CDS protection fell on insurance companies, leading them to file for bankruptcy protection.

THE GLOBAL FINANCIAL CRISIS IS NOT FINANCIAL

As more investors bought CDS protection against defaults, the CDS market showed an interesting paradox. The investors would buy CDS protection and the spreads would increase if the probability of default increased and vice versa. This meant that the CDS market grew with the perceived weakness in the environment to $45 trillion in 2007 (International Swaps and Derivatives Association, 2010). Investors in the CDS market were benefiting from the higher risk and defaults in the market. If there was no actual default, at least speculation and sentiment supported the default.

The banks shouldered nearly half of the losses due to exposure in the sub-prime mortgage crisis because it had a negative impact on the valuation of the assets, which reflected both in the balance sheets of the banks and the investors. In turn, it lowered capitalization and profitability, consequently facing challenges of squeezed credit multipliers based on weak collaterals.

Result

Governments had to use their resources to support the private financial institutions. In turn, it did manage to lower the severity of the recession but now carried the burden of higher debts and perils of fiscal failure (IMF, Global Financial Stability Report, Oct, 2010). Further, effects of the debt burden and fiscal failure continued to be seen in the current economic failures in the UK, Iceland, Ireland, Greece, Spain and others. Also, recent turmoil in sovereign debt markets in Europe highlights the vulnerabilities of bank and sovereign balance sheets are shaken up by the current crisis.

Conclusion

As one is reading through this chapter, it would seem as if nothing worked in the financial system. But that is not the case. It is a case of dysfunctional entities in the system that was most crucial to the success of all other systems. The author has questioned the working of these gigantic institutions with an argument that responsibility increases with influence parted and in this instance, the influence was global, widespread, long lasting and eventually, disastrous. Therefore, there was every reason for these institutions and their regulatory authorities to tread carefully, bearing in mind the consequences of their actions, especially when they are called 'too-big-to-fail'.

The Current Crisis – seems everlasting

There is so much attributed to the current crisis that it will be very difficult to pinpoint one single factor. It only suggests that the financial community and players were allowing things to happen intentionally or unintentionally without perceiving the future consequences. It is about the nature of this gross blind spot that the regulators and other players were driving the financial system. This forms the basis of this book's main argument and the search for answers.

It is apparent that the regulators, the government and financial institutions were not able to foresee the degree of problem that was residing in the US housing market. Neither were they able to simulate the default in terms of its magnitude and rapidity nor were they aware that defaults would lead to a chain reaction into other sectors of the US and global economy. Since the inability is due to lack of information or poor quality of information, the author is very emphatic in claiming that the **"global financial crisis is not financial"**.

Where is the ray of hope?

Although, there is conflict between the monetarist and the information systems view, it is the author's conviction that both views are required to run the financial system. **The 'monetarist' view provides for doing the right things in the financial and the 'information' view provides for doing those things right.** The two views are complementary to each other and in the current crisis; we have seen an imbalance of them.

There are cases which are discussed later in the book using an analytical framework, where the financial system's information units such as credit rating, risk factor, disclosures, financial reports, OBSEs and others are considered part of a constructive financial system. The outcome of these informational units failed to reach the intended player in the right form and this is another important factor that has contributed to the current crisis.

This gives rise to a need to possess an information system, as a strategy, that could fulfill the shortfall in these informational units. Had these informational units functioned in compliance with their objectives, it would have restricted excessive risk taking in the financial system and sustained the system with information as a positive ingredient of entrepreneurship. Also, it would have enabled financial engineering as a productive tool in this new age financial system with prudent regulation, preventing a systemic failure.

When there are numerous factors to consider and one seems more important than the other, then the solution must be based on principles. Hence, it is a need to run the financial system based on principles such as optimization of human intervention and computational abilities without risking market stability. In the chapters to follow, the book will analyze in detail the shortcoming in the financial system and simultaneously, build principles to reconstruct the financial system architecture.

Chapter 2

Information Asymmetry

THE GLOBAL FINANCIAL CRISIS IS NOT FINANCIAL

What is information Asymmetry?

Information asymmetry is unequal distribution of relevant information between two transacting parties so that one party has an advantage over the other. There could be multiple reasons for information asymmetry, some natural and others, intentional. In any system, inequality is bound to happen because the level of expertise and resources differ between any two transacting parties.

The doctor knows more about medicine than the patient and the lawyer knows more about law than the client, yet they transact (Council of Economic Advisors, 2010). This means that in the case of a doctor, lawyer and others there exists a boundary condition where reduced information creates asymmetry and additional information can be considered redundant for that transaction.

The doctor is not required to discourse the entire medical science to the patient nor is the lawyer required to share all that is in the books of law.

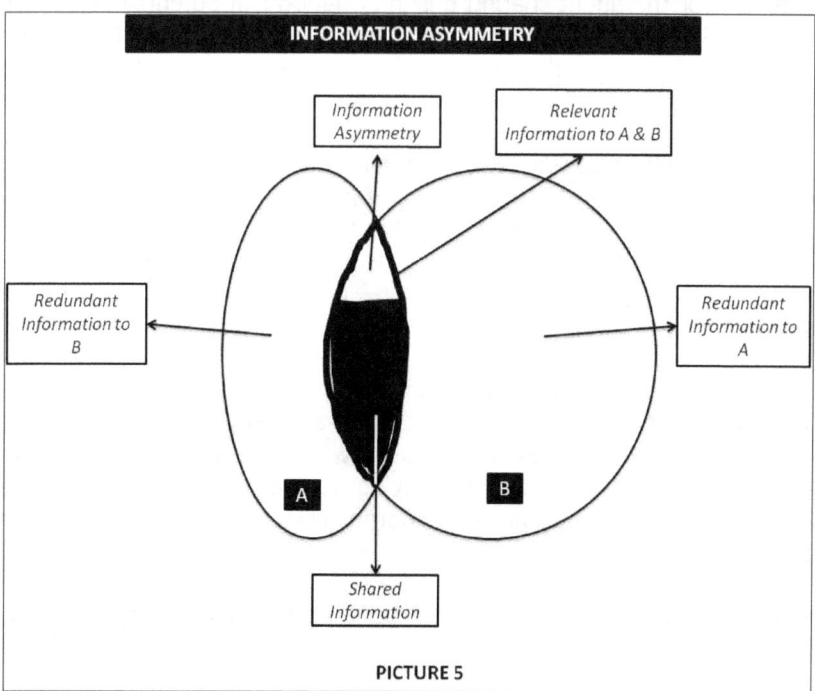

PICTURE 5

Information Asymmetry

In the same example, if the doctor knows about the side effects and does not share that information with the patient before administering the treatment, it amounts to information asymmetry. If the patient knew about the side effects, he might have chosen not to take the drug. The decision could have been either way.

If you were to buy a house and were negotiating with an estate agent, you would like to know all about the house: price, local tax, legal issues, financial liability on the title, history of repairs, general condition, neighbourhood, distance from major amenities, etc. On the other hand, the agent has an objective to sell the house because he will earn commission and that is his business. In the capacity of being an agent, he is also in possession of information that is both in favour of and against the property. As a case, the agent might know that even though the property is in good condition, the neighbourhood is not very peaceful or during the winter there are problems with the water clogging due to melting snow as the slope tilts into the house. Sharing this information may or may not influence the decision-making of the buyer but for the agent sharing this information is a potential risk to his deal. Hence, for the agent it is convenient and beneficial not to disclose any information about the property that is potentially negative and not legally binding.

In this example, also the status of information sharing between the agent and the buyer of the house is unequal. The buyer knows less about the property than the agent because the agent has not revealed relevant information. Between the two transacting parties there is information asymmetry because there is a difference between the 'known' and the 'actual'.

Since the buyer did not have symmetric information on the property, the deal seemed appropriate and the buyer may proceed to make a purchase. In future, when the property would create difficulty for the buyer, he would then realize the buying decision was not suitable and also that he could have made a different choice, had he known more about the property.

Does it also mean it could have been different if more information was shared?

So what is 'more'? 'More' is the additional relevant information that the agent possessed but chose not to disclose to the buyer, in deficit of which this buyer made an adverse selection. The information asymmetry led to the behaviour of adverse selection by the buyer and moral hazard by the seller. The result is a toxic transaction and a potentially toxic asset. Thus, the information asymmetry changed the transaction behaviour of both participants.

For a transaction, the distinguishing factor between 'knowing less' and 'information asymmetry' is the mandatory possession of relevant information.

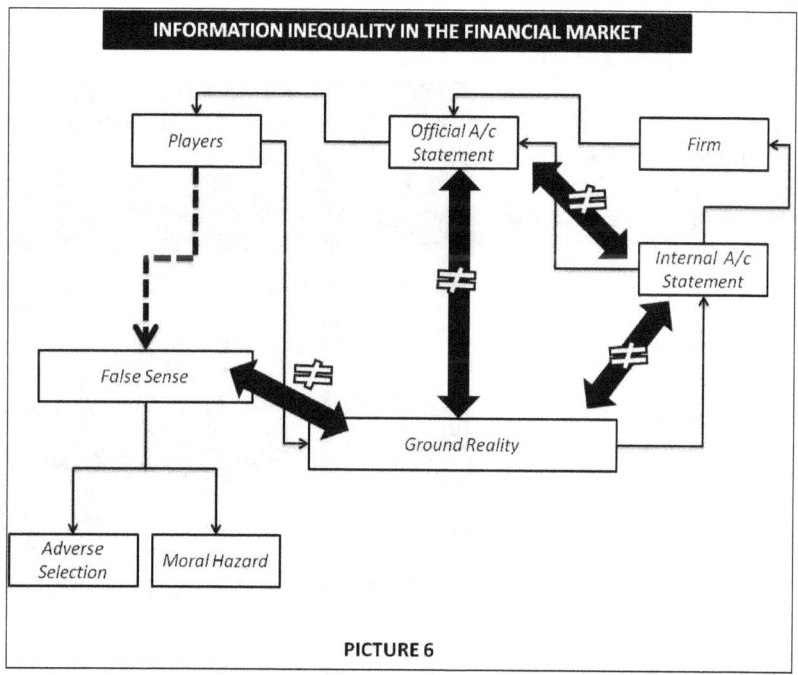

PICTURE 6

Financial Crisis: The role of 'mismatch'

In the build-up of the crisis, the information available to the players was different from the actual ground realities. Hence, the players were relying on a false sense of market conditions to make a business decision. Firms, before publishing an official and legally binding statement of account, already process an internal statement which in most cases captures a more realistic picture of ground realities. With

Information Asymmetry

this possibility, there exists inequality between the two information units, the official and internal statement of accounts.

When making an official account statement, firms disclose only that which is legally necessary leaving interpretation and analysis to the players, to assess the ground reality. If there is a difference between the reality and what the official statement of account suggests, then the players are directed to a false sense about the firm.

These multiplicities of inequalities in the system are sources of information asymmetry as the difference in information exists between the 'known', as held by firms, and the 'actual'. Consequently, a toxic transaction becomes highly probable.

According to the author, it is neither liquidity nor housing market slowdown that is responsible for the current financial crisis, but the crisis is a result of an imperfect interaction between players due to information asymmetry in the financial processes which was contagious during that period.

> There are known knowns; there are things we know that we know.
>
> There are known unknowns; that is to say there are things that, we now know we don't know.
>
> But there are also unknown unknowns; there are things we do not know, we don't know.
>
> ~ (Donald.H.Rumsfield 2002)

With reference to the current crisis, this book discusses how information asymmetry has become a by-product of processes such as accounting, auditing, regulation and seven other key processes in the financial system. It also analyses how they affected the behaviour of market players such as investors, regulators, financial intermediaries, legislators and central banks. In the financial system, if one of the counterparty is devoid of information relevant to the transaction, it is information asymmetry. This could mean that the true value of the product is not disclosed to the investors and the risk defined was understated or the regulators were not provided with access to relevant information.

If the environment prevails with information asymmetry, it will be riddled with scrupulous decision-making (adverse selection) and malicious influences (moral hazard), as seen in the previous example of buying a house. In a symmetric transaction, the buyer of the product needs to share in equality, the inherent risks, built into those products. As a check, if the seller is in possession of additional information, whose disclosure could have changed the buying decision, then information asymmetry prevails.

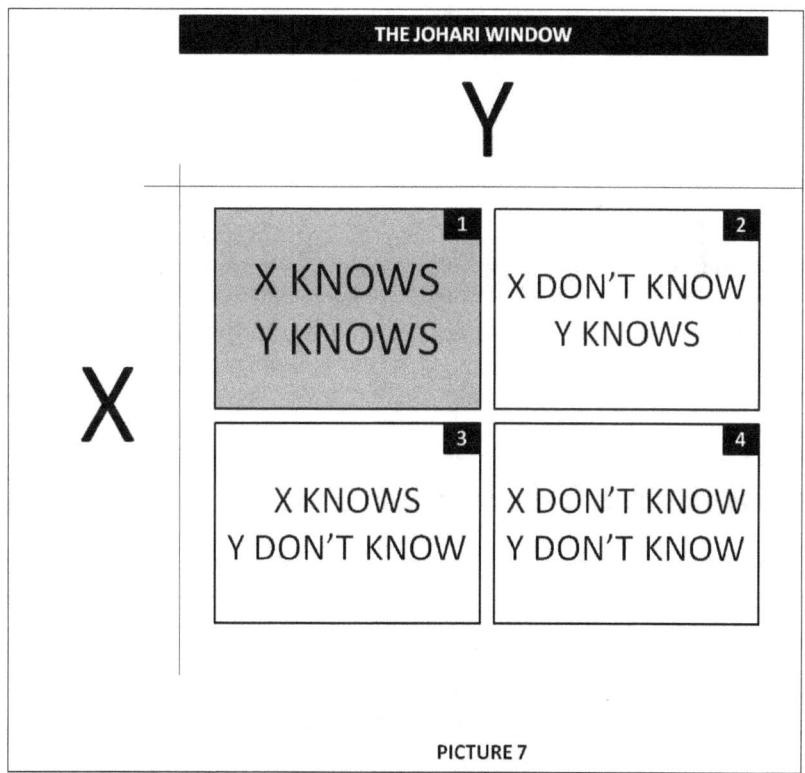

PICTURE 7

Information Asymmetry using the Johari Window

The Johari window has been instrumental in bringing to the forefront the idea of transparency between two transacting parties and the process of 'knowing'. It is a conceptual model in personal communication which is very apt to the concept of symmetric information. In this book, it is referred for studying information systems underlying the global financial systems.

There are four quadrants to the Johari window as shown in picture 7. In practical terms the best scenario for entities X and Y to interact and transact business will be in the first quadrant where both have equality of information. This quadrant is referred to as the quadrant of information symmetry and all other quadrants are in the space of information asymmetry because one party is in possession of more relevant information than the other.

The symmetric information sharing as in quadrant 1 not only has the consequence for a live transaction but also for a potential transaction as the investors must know the performance of the investment opportunity.

Since information sharing is the key to a transaction or a potential transaction, the challenge of information asymmetry will have to be universally addressed in all financial processes. For example, the credit rating of the product needs to equate with the true risk as seen on the ground. If for any reason the credit rating is unable to equate, then the transaction based on the rating will be toxic, as it happened in the current crisis.

It is a crisis of information

Information asymmetry in information exchange creates a potential risk in that transaction and the quantum of risk is consequential to the size of the information asymmetry. In a system where information asymmetry is inherently built in each financial transaction due to various reasons, as discussed in the later part of the book, a high volume of transactions in the global financial system only aggravates the cumulative risk in the entire system. It is depicted in the picture 8.

The world of financial markets has become more complex, highly interconnected, global and less predictable (Chapman, 2004). Important decisions in respective functions such as investment, regulation, market making, credit rating or analysis are dependent on extensive information exchange. Comparing the information required and available, there will always be a shortcoming as the information available to the market players may be limited due to one or multiple reasons as discussed in Chapter 1

THE GLOBAL FINANCIAL CRISIS IS NOT FINANCIAL

Handling financial products: Information Black Box

The information available to players was like a collage; patchy, incomplete and flowing from all directions, unable to provide correct information on the realities. In such an environment, it is natural that governments throw up surprise sovereign debt reports and financial institutions file for bankruptcy protection.

Here is a simplistic account of how information asymmetry accumulated risk with financial intermediaries dealing with the US housing mortgages. It involved various levels of management hierarchies along with the inability of the regulators to have an effective regulation.

While managers in the financial intermediaries, with inside information about flawed business practices in sub-prime mortgage dispensation, failed to persuade seniors to correct the processes, the senior executives failed to convey the dipping numbers to the shareholders. Instead, they managed to evade the critical eye of the shareholders by window dressing the accounts books and the financial results. The regulators were unable to detect the window dressing with alternative accounting techniques because the information shared by these firms had already met all legal requirements or sought additional information as regulation is different from investigation. The only choice that the players had in this high-speed financial system was to accept financial disclosures at face value. Also, these financial intermediaries had novice customers who were unable to understand critically the terms and conditions, and there were no alternatives in those voluminous contracts as a choice. Therefore, as a 'no choice option' the mortgage borrowers accepted the contracts even though they did not understand them.

| Information Asymmetry

Importantly, the excitement of owning a home had opiate and diverted from the scare of falling into the debt trap.

As seen, the financial system that is interconnected by an intricate network of information systems, the information asymmetry crept at key organization levels of the financial intermediaries. From a system's point of view, the holistic information became severely flawed and asymmetric when compared to the ground reality. It was so, because the information in the entire financial system was more asymmetric due to contagion (information effect) than the sum of its asymmetric parts.

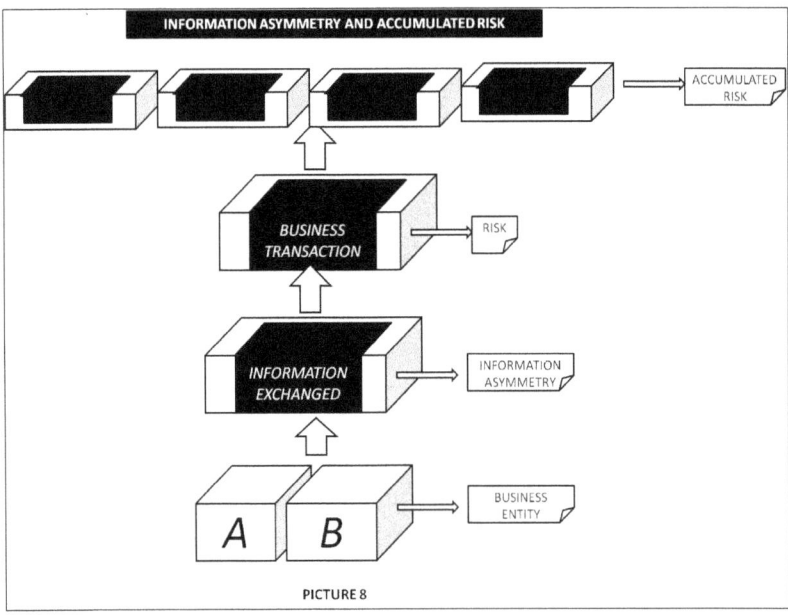

PICTURE 8

The nature of Over-The-Counter (OTC) transactions is another example of widespread information asymmetry prevailing in the financial market which is to the tune of a few hundred trillion dollars. OTC transactions contain serious information inequalities and disclosure discrepancies purposefully hidden from other market players. It is not because of any technical or legal reason but as part of the conventional business practice which thrives on perceived arbitrage. In fact, the OTC market can be considered as the most opaque side of the global financial system. If the volume of OTC business was miniscule and the inherent risk was only limited to a few individuals or small firms, it could have been ignored as an exception. Since its turnover is twenty to thirty times the global GDP, hence their potential risk to the entire global financial system cannot be ignored. As the financial system consists of systemic parts, they are always ready to flare up.

Mitigating information asymmetry with Quality of Information (QoI)

The nature of information in the global financial system is dynamic and emergent. Players are always on their toes in their desire for additional relevant information to be symmetric with their counterparties. The information is accumulated from multiple sources through statistics, cognition or other subjective mediums. Even though the information created is based on a mathematical model and cognition of the financial environment, ultimately the decision requires a high sense of judgement. Therefore, both qualitative and quantitative information exchange define the functioning of the financial system.

To overcome information asymmetry, **'What ought to be known must be known'**.

Among different players in the financial system, information is sought, created, viewed, verified, analyzed and distributed to suit different business objectives. One guiding principle common to the entire business objective is the nature of information processing which determines the efficiency and effectiveness of the decision taken. Blackout or partial eclipse at any one part of the information supply chain would lead to a conceptual failure of the information system. In any healthy information system, the primary objective is not only to continuously carry the information between destinations such as two transacting parties like potential investor or governing authorities, but also to strive continuously to achieve information symmetric between the counterparties. All players in the financial system need to 'symmetrically know' to enable better decision-making in pursuit of profits. For a financial system with an underlying healthy information system, even though the returns may not be glorious, information asymmetry is a no go. It is worthwhile to disclose poor financial results now and make business corrections than to file for bankruptcy in future.

According to Schwakopf (1999), the failure in the information system leads to adverse selection and moral hazard which may contribute to the market failure, if left unchecked. The failure in providing information

Information Asymmetry

to investors about investments and solvency also leads to inefficiency in the business. Summer (2003) indicates that the theory of banking regulation and systemic risk addresses information asymmetry for negative externalities. Hence, he had argued that there is a strong dependency of information symmetry on the successful running of the financial market.

The key to mitigating the current financial crisis lies in elaborate and symmetric disclosures in the balance sheets, as it forms the nerve centre of all financial information. Today, if one was to undertake a suitable analysis of preventive systemic liquidity risk, the market data is scarcely available. It is available within the circle of a few participants who share the information with each other to a degree that is just appropriate to their business (IMF, Global Financial Stability Report, October 2010). This varied opaqueness and asymmetric information structure is not conducive to the long term and healthy survival of any system.

In the reconstruction of the broken financial system, one of the approaches to help mitigate the sovereign risk and stabilize funding market by the national and international organizations, is to get in-depth information on their balance sheets. At a given time it is found that the bank balance sheets were not revealing enough information to plug the upcoming crisis and therefore to mitigate the impeding risk, more quality information was required (IMF, Global Financial Stability Report, October 2010).

This suggests that the crux of the solution to the current crisis is in mitigating information asymmetry. This can be addressed by ensuring high Quality of Information (QoI) in the financial system. With information as raw material in the assembly line of financial decision-making, determining the QoI becomes the critical success factor for the financial system.

Further, it is up to the QoI which determines the overall health of transactions, decisions and overall, the financial system. Extrapolating the objective of QoI, it is vital to any functioning system such as economic, judicial, political, and democratic among others.

The subject of QoI has somehow been overlooked in the speed and excitement of developing information technology. ***It is a mistake made by experts in the field of information technology when***

THE GLOBAL FINANCIAL CRISIS IS NOT FINANCIAL

they interchangeably use quality of data with quality of information. There have been tremendous improvements in the science of achieving quality of data but equal emphasis is required to achieve high Quality of Information.

As the book progresses, the author will identify the sources of information asymmetry in various financial processes and practices to construct the concept of QoI.

Lessons for non-financial sectors

The non-financial business sector also faces the same issues as the financial sector when it comes to symmetric information systems. Though it is simpler in the case of the non-financial sector because the core function is not based on arbitrage and speculation, yet information asymmetry may well get built into the system for the same reasons as found in the financial system. Mostly, the risk of the asymmetric information system points towards their internal information systems and its management, as the information landscape is bulkier than a financial firm. This means that for the same turnover, a non-financial firm has to create, corroborate and communicate more information when compared to a financial firm; hence there is more risk of incorporating information asymmetry into the system. This book will continue to touch upon the issues of information asymmetry in the non-financial sector as learnt from the mistakes of the global financial system.

Chapter 3

Quality of Information (QoI)

THE GLOBAL FINANCIAL CRISIS IS NOT FINANCIAL

Quality of Information as a remedy for information asymmetry

Information moves in the system providing the necessary ingredients to carry out the core activities intended by that system. All systems are an integration of multiple parts, each part having a specific function to perform, and need to be in **informational harmony** with each other. For a system as complex as the financial system, all working parts are primarily dependent on the availability of information as its raw material. It is common sense to understand the crucial nature of information feeding the financial system which survives solely on informed decision-making. Experts have also reiterated that a perfect competitive market needs symmetric, emergent and high quality information (Pelaez, 2009).

The importance of information is nothing new that is being discovered. For ages, the world's important religions have spoken immensely about the prime importance of information quality such as "knowledge is power" or "improper knowledge is the root of all problems". The author is only contextualizing this ancient understanding of 'knowledge' with the new age working of financial systems and their role in the making of crises. The book analyzes the relevance of this high quality of information to the information system whose failure led to the current financial turmoil.

Previous chapter of the book discussed various ways in which information asymmetry can creep into the system, leading to adverse selection and moral hazard. When the financial system is riddled with information asymmetry to an extent that the global financial system and other systemic systems are failing, it is important to mitigate information asymmetry with a universal and corrective principle, the principle being 'Quality of Information (QoI)'.

Prior to writing this book, many industry experts had defined 'Quality of Information' or 'Information Quality' using definitions of quality as in product quality. The author agrees with their approach since information is similar to a product. Interestingly, none of the experts have correlated information symmetry as a function of QoI. When this book discusses QoI, it is with the intention of correcting and preventing information asymmetry in the financial system. The variations of information asymmetry have already been discussed in Chapter 1; section 'Information Black Box'.

What is Quality of Information (QoI)?

In simplistic terms Quality of Information (QoI) means the fitness of information for market players such as investors, creditors, regulators, financial institutions and governments. The definition is inspired by Shiba's concept of levels of quality (Shiba & Walden, 2001). In terms of fitness the information flowing in the system has to meet:

Fitness to requirement

- Correct
- Compliant to standards
- Comprehensive
- Timely
- Symmetric

Fitness to use

- Simple and user-friendly
- Easy access
- Multiple outlooks
- Transparent
- Analytical flexibility

Fitness to cost

- Inexpensive above (say) 5th percentile of income group

Fitness to additional requirement

- Exploratory options

This is not the complete and final list defining Quality of Information. It is an ongoing process to reach a desired state where the system has perfect information symmetry with infinitesimal time lag and that is the highest QoI.

There are large IT systems installed across firms to record and collate data. Then there is analytics software that is used to create simulation of the business environment which can help management in decision-making and watchdog authorities to correct the glitches in the system. So there is a base system to record business transactions that is current in time, upon which sits the analytics, to create 'may be' scenarios in order to prepare for future situations.

THE GLOBAL FINANCIAL CRISIS IS NOT FINANCIAL

It is not a necessity that firms, who have an installed base of sophisticated information technology will get high-quality information about their business environment. The quality of information represented by an Excel sheet can be better than those churned out by the most sophisticated databases. The author has seen organizations drawing financial reports from the enterprise database and then making the final analysis on an Excel sheet. There is nothing wrong with the practice. However, it raises a serious question of the inability of the most sophisticated IT systems to deliver the last mile information with the highest quality to provide the most crucial foresight into key business decisions.

There is information coming from different directions in the financial environment, not only from rumours but also from authentic sources such as investigative authorities or research- based media. In September 2004, the FBI raised the alarm on the large-scale fraud in the mortgage business and indicated that it could be on the scale of the S&L crisis. Then in 2005, the well-known magazine 'The Economist' indicated the end of the housing boom which could affect the world economy.

Are these information sets, considered just another informational noise in the system or the information not considered of good enough quality that can attract response from the custodians of the system?

These are also pieces of quality information that need to be considered with foresight. The curious thing about the current crisis much before 2008 (the actual crisis was declared with the collapse of Bear Stearns in 2008) was the inability of any authority to recognize this information and respond with a suitable reaction.

If there is a measure of QoI, it has to be benchmarked with the response from the intended recipient. With hindsight, since there was no visible response from the recipients such as regulators, central banks and legislators, it can be concluded that information flowing in the financial system was missing the quality mark. No driver would continue driving knowing the map was indicating a wrong direction. Either the information in the system was misleading or the players were deliberate. Hence the quality of information (QoI) needs to include a parameter to gauge and measure the timeliness of response from the recipient as a function of preventing any kind of loss, minimal or substantial.

| Quality of Information (QoI)

Conceptually, a stable and running system requires a high QoI which can be achieved by following the 'information execution model' as argued in this book. The author is not only suggesting the availability of high-quality information to the top and strategic layer of management, but also to all those who are remotely affected by the system. As QoI, it will define the right players in the system.

Does high - quality information mean more information or correct data? The answer is 'no'. The book did answer this question in the previous chapter when the author discussed the topic of 'relevant and redundant' information. Ironically, terabytes of data are created every day by firms in pursuit of quality decisions, yet in terms of getting the high quality of information to prevent insolvency, the 'Right Information' is still not there.

In terms of QoI, it is the 'Right Information' that is important rather than the quantity of data. For a system with multiple players at multiple levels of organization with numerous objectives, the information requires customization. The slice and dice of information, from being collective information in the environment, to being focused information for the complex set of users, is a necessity if the system has to sustain the objectivity of providing the right information for the right player.

> "The standards themselves must be of high quality. By that I mean useful to investors in a way that provides transparency, consistency and comparability in the way companies report in a global capital market. It is the CFO who ensures the quality of the financial information provided to investors -- information that is high quality because it is accurate, and provides a complete and balanced picture to the investors (Turner, 2000)."

What will QoI achieve?

As an outcome, high-quality information (QoI) in the financial system will create transparency which in turn will create trust and righteous confidence with the players to participate as entrepreneurs. This leads back to our discussion about the risk taking by the players and the topic of moral hazard. A system with high-quality information, symmetric to participating players, will bring with it a natural check and balance to curb moral hazard and excessive risk taking.

THE GLOBAL FINANCIAL CRISIS IS NOT FINANCIAL

In the same stretch of extended reasoning, it is simple to understand that the **Quality of Information (QoI)** will bring parity of information to the financial system. All players will possess information that is most suited to a transaction and one particular transacting party will not be at an advantage over the other. The outcome of the business may vary because that is dependent on the business motive but QoI will ensure that decision-making is based on all the necessary information.

High QoI can be achieved if and only if the financial system achieves quality at each stage of its information life cycle. In this book, quality of information is introduced as an overarching outcome of all the stages of the information execution life cycle. The stages of life cycle, as defined in the **Information Life Cycle,** are

- **Information Creation,**
- **Information Corroboration and**
- **Information Communication.**

Each stage of the life cycle is to be enabled by **Information Enablers** who facilitate symmetric information created, corroborated and communicated.

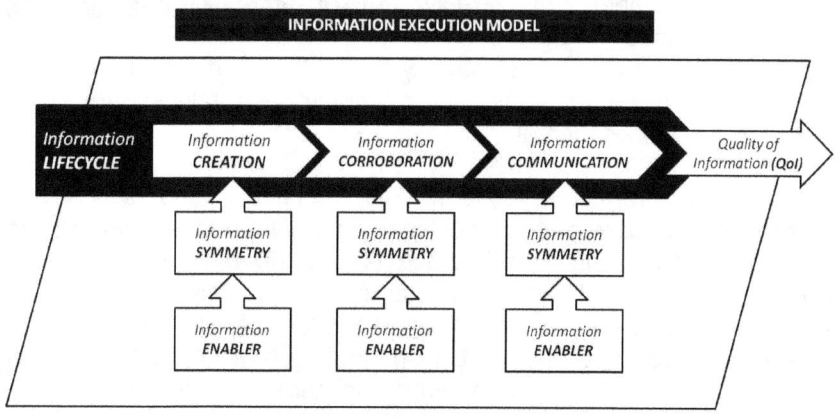

PICTURE 9

The enablers have their own operating method and together multiple enablers make it possible that information symmetry is maintained in each stage of the life cycle. The enablers act independently of each

Quality of Information (QoI)

stage of the life cycle with a common objective of attaining information symmetry. Together the interplay of information creation, corroboration, communication and enablers form the **Information Execution Model**.

What is the failure of information system?

The primary objective of the information system underlying the financial system is to execute the information life cycle to achieve QoI. For any information system, failure is when one or more stages of the life cycle operate with asymmetric information. It will break the information life cycle and therefore the outcome will be information that is not suitable for the right decision-making. Players in the financial market will be continuously operating with a false sense of reality, making decisions that will end up being toxic transactions. An asymmetric information life cycle will fail the underlying information system and the financial system will struggle to stay afloat. It is also important to differentiate between information symmetry in the transaction and the content. In a transaction, two transacting parties have to be in sync with the information available to both of them. In content symmetry, the records need to reflect with accuracy the status of the reality. Content asymmetry may lead to transaction asymmetry and influence the chain of financial activities thereon.

> Within 30 years, we will have the means to create superhuman intelligence. Shortly after, the human era will be ended – Vernor Vinge
> (The coming technological singularity)

In a failed information system, the regulatory and supervisory authorities will observe redundant information which in turn will attract irrelevant actions. Since each stage of the information life cycle is linearly consequential, information asymmetry in any corner of the stages will affect the entire execution model and ultimately QoI. In perspective, the successful global financial system is a function of a successful information system, which in turn is a function of the successful execution of an information life cycle. Many authors have mentioned informational efficiency like the Hurst Exponent, which is one aspect of QoI. With QoI, both, effectiveness and efficiency of information are being addressed.

Symmetric Information Execution Model – Analytical Framework

The author follows an analytical framework using the Information Execution Model, as linearly connected stages in the information life cycle (creation, corroboration and communication). For each stage the model dives deep into the processes and practices of the financial system such as accounting, credit rating, auditing and others. The proposed analytical framework then analyzes the enablers to this information life cycle.

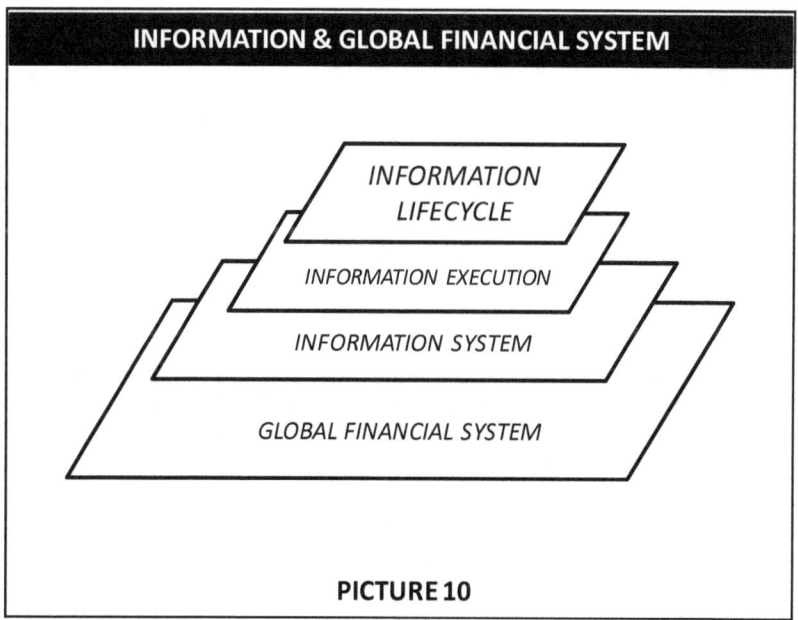

PICTURE 10

Irrespective of any kind of system – financial, judicial, democratic, business and others – the information execution framework is a generic model for the information system. In this case, readers will find how the financial system failed because of its failed information execution model.

The financial system has advance users of both mathematical methods and technology to create information who use human judgement to make decisions. The information execution model needs to strike a balance in the mix of both scientific method and human judgement. Lately, the financial system has become technology centric and the

Quality of Information (QoI)

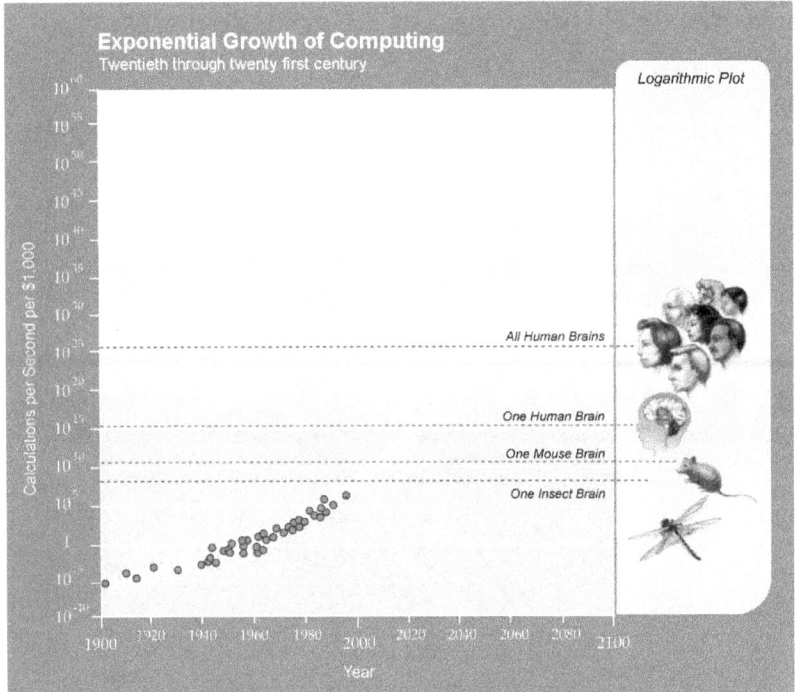

author argues against this trend. Technology is only an enhancement to the computational abilities of humans and works with a given set of rules. This means that the results from the technological tools are not enough for sound decision-making equivalent to human judgement. It is possible that in the future (The Singularity is Near) more and more human judgement may be overtaken by technology but for now, the human judgement is required which still reins supreme.

Source: The Singularity is Near, Time Magazine, February 2011

3 Cs of the Information Life Cycle
Information Life Cycle in the Financial System

For this book the following are the components of the financial system that are being analyzed. This financial crisis is a lethal failure of these elements, not necessarily in a sequence.

	Information Life cycle		
Components	**Information Creation**	**Information Corroboration**	**Information Communication**
	Accounting	BASEL Framework	Reporting
	Financial Modelling	Regulation	Interconnectedness
	Credit Rating	Audit	Disclosure
	Valuation	Moral Hazard	

Creation

The information creation phase consists of analyzing a fundamental function where the financial information originates. There are many tools, statistical and mathematical methods used to create financial information and the mother of all these methods is accounting. As it is known, all accounting practices followed by firms, governments and individuals are based on the accounting standards, majority of them are universal, while others follow country or regional standards. Accounting creates primary financial information, and all other sources of financial information are further developed over this primary information. Annual reports containing the balance sheet, income statement and disclosures are official documents of the firm and are the starting point for all financial decision-making. Credit rating, financial modelling and valuations are derived information from the account statement. Hence, accounting and its standards are mandatory for achieving information symmetry in the system and hence high QoI.

It is very important that these documents are made with high QoI and all the key processes that go into making them are rigorously designed to suit information symmetry. We will see in detail, the practice of accounting and understand how it resulted in creating information asymmetry in the financial system.

For any sailor on the high seas to survive, he must know the direction of the sails. The right information about his sails sets the ship in the

Quality of Information (QoI)

right direction. Similarly, the creation of the right information is a key to the navigation of the financial system and therefore the focus of doing business is also to create and record the right information. In the financial system, where volumes of information are created, managing the sources of information is of utmost importance. Reliability is a characteristic of symmetric information that includes accuracy, correctness and timeliness. To achieve a reliable source of information, the underlying process and methodology followed by the source are crucial and this points to the standards that govern the practices of creating the information in the system.

Even though some sources of information are regulated and are required to meet the statutory requirements, they are mostly macro in nature. The constituents of information at micro level are not regulated, and this makes them potential sources of information asymmetry.

While the financial institutions and banks are responsible for the accurate consolidation of the micro information of the housing mortgage market, there were disruptions in the information supply chain. As it happened in the case of the US housing market, where the mortgage collection was done by third-party agencies, the information on a successful collection rate took time to reflect in the financial reports of the financial intermediaries and financial institutions. Overall, this multi-tier and sluggish operating structure of capturing the information from the ground failed in timeliness of the information creation at the macro-financial system level. After realizing the sluggishness in reconciling this micro information, there were strategic acquisitions of these agencies as consolidations by the US banks but the move was too late; mortgage default as a crisis had already crept into the system due to asymmetry between the ground reality and the financial statements. The conclusion reached is that sources of information origination are as important as the tools for information creation.

In the case of the present financial system, the accounting standards are assumed to produce reliable financial information. With this assumption the feedback from auditors and regulators to the accounting standards bodies was weak. It resulted in accounting practices that were misused by the financial firms to cook their accounts books. For the standards-making bodies this channel was an important contributor to the reliability of the financial information created in the system, which ultimately failed.

THE GLOBAL FINANCIAL CRISIS IS <u>NOT</u> FINANCIAL

The information creation phase is the starting point for all the ills in the system, should it go wrong. If the information created is asymmetric, all the information used in the system for subsequent purposes will be asymmetric, not only for any financial transaction but also as a misleading influence on the financial decision-making.

*C*orroboration

Information Corroboration is a process for review and validation of information to ensure that the transaction occurs within stipulated guidelines. Even though the guidelines are established, in practice, all the guidelines are not followed either intentionally or unintentionally; it is no wonder that firms have made provisions for fines and penalties in their budgets. In order to keep an eye on non-compliance there are functions such as audits and regulations which keep tabs on the financial activities. Fundamentally, a strict and smart mechanism of checks and balances is important for the system to comply and ensure that the credibility of the system is maintained not only as a function but also in spirit. There are multiple methods and approaches to corroborate the information in the system including regulations, audits and checks on moral hazard.

There have been debates about regulations and the extent to which regulation needs to prevail into the day-to-day functioning of the system. To assess the objectives of the regulators the following questions need to be asked. Should regulation be for the purpose of guidance only? Should the regulators intervene if there is a fundamental deviation from standards and leave the review of business transactions to the process of audit, or should the regulation be involved in correcting the nature of financial business?

In the US even those practitioners in favour of a deregulated market should have considered those large-scale crises such as the S&L crisis and the P&G derivative scandal, though the scale was not global at the time before propagating deregulation. But it is only after going through the scale of the current crisis, which is both macro and micro in nature, that market players are talking in favour of prudent regulation, realizing that failure of regulation was one of the reasons for the current crisis. With these multiple and diverse objectives set for the regulators, both by statute and natural forces of the market, the process of corroboration is the key to the success of the financial system and hence the question; who regulates the regulators?

| Quality of Information (QoI)

Audits are a method of validating the procedure followed and are usually able to trap any financial wrongdoing. The question to be answered here is about the correctness of the financial procedure and standards that are being audited. If the standards laid for the procedures themselves are faulty, then audits will continue to certify those faulty procedures. It is because the process of audit is more about the verification of compliance rather than verification of these procedures. Ideally, the audit findings need to feedback to the accounting standard agencies, but that part of the circuit is rather loose-ended, as accounting standards are not laid down as national legislations.

The corroboration process is complicated. If the entire financial system depends on audits for primary corroboration, audit then becomes a single point of failure for the system. There is no doubt that the audit for compliance is important in order to hold the relevance of accounting standards but the question is; who audits the auditors?

The primary ingredient in the process of corroboration, regulation and audit, is based on QoI. Whenever experts talk about the success of regulation and audit, they invariably assume that the information shared by the firms to the regulators and auditors is symmetric and high QoI. Therefore it is important that this assumption is sustained throughout the process of corroboration and there exists a process to ensure information symmetry in the financial system. As mentioned previously, if regulation, audit, stress tests and other methods of corroboration were to run successfully, it has to be on a robust platform of sustained information symmetry.

How else can the information created in the system be corroborated? House committees, stress tests, auditors, regulators, legislators and central banks are all part of the same system, varying only in the scope and depth into which they can dive. That questions the reliability of the process of corroboration that is based on the same recycled set of information. It is an extensive debate: whether to assign the process of corroboration to an agency outside the financial system and risk both efficiency and effectiveness, or leave the system to operate with flaws in plain sight?

Also, somewhere the process of corroboration has to avoid being an investigator.

THE GLOBAL FINANCIAL CRISIS IS <u>NOT</u> FINANCIAL

Even though the system may facilitate having perfect information symmetry between the transacting parties, it could be faulty information on which basis the business is transacting, and history (in the making) shows that repercussion of faulty information can be serious.

Here is one piece of latest history. Assuming it was unintentional; subsequently the Greek government were responsible for the Eurozone crisis because official accounts relating to Greek public debt were incorrect. The consequence of uncorroborated information in the Eurozone is now threatening the existence of many other countries in the Eurozone. Since, the underlying Euro, as a unique international currency, is under severe strain and threat. This situation could have been avoided if information in the Greek financial system and the Euro financial system was effectively and efficiently corroborated as a process and practice.

While the process is an established method of doing things, the practice makes it consistent and compliant. In this book, the author is questioning the flaws in both the process and practice of corroboration as followed in the global financial system.

Extending the concept of corroboration, both as a process and a practice, corroboration is an entry criterion for making information symmetry work in a system. As seen by the Greek debt crisis, since the information was incorrect, the European Central bank account statement reflected differently from what was a reality. Information asymmetry comes into play if the information is not verified, tallied and cross-checked with alternative methods and sources. The concept of corroboration, therefore, is necessary to bring parity to the content which enhances the symmetry between the records (books) and the ground reality.

A successful information system has to undergo a rigorous process of corroboration to prevent information asymmetry without which asymmetry will spread unabated to other systemic nodes. The cascade becomes so subtle and natural that it may appear to be logically correct but in fact may be a misrepresentation of the reality. As an example, readers might like to refer to the UK's Payment Protection Insurance (PPI) case, where PPI was being wrongly sold to millions of customers (Financial Ombudsman Services, May 2010). It was a practice followed for years, the process never being corroborated till the time it was taken up as a complaint and investigated. If the process and practice of corroboration was in place, millions of UK customers would have been saved from financial loss and the banks would have been saved from financial distress due to counterclaims and compensation.

Corroboration is an important second step in the logical sequence of the information execution chain and therefore finds a key place in the Information Execution Model. The system might create asymmetric information for various reasons, but the ***process of corroboration has the ability to reset the contents to reality.***

Communication

The third stage in the Information Execution Model is Information Communication, whose purpose is to ensure that the right information reaches the right destination. Information symmetry also means that the right people in the transaction hold the information and therefore the channel of communication needs to originate and terminate at the right places. In the financial system, there are many mechanisms such as Annual Reports, Balance Sheets, Disclosures, Disclaimers & Warnings and others, which ensure that the information is communicated and the correctness of the information is assured. Most of the effort by the firm is focused towards the timeliness and content while the responsibility of distribution is not clearly fixed. If the news is positive, the firms would like to make the information louder and wider so as to expand on their business interests. If the news is negative, the firms are reluctant, obviously, to avoid a slide in reputation. So there is an unequal treatment of information which in true sense is reality. This leads to asymmetry, as more information is known about one kind of reality and less about the other.

The mode of information communication in the financial system is more of a 'broadcast' than an actual delivery. In a broadcast, it is voluntary to the receiver to take it or leave it and has no status in case the receivers 'miss it'. In case of delivery, the recipients are in confirmation of receiving the information and that reduces the incidence of asymmetry. A signed contract is a typical example of 'information delivery'.

The communication channels in the financial system are well defined but are restricted to only a few times a year. The statement of accounts is made available to all players only four times a year. All other information regarding the finance of the firm is communicated as news or as a declaration to regulatory authorities such as the SEC. There are arguments about the frequency of the communication in subsequent sections of the book.

Prima facie there is a gap in the execution of information, and the objective is to seek a solution such as having an information-distributing authority like the regulators and auditors play in their respective scope of work. For information sharing, someone in the system needs to ensure that information distributed to the players is symmetrical and that no player has an undue advantage.

As in previous sections, the author closes the introduction to this stage of information execution with another question: **who owns the financial information distribution?**

Information Enablers

Components	Enabler
	Information Views
	Real Time
	Systemic
	Foresight

The enablers accelerate the information execution cycle and act as a catalyst to the participant's activities. Based on these enablers, the players can develop a reactive, proactive and analytical perception of the market information. There are multiple enablers, and while the list is not comprehensive only the important ones are discussed. The enablers are technology centric, as the information needs to be provisioned to the users in a particular way.

The enablers like real-time access to the information, addresses the challenge of Quality of Information (QoI) with respect to information's fitness to use. The consumers of information will not be left without information because there is a time lag between origination and consumption. The real-time enablers in the system would enhance the momentous availability of information for decision-making. In a global financial system, events across one continent can influence decision-making in another. This is to highlight the systemic nature of the financial system. Along with exceptional events, even activities classified as business-as-usual, including declarations, quarterly results and new business orders, when made in real time, enhance the information symmetry. A lot is being done today at macro level due to the advent of the Internet and World Wide Web, but more needs to be done at micro information level.

Quality of Information (QoI)

A suitable view to the information is an enabler to information symmetry. In a nutshell, the author has introduced three views as enablers. The view to the current information is 'real-time' view, the view to future anticipations is 'foresight' and the view to comprehensive information is 'systemic' view. They are discussed in detail in subsequent chapters of the book.

These views by themselves do not guarantee a successful and profitable business because it depends on many other factors, but certainly these views do prevent the business running aground.

Information Outcome

	Outcome
Components	**Quality of Information (QoI)**
	Unification
	Transparency
	Trust

The outcome of the information execution model is to meet the sole objective of achieving high QoI. As a consequence of this analysis, the list of these outcomes is a natural path and a checklist to a remedial course of action to mitigate the current financial crisis. The author argues that not only can the list of these outcomes be a checklist of high QoI, specifically to the financial system, but also generic to any other system.

The list of these outcomes is based on the research of the current financial crisis and other man-made disasters where the system has repeatedly failed to meet these outcomes. Rather, it would be appropriate to say that the inability to meet these outcomes led to system failure. Of course, this list is not claimed to be complete and final; it is rather an emergent list. But for the current financial system these are the mandatory checks to the outcome of the information system. It needs to be measured and quantified in order to mitigate the crisis and prevent another one in the future.

These are arguments in favour of running the financial system on information based on the execution model. There could also be arguments against this model which may suggest a risk in the pursuit of these end results on the grounds of gigantic effort in governance. Those are recognized risks categorized more as inconvenience and they should not hamper the construction of high QoI in the financial system.

THE GLOBAL FINANCIAL CRISIS IS NOT FINANCIAL

In the chapters to follow, each of the components of the information life cycle is discussed separately. They are analyzed for reasons of information asymmetry in the financial system which led to blind spots and poor QoI. Not one authority or agency is responsible for the containing asymmetry. *In a holistic picture, this financial crisis can be seen as an assortment of processes and practices with information asymmetry as its intrinsic characteristics.*

Chapter 4
Information Creation (1st C)

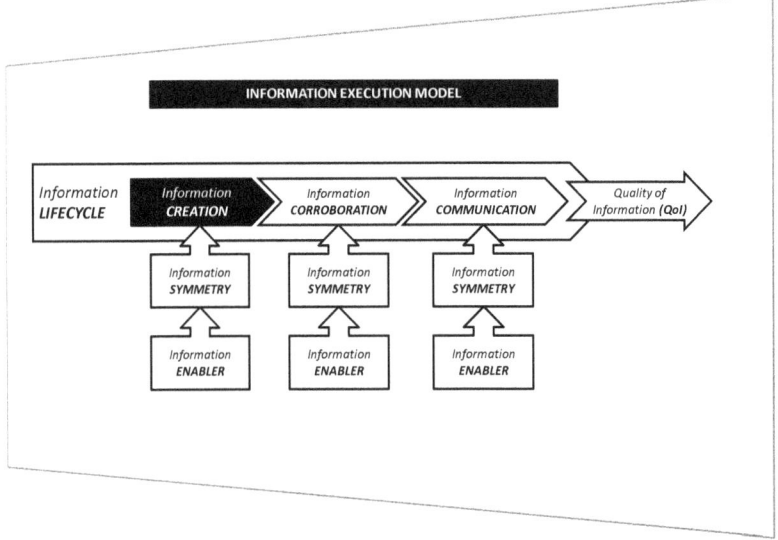

THE GLOBAL FINANCIAL CRISIS IS NOT FINANCIAL

Accounting: Far from true value

As a principle, the purpose of accounting is to create records of business transactions and generate information for sound decision-making by investors, creditors, regulators and tax authorities. The main financial information comes from reports, such as the annual report containing balance sheet, income statement and directors' notes, which reflect the firm's performance on a periodic basis. Many countries follow their domestic accounting standards, but at the time of increased globalization and cross-border capital allocation, it is important that investors and managers have a financial view that provides unbiased information to players across the borders. In doing, so the current structure of the accounting standards has a domestic tier and an international tier which is in compliance with the International Accounting Standards (IAS). There are more than 100 countries that follow the IAS and more are required to do so in future, including the US. Currently, the US follow the Generally Accepted Accounting Principles (GAAP) and intend to converge with the IAS by 2015 (Lindberg and Seifert, 2010).

There have been debates about the standardization of accounting standards across the board and different metrics have been created to evaluate their respective benefits. From an information content creation viewpoint, the author has questions regarding the current accounting standards and practices.

The author's view is that standardization of accounting standards would restrict taking advantage of one standard over the other, as it would provide an added perspective. So it is important to open up all the standards for accounting as alternatives. While reporting earnings, with reference to all the standards, investors will get a second or multiple perspectives and the financial system will reduce the risk of using wrong information. The economic environment, which is derived from financial statements, will be more comprehensive with varied views and perspectives on the financial earnings from a firm.

Enhancing the quality of accounting, hence the quality of information created, is a pursuit that is emergent and everlasting, so there is no harm in making a secure experimentation of creating more and more information that is fundamental to the system.

Information Creation (1st C)

There are wide-ranging conceptual differences between the International Financial Reporting Standards (IFRS) and US GAAP, and those differences are making an impact on the global financial system in multiple ways. On one side, there are more than 100 countries that follow IFRS guidelines and the number of countries is continually increasing. This is going to be nearly 150 countries by 2013. On the

Issue	US GAAP	IFRS
FRAMEWORK LEVEL DIFFERENCE		
Conceptual Framework	More Rule Based	More Principle-Based
Industry-Specific Guidance	Extensive Guidance for certain industries	Little industry-specific guidance
Judgements and Interpretation	Requires less judgement as extensive guidance (Bright Line rules exist)	General guidance requires more judgement
Disclosure	Requires some disclosures, but they are not extensive	Disclosure requirements are extensive
Accrual accounting approach	Income statement is the focus through matching principle	Balance sheet is the focus through fair value measurement
ACCOUNTING LEVEL DIFFERENCE		
Depreciation	One depreciation rate is used for a single asset	Components of single asset can be depreciated at different rates
Long-Lived Asset Valuation	Long-lived assets are recorded at cost	Long-lived assets are recorded at choice of either cost or fair market value
Contingent Liability	Recognized when probable (greater than 70% to 80% chance) if can be reasonably estimated	Recognized when 'more likely' than not, so greater than (50%) chance
Impairment of Assets	Assets written down when the current value exceeds undiscounted cash flows associated with the assets. No reversal of write-downs allowed.	Impairment recorded when the current value exceeds the fair value of the assets. Impairment charges can be recovered, up to the original price of the asset.
Leases	Four specific conditions to consider capitalization	Lease is capitalized if 'substantially all' of the major aspects of the lease have been transferred to the lessee.
Research and Development Cost	Expensed as incurred	Allows capitalization of R&D costs under certain conditions.

Source: Lindberg and Seifert, 2010

other side, the US (where the financial centre of gravity lies) is nowhere close to adopting IFRS. As reported in the media, the convergence of standards is expected to be in 2015, if the Securities and Exchange Commission (SEC) pulls it through. That makes a polarized world of accounting and reporting standards. The complexity is further enhanced when global firms are reporting across these accounting poles, making it necessary for an investor to be an expert at reading between the lines before making a sound and informed financial decision.

The two polarized accounting systems (US GAAP and IFRS) not only are discrete by volume of transactions and ability to influence global economies but also vary in the broad framework and principles of accounting treatment. Refer to the summarized table to compare the two polarized accounting systems.

GAAP requirements are generic: choice is with the managers

Which one is the better of the two, makes the debate interesting. There will be no answer to that, so why not have both. With these many variations in the two systems of accounting, it will be inappropriate for the two to converge and arrive at a single accounting standard. Instead, it will be wiser to harness the perspectives provided by these two systems for a wider and in-depth financial outlook. To repeat the argument previously made, both methods need to coexist in the system, but conditional to being done simultaneously, so that no information asymmetry is created by the use of one method while avoiding the other.

The firms in question, who are considered responsible for the financial crisis, had been consistently reporting the financial results and there was no major concern till 'that day'. The importance attached to this situation is the relevance of the financial reporting, even though it was being done periodically but was inept in providing an insight into the financial status of the firms' value. There is some baseline research that suggests the relationship of a firm's higher value relevance with the faithful representation of a firm's economic value by restricting the manager's opportunistic and discretionary accounting for earnings (Barth, Landsman and Lang, 2008). This means the value on the ground cannot be equated to the value in the books because a gap exists which is managed by the practice of window dressing.

If the financial situation on the ground is different from the financial statements as recorded in the account books, then there is something wrong in the basic approach to the creation of this financial information. Financial statements are an aggregate of accounting journal entries, following the rules of financial accounting. If the practice of accounting in its current form does not reflect the true condition of the firm, then

Information Creation (1st C)

the practice needs to be questioned for its effectiveness. When the manager of a firm starts to manage the earnings with discretion to cater for the opportunities in the economic environment, then accounting, though argued to be providing general flexibility, creates inconsistency in the system. The idea of accounting is to provide true value rather than providing value to the economic environment, contrary to what is happening today. Therefore the objective of **true value** as a result of accounting practice needs to be the guiding principle for the new financial architecture.

Moreover, the accounts are prepared for a different audience, such as investors, tax authorities and internal management or another, may be, the real one. For a firm in the globalized trading environment, complexity is unimaginable if a firm is preparing these objective-serving accounts in different countries using multiple accounting standards. The true value of the firm certainly lies in the tangled mix of these objective accounts adding and truncating numbers, all to the disadvantage of the true value of the economic environment. The practice of earning management also is prevalent in all businesses and especially where stakeholders are aggressive. The activities are called by different names, such as Creative Accounting, Banking income for the future, Financial Statement Manipulation, Re-engineering the income statement, Financial Statement Management, Borrowing income from future (this is the author's favourite), Income Smoothing, Window Dressing, Accounting Alchemy and many more. These practices are both legal and illegal, depending on the situation, so it is appropriate to call them 'amoral'. They are legal because in the past, Fortune 500 companies have used these practices for years without being questioned by any authorities, while in some cases the practices have crossed the line into being considered fraud. Similarly, one is not sure if accounting for the Greek sovereign debt, which led them into the Euro crisis, can be considered legal or illegal.

In this section there are several accounting practices that are discussed which had an impact on the financial transactions of the firms involved in this global financial crisis.

A particular accounting practice had slipped past the critical eye of the regulators, and certainly showed the failure of the balance sheet to reflect the correct loan quality for firms in the business of loans and mortgages. For the regulators to monitor the net realizable value, the balance sheet needs to account for loan loss allowance as a contra

THE GLOBAL FINANCIAL CRISIS IS NOT FINANCIAL

account. For solvency, the contra account is supposed to support the credit risk during economic slowdown. As it happened during the times before the crisis, the credit risk was growing due to bad mortgages, while the balance sheet did not account for the loan loss allowance. Although loan loss allowance is a measure of credit as seen by the regulator, it was still not accounting for the real credit risk. As the regulators monitored the credit risk on the official balance sheets of numerous firms across the business, they were misled by the figures there and the crisis was conceived.

Hence, one needs to question the ability of current accounting principles as in bookkeeping to represent accurately the measured credit risk by the balance sheet into the real credit risk to reflect the true value of the firm.

In a similar case, an important reason for regulators, having a blind spot on credit risk for securities, lies in the method of accounting. While the losses on loans are based on the shortfall in the projected cash flow and are accounted for on the balance sheet, losses on securities are based on changing market conditions. The market condition is measured by ABX indices for derivatives and changes frequently during trading sessions. So the losses in securities may have been accounted for, on a daily basis, but only for internal management reporting and not for the regulators. As a system it fails to find an audience with the regulators on a daily basis or more periodic basis which could have been more effective than being reported along with the loan losses as part of the quarterly reporting (IMF, Containing Systemic Risks and Restoring Financial Soundness, April 2008).

As a case of information asymmetry, in this situation there exists a set of information, one for the internal management and none for the others. The information that is available for the others come quarterly which can be considered sufficient delay in today's world of robotic and high-frequency transactions. One can also argue that the accounting treatment of loan losses and securities losses using the same principle is flawed, as the periodicity of the realization in both cases is vastly different because of the character of these products (loans and securities).

Information Creation (1st C)

Validate the process of securitization

The loans are one direct transaction between the buyer and the seller and so are the securities, also one direct transaction between a buyer and seller. But considering the nature of the product and their individual transactions, the securities are a bundle of many transactions. Securitization of the loans would include multiple loans and each loan, even though the same in financial terms is socially different. Each loan has risk factors that are unique because they belong to a different set of owners and their financial conditions, so bundling the loans or securitization tries to equate and generalize the risk perception in each loan. This process chops off the non-equated risks as unique. Still the risk is discretely and invisibly accumulating in the bundle. It remains away from being part of the holistic calculation. Therefore, there is both a calculated and chopped tail-risk in the process of securitization. As a case of information asymmetry, the securitized product is inherently built with risk because the information of the product appears to be what it is not. *If securitization was working all this time, the financial system was 'lucky'.*

Relaxing fair value accounting

Since the balance sheet reflects the state of the financial standing of a going concern, during the current crisis and subsequently in the period of slow down, the market value of the assets would show lower values. This would further depress the market outlook. Therefore a temporary provision has been made in the IFRS in order to 'relax' the fair value accounting of the assets so as not to reflect the depressed value of the assets (Herz, 2010).

Following the basic concept in this book, it can be termed to be officially building information asymmetry into the system. In the near future, whenever the relaxation would be removed, the market price of the assets will rebound for a short duration and then stay depressed due to the non-uniform response to recovery, across the globe. How long the relaxation will last is anybody's guess, but there will be at least one annual report that will bring volatility into the system because the firms will readjust to the fair value accounting (whenever). Although this is not a 'revaluation' the relaxation of the policy seemed a necessity as part of fine-tuning the financial system for efficiency, otherwise, the balance sheet would reflect a true value, a negative investment picture, which could deter investors and current stakeholders. It is a sort of giving a freehand by creating leniency in accounting standards to drive the market positively so that all firms with depressed assets can show themselves in green to attract investments. Too much fine-tuning of accounting standards will leave the system more vulnerable to flaws. Market behaviour is not predictable and it is possible that it becomes a permanent feature or practice, something that scrupulous players would like to exploit repeatedly. It is very close to the example where making students look attractive in the employment market by lowering their grade requirements because most of them were struggling to cope with the curriculum that year with some students taking advantage of the leniency.

The question is whether the duration of this deviation and the process to restore confidence using this methodology is a correct solution. The author is convinced that it cannot be a dependable option because the information asymmetry is being officially injected into the system. In future, the firms will look forward to this practice which will create a false sense of security like too-big-to-fail.

Regulating the misinformation

The US GAAP has guidelines for accounting the transfer of assets. A typical financial institution would sell a security and repurchase the same at a later date. This is called 'Repo 105 transaction' for secured borrowings. Instead of accounting Repo 105 transaction under secured borrowings, one of the financial institutions treated this transfer transaction as sales while taking the asset off the balance sheet and booking the profits (Kroeker, 2010). This way the institution was able to bluff the accounting system, temporarily glorify the balance sheet and profit from it. Using this method is like intentionally creating information asymmetry in the system.

The regulator depends on the reported figures for regulation and in this case they were regulating the asymmetric information created from the abuse of the Repo 105 transaction.

The problems identified in the case of Repo 105 are as follows: First, misinterpretation of accounting practices for the benefit of one party. Second, audits were not able to detect the flaws in the accounting practices nor were they able to alert either the accounting policy body or the regulatory authorities. Third, the firm was able to conduct,

Information Creation (1st C)

unabated, very large financial transactions knowing that the ambiguity in the accounting exists. This in turn falsely influenced the market.

The argument is less about the inability of the audits but more about the inability of the accounting system to create interlocks in the process which allowed this ambiguity to be used for trading large volumes in business.

These transactions had been done in plain sight of the auditors and regulators, and the feedback from the ground to the policy-making stood silent. The process of feedback is for the purpose of refreshing the system and flushing out inadequacies. If feedback is ineffective the system becomes prone to undetected problems and that is the learning from the current crisis. Hence, there is a need to have new thinking in the way accounting and accounting standards are embedded in the financial system.

It is not to suggest mistrust in accounting practices, but incident like this, which is a deliberate misuse of Repo 105, committed by reputed firms, do not create trust either. Trust as discussed previously in the Information Execution Model is an outcome of high QoI. The flawed accounting system had created faulty markets, and the market risk had grown with time. With more funds coming into play from the fiat monetary system, it has spiralled into a complex and latent form of crisis, only to be discovered when prevention was not possible.

As we read this section, one would never know which accounting practice is being currently misused in some corner of the marketplace which could potentially lead to another significant crisis like the current one.

The learning from the case of Repo 105 is to strengthen the feedback loop from the transaction to the standards using alerts from audit, regulation and transaction volumes. In this case, the connection between the practice and the process is found to be weak. As a system, if a section of the feedback loop is silent or too active, it is not guesswork that something in the system is getting built as a potential hazard. Therefore, appropriate sensors need to be entrenched in the system that could alert potential deviations and hazards.

There had been numerous changes to the accounting practice over a period of time but fine-tuning the accounting practices and plugging

THE GLOBAL FINANCIAL CRISIS IS NOT FINANCIAL

fundamental flaws are two different things, especially when the risk of having a major crisis has resulted from both these kinds of flaws. A case of each is seen in the previous examples of fair value accounting and Repo 105 transaction.

The relaxation to fair value accounting is fine-tuning of the system while the abuse of Repo 105 transactions was clearly a flaw in the system. Fixing a flaw is to maintain effectiveness of the system while fine-tuning enhances efficiency. Flaws hurt the strategic ability of the system while fine-tuning smoothen the tactical irritants, but both require a robust feedback, channelling information to the guardians of the system. While the global financial system tries to come out of the current crisis, a difference in approach is required to prevent mixing the issues.

Accountability of Accounting and Accounting Standards

Accounting is the practice of recording transactions while accounting standards are the rules and guidelines for the process of accounting. Both accounting and accounting standards exist in a system but are miles apart if their ownership were to be identified. While accounting is a financial activity of the firm, accounting standards hold a spirit of responsible financial behavior. Accounting standards are needed so that financial statements reflect fairly the performance of the firm and bring about the correctness and consistency in bookkeeping. Setting responsible behavior in the accounting system requires perpetual feedback from the accounting practice. The objective is to flush out any activity that could be part of the practice but is irresponsible and hampers the conduct of business. Based on the study of the financial crisis, it is evident that the feedback loop from the centre of accounting activities to the accounting standards body was ineffective. This is one of the reasons for poor QoI in the financial system and following are a few examples.

> "It may be illustrative to use a rough analogy in opening our discussion of this very complex issue. International accounting standards used in the preparation of financial reports throughout the world are somewhat like international rules of driving. Both establish a fundamental, commonly understood language (Elliott 2001)."

The role and responsibility of accounting standards Getting the liabilities off the balance sheet is one important focus of finance managers. There are many methods to do that and it is called transaction restructuring (Jamal and Tan, 2010). The firm achieves financial objectives by making different kinds of accounting treatment to the transaction. Off-Balance Sheet Entities (OBSE) is a live case of transaction restructuring which had put the financial system on a tailspin. These transactions are neither covered under the regulation nor are in the scope of auditors. They are completely at the discretion of managers to maneuver the financial numbers without being questioned by an authority. Transaction restructuring is a known practice and it is surprising that the standards authorities had kept silent on it, knowing that the financial system had gone on a tailspin as a consequence.

During the period of high growth and credit expansion the risk of defaults was hidden in the shadow financial system of OBSEs. This skewed the fundamentals of the investments by the holding banks, even though they were being done in strictly accounting terms, as allowed in the accounting standards. Until the crisis there was no clear definition of a shadow financial system or shadow banking which only suggests that the activities that are now termed as 'shadow' were considered part of the mainstream financial system.

The Financial Stability Board does mention the shadow banking system as 'mutation' in the credit intermediations, which can pose a risk to the financial system (Financial Stability Board, 2011). Also, it characterizes the activities under the shadow financial system as evolving over a period of time which depends on financial innovation and regulations. The argument here is that a shadow system develops using financial innovation techniques around regulatory arbitrage. Therefore, the information in the balance sheet gives a false sense of value of the firm.

One can argue about the fundamental fault of the accounting standards in the first place but the argument puts responsibility on the regulators for overlooking the problem because they were ignorant, similar to legalizing the robbery when the policeman is sleeping. Can this deviation be treated as a moral hazard? The book will deal with this syndrome of 'moral hazard' later in a separate chapter. In the light of the same argument it is the same audit standards which failed to trap the flaws in accounting standards, and it is attributed to the laws in many jurisdictions which do not prescribe sufficiently rigorous audit standards (Levitt, 1999). Based on this evidence, in the last decade the failure of audit standards to mind accounting standards has been a catalyst in creating information asymmetry in the balance sheets. Also, accounting guidelines on securitizations (FAS 133, 166 and 167) and regulation AB on ABS contributed to this trend. As the IMF (Containing Systemic Risks and Restoring Financial Soundness, April 2008) suggests, and one can agree, an important lesson from the current crisis underscores an urgent need to redefine and update the implementation of more robust accounting standards.

Examples of differences in definitions in accounting standards and effects

Capital Adequacy Ratio (CAR) has been interpreted in different ways, and multiple concepts exist. Not only do different concepts exist, but also there is a difference between CAR and Federal Deposit Insurance Corporation (FDIC) 'Well-Capitalized' requirements. There is a variation in monitoring bank capital in Europe and in the US; the two global financial poles. While in Europe it is core tier-1, in the US it is tangible common equity/total assets, better known as TCE/TA. This variation leads to a problem in cross-border bank comparisons.

Another example is the disclosure of certain derivatives and Repo transactions in the IFRS while it is being shown as net in the US GAAP. Therefore, the US GAAP can be considered to have more lenient guidelines for disclosures than the IFRS (IMF, Navigating the Financial Challenges Ahead, October 2009) and aptly it becomes a source of disclosure arbitrage. Multiple definitions end up in contest with the authorities because they are interpreted differently as a consequence. A lot of national resource is wasted in the legal battle and arbitration and mostly the regulators are consumed in this effort.

It is the principle of **true value** that has been defied with the concept of accounting standards. Different parts of the same global market use different definitions and therefore enhance the scope for disclosure arbitrage, misinterpretation and ultimately information asymmetry. Not only limited to this, but also these are natural sources of moral hazard in the system. It would be an assumption that information asymmetry is unintentional and does not include cases of moral hazard.

The other side of the coin is that a unified accounting standard is like putting one peg into different sized holes. It will be impractical for the global financial system to maintain one standard across international boundaries. The nature of business is different, the risk appetite is different across nations and there are regional legislations and regulations. Finally, the sophistication in recording the transactions is varied. In short, it is about taming the entropy in the system that will define the future of accounting standards.

Socio-financial system and accounting

By principle, financial accounting needs to be done differently for different parts of the social system. Households, Main Street (High Street) and Wall Street represent different attitudes and putting all of them under the same accounting standards create risk of relevance. Following here are a few differentiating factors. Household financial activity, and hence balance sheet, is based on realistic cash flow. A realistic cash flow then describes the financial status of the household and therefore reflects their risk appetite. The Main Street balance sheet is a mix of both realistic cash flow and entrepreneurial outlook which usually defines their investment decisions aiming at low-risk cash flow. The Wall Street balance sheet is a daily reflection of complex, speculative and risk-modelled finances for the next day's investments. If the accounting standards prescribe the same set of practice for these three layers of the financial system then there are bound to be mismatches in what the financial statement reflects. The generalization of these economic segments and layers hides the micro risks which can be a potential for failures that are deep seated.

Not all numbers in the financial statement will reflect the true condition of these layers of **socio-financial system**. The accounting standards are inherently including information asymmetry in the system by standardizing the way Household, Main Street and Wall Street financial statements are created.

The primary objective of accounting standards is the true reflection of an entity's financial status. There will always be socio-financial layering in the financial system; therefore the standards have to be more accommodating to this categorization rather than social systems adjusting to the standards.

The current financial crisis is a typical case of one socio-financial layer affecting another. Home mortgage borrowers were backed by their household income, and thence their balance sheet reflected a certain degree of risk appetite. If aggregated, this risk appetite should reflect a consolidated risk of the home mortgage industry sector. The Wall Street

THE GLOBAL FINANCIAL CRISIS IS NOT FINANCIAL

firms did have a risk appetite as reflected in their account books but was certainly different from the aggregate of individual home owner's risk appetite. In simple terms, it should have been a summation of risk appetite in proportion to their exposure to household risks. There is a logical mismatch visible here. No one knows if that was reflected clearly or whether it was only after intense analysis that a meaning could have been derived from the Wall Street balance sheet. Since risk appetite is different for different layers, the accounting methods for these socio-financial systems ought to be different in order to avoid any future mismatch of risk assessment in the system.

Times have changed since the modern financial system took to the helm some six decades ago, and now there are more players than ever in the market. More and more financial products are getting onto the market to benefit from micro and macro parts of the economy. It is an era of financial activism, and risk appetite globally has changed discreetly. Hence, it is more than an opportunity but a necessity to look again at the rules that govern accounting in the financial system. It is a good time to reconsider the three distinct layers of the socio-financial system (households, high street banks and financial institutions) and have discrete and objective accounting principles to reflect their **true risk appetite**.

The New Architecture

The new architecture will have a significant layer called **frameworks** that will help exploit the convergence and divergence of the accounting systems. Over and above the advantage of information symmetry across the system, not only will the accounting principle used, be visible to the regulators, but also to the competitors which will help in raising fundamental alerts in the system. This will tend to make the system more self-governing.

| Information Creation (1st C)

Asset Valuation: Too Complex

Asset Valuation is where life begins in the financial system, and therefore it is important that all assets in play are accurately valuated and recorded in account books, with a frequency that makes the books synchronous with ground realities. The process of valuation is primary to financial activity and the information created by valuation is the pulse of the financial system (that is at least learning from the current crisis). Asset valuation is also primary to the sentiments of the market player and the information that the valuation relays is not just financial but has a long-term bearing on the general health of the market. In a way asset valuation as a process is a common sentiment for both financial and economic activities and any disruption in the creation of this information has a direct bearing on both the financial and economic system. Hence, asset valuation as a process has systemic bearings by its very nature. Because of the complexity and the tedious nature of creating this information, the information is not created as frequently as it should be, especially in these fast-changing markets.

With a securitized asset the challenge of valuation is even more complex as assets do not appear individually and are evaluated by the risk associated with it. It has happened in the current crisis that an underlying asset in the structured instrument was valued differently because it was securitized. Structured instruments have added more complexity to the process of asset valuation in both the upward and downward economic cycle, as the gains and losses are undistinguishable, respectively. Since information on valuation is absent, still the investors have the inability to accurately identify losses in the securitized product and therefore it makes things difficult for the market players to also identify the counterparties. Thus the valuation process is marred by the opaqueness due to securitization.

> **Any fool can make something complicated. It takes a genius to make it simple.**
>
> — Woody Guthrie

Capital ratios will paint an incorrect picture if the assets are valued inaccurately, and whatever the state of disclosures and transparency is, the balance sheet will continue to be faulty (Crockett, 2001). The financial crisis was a result of accumulated assets which were valued much more than at market price. In financial parlance they are often called 'toxic assets' and the primary reason for accumulated toxic assets is the incorrect valuation of the assets at the time of the transaction, even though there are standards laid down for valuation in International Financial Reporting Standards (IFRS) as International Valuation Standards (IVS).

In the scenario where the tradable instrument is not a primary asset but a pool of return on assets, the valuation of the instrument becomes complex. For example, a typical pool has 7000 home loans with 70 different credit attributes (categorization). In order to evaluate different home prices and risks in that pool, numerous risk scenarios need to be simulated. The scenarios could be as many as a number of individual home loans on one extreme (very tedious) to as many as effective categorization, one can logically derive.

In principle, categorization on one side identifies similarity in the individual entities and on the other side ignores the differentiation in those entities. The process of ignoring the differentiation in the category suppresses a kind of information in the system and as a practice; it becomes a factor of information asymmetry by design. In categorizing the fruits in a large basket, it is a common practice to pick up all the apples, then bananas, strawberries and so on. In this action the similarities are the key focus while ignoring the fact that there could be apples of different sizes. The categorization could also have been on another factor such as sweetness or natural shelf life, so there are various ways in which categorization can slice and dice the pool of entities. It all depends on the considered effectiveness of the chosen criterion. In each exercise there is a factor that is being ignored about an individual entity after being considered ignorable. Paradoxically, the process flattens the uniqueness of the entity while trying to create commonness in the group (Angell and Demetis, 2010). In the current crisis the 'capacity of the borrower to pay back' was ignored over the categorization of 'projected return on asset' and that is where the basics of asset valuation, which also includes the losses due to the default and recovery charges (4Cs of Risk Layering in the next chapter), got overwritten by the valuation of the physical asset only.

Further imagine, consolidating a few thousand pools of home loans, and the information that is being ignored because the guiding principle does not encapsulate the information, considering it ignorable or outside the purview. According to research (Rajan, Seru and Vig, 2008), the borrower has two sets of information: hard information that banks or lenders had acquired and generalized that information, and soft information specific to each borrower. To acquire soft information requires a high cost and effort by the lender, hence it is convenient to ignore, in the business model of securitization and originate-to-distribute.

Two standards form the guidelines for valuation of structured financial products. They are the US GAAP section FAS 157 and IFRS 7 for the European Union and European Economic Area. In describing fair value, a hierarchy of methodologies is used. The products move between the hierarchies based on the least loss assessment or depending on the situation at the time of recognition, such as available for sale, held to maturity and trading, among others. One also finds that both FAS 157 and IFRS 7 do not prevent a firm from changing the method for calculating the asset's fair value. It is also observed by the IMF (IMF, April 2008) that in the case of assets such as mortgage-backed securities (MBS), no fixed pattern of transaction prevailed and the firms used ABX indices for the valuation. As an argument, it can be said that since MBS are a composition of assets, the valuation method based on each asset makes sense. While the argument for this method as tedious may be valid, some experts in the field have argued a different method of using ABX indices, since MBS are traded as derivatives. In light of this duality and unregulated flexibility in the usage of valuation methods, the valuation process remains discretionary and investors are asymmetric to the information about the risk due to various valuation methods used.

Alternative Valuation

Another case of an alternative valuation technique is used in interbank lending. The interbank unsecured market is the most prominent and longest existing component of the money market. Banks use the Over-the-counter (OTC) market to lend and borrow funds from their peers. They open credit lines only to creditworthy and well-established counterparties. Money market indices, such as the LIBOR, which were initially meant to provide benchmark rates to the unsecured interbank market, over a period of time started to be used increasingly for the indexation of short-term derivatives and securities. If the index starts to become a reference in valuation techniques then these indices bring to the system secondary information, based on and derived from another source. In the process the fundamental information becomes truncated and is a risk to market perfection.

In the practice that prevailed in the period of build-up to the crisis, the disclosure about the valuation method and techniques used was made

THE GLOBAL FINANCIAL CRISIS IS NOT FINANCIAL

only once in the annual report, except for US companies where the SEC has mandated quarterly disclosures. Information asymmetry, as an imperfection still stays embedded in the system because the SEC requires firms to furnish additional disclosures outside of the FAS 157. It creates further an inconsistency and non-standardization in the financial disclosure framework. Thereafter the timing of the disclosure of the revaluation is left to the discretion of individual firms, following either FAS or US GAAP, which along with the use of valuation techniques, leaves more scope for partial information to the market. Since the revaluation of assets and their disclosure was not standardized during the current crisis, that may have added to the chaos and uncertainty (IMF, April 2008). Although it makes sense to secure and maximize the shareholder's wealth, as a primary objective the discretion to choose the timing and the technique supports the primary objective. However, in the larger picture of market function, the information created in the system was asymmetric.

The credit rating of structured instruments had overwritten the valuation as an aggregate of the underlying assets compared to each of them, if they were to be individually evaluated. The credit rating gave a composite valuation to the securitized instruments. This reflected differently from the reality because the model for valuation used was different from a conventional method. Moreover, the valuations of these structure products were not frequently adjusted to the valuation of the underlying assets, as there was no mechanism existing to do that. While the credit rating made the valuation complex due to mixed-up assets, the accounting framework added confusion to the valuation techniques used for the structured products. The framework allowed use of fair value to include unobservable inputs to the valuation, in case there was no active market. So during the crisis, when the assets were on distress sale, the framework allowed scope for giving different valuation results for similar situations. On the other hand, mark-to-market conventions forced lower valuations, which in turn led to fire sales of assets and resulted in a self-fulfilling vicious circle of lower valuations and higher volatilities.

As an alternative way of thinking, what if the structured financial products were evaluated as a simple summation of the underlying assets? Then at no point in time would there be a mix-up of valuation techniques, and a realistic value would have existed. This true value would have denoted the **true risk appetite** of the instrument. Of

Information Creation (1st C)

course that would not have guaranteed anything about the volatility of the markets.

The process of valuation is stung by multiple problems. There is an inconsistency in the valuation method therefore a loan can be shown in a different light. The methodologies for the valuation are not regulated, though the standards are applicable, often to the debate of the auditors. It is at the discretion of the firm to disclose the evaluation methodology used. So for an investor or even the regulator, the sources of information are like shifting targets. The firms withhold the details of the valuation method and techniques because it is claimed to be their propriety. With the non-standard method of valuation, firms unwilling to disclose the methods, techniques, frequency and disclosure, one can only conclude that the process of valuation, though sophisticated, requires rigorous process to create high QoI in the financial system.

THE GLOBAL FINANCIAL CRISIS IS NOT FINANCIAL

Credit Rating: Not same as credit worthiness

The credit rating in its position as a crucial contributor to the financial crisis is analyzed from the perspective of being both a process and practice failure. Here in this chapter, the credit rating and credit rating agencies are seen to be a single point of failure in its vertical.

Process Failure

Blind faith on credit rating

Credit rating is a grade that each financial product scores by way of modelling its risk, and is awarded by credit rating agencies. There are acronyms, such as AAA, BBB, BB+, to identify the credit quality of these financial products and they represent risks in expected returns with probability of default. Referring to the attached credit rating for the financial product, an investor can decide on the investment based on the risk associated with that credit rating. That way, credit rating is an integral part, as well as the face of the product, as it characterizes its inherent properties.

> The United States can destroy by dropping bombs and Moody's can destroy you by downgrading your bonds. And believe me; it's not clear sometimes who's more powerful"
> (T Friedman. "News Hour", PBS. February 13, 1996)

So what went wrong?

The credit rating agencies insisted, according to the IMF, that investors were unaware of their warnings and disclaimer that the ratings were only a measure of default risk and not the likelihood of downgrade or mark-to-market valuation losses (IMF, Containing Systemic Risks and Restoring Financial Soundness, April 2008). The confusion, rather misleading credit rating information in the system, still is the source of reference and the blind faith persists. For the last hundred years credit rating agencies have played an important role in the function of rating. Investors usually are highly dependent on the ratings. They consider them reliable and base their decision to buy or sell without making further product-specific analysis.

Information Creation (1st C)

The concept of credit rating had left investors with a paradigm of reliability due to these reductionist and simplistic acronyms, so there was an auto dependence on these credit ratings. These acronyms are profound in content, as they represent a result of volumes of risk calculation and related information. In them they encapsulate the properties of the product. For an investor, it is like outsourced due diligence with an assumption of utmost reliability. As a root cause of the financial crisis, this failed market culture of reliance on credit rating is considered one of the major factors of the crisis.

Conflict of Interest and Business of Credit Rating

As per the original design of the credit rating business model, the credit rating agencies were to generate their income by selling credit ratings to investors. This meant that the rating would be supplied to potential buyers (investors) of the financial products, and this prevented the issuers from misleading and incorrectly selling the credibility of the product. In this business model the issuer, buyer and evaluator (rating agencies) had independent objectives and therefore there was no conflict of interest in the system. It was by this design of the credit rating business model that the ratings of the products were made as unbiased as possible and highly reliable. As of 1975, the Nationally Recognized Statistical Rating Organization (NRSRO) was formed and the buyer-pay revenue model was changed. The US Securities and Exchange Commission (SEC) made it mandatory for financial institutions to obtain the grade certification by the credit rating before issuing the product on the market. This made the issuers of the products pay for the credit rating rather than the investors paying the fees, as in the original design. According to the new business model, the credit rating agencies became a natural 'toll gate' for the entry of the products onto the financial market. The model did not remain as simple as when it was conceived earlier. Agencies received fees from the issuers for rating their products, which developed into a practice of providing a more favourable rating, since it made the issuer more likely to return with repeat business in the future. It became a cyclic correlation of rating, fees, favourable rating and repeat business. Tailored rating directly affected revenues, and when the credit rating agencies had been competing for a share of business in the limited players' market, this vicious cycle became an unsaid competition for favourably rating the products for gains due to repeat business (Shelby, 2006).

Further, since the financial institutions were always eager to get the most favourable rating for their products, the credit rating agencies not only were engaged by financial institutions (FI) to rate the products, but also to assist the issuers (FI) in creating and tailoring products to best suit the market. In case the ratings by the agencies did not match the expectations of the financial institution, there was always a chance that the rating agency would lose their future business (Cox, 2008). This meant that the rating agencies were not only paid for the rating, but

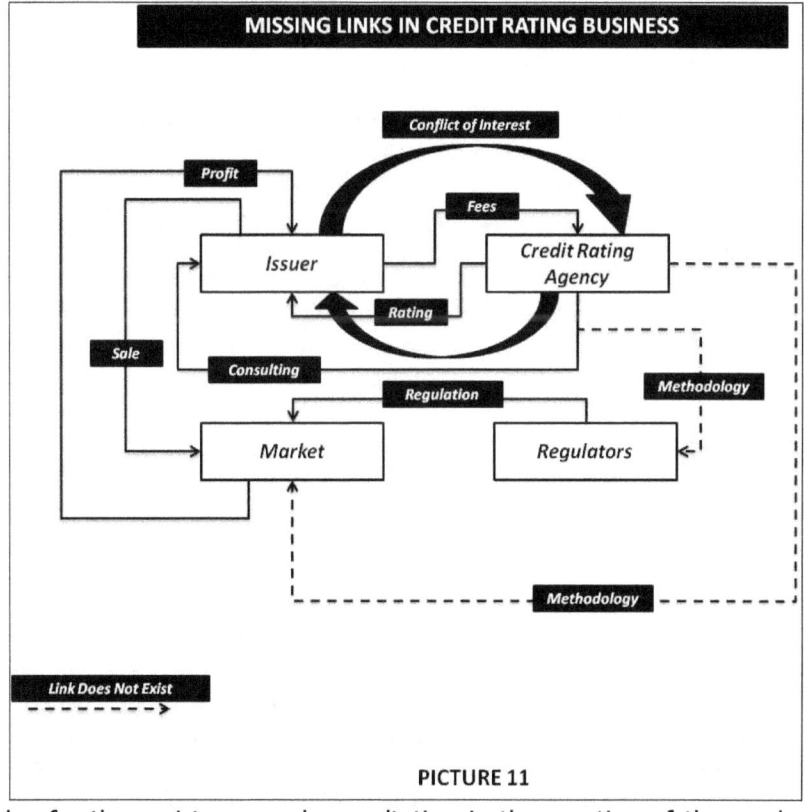

PICTURE 11

also for the assistance and consultation in the creation of the product for a favourable rating. If one looks at the list of services that credit rating agencies offer, it is much more than credit rating alone.

At the time of the crisis virtually both issuers and rating agencies were on the same side; the seller's side, while prior to 1975 the agencies were designed to be independent and neutral. Credit rating as a process was envisaged to be unidirectional and the product created by the

Information Creation (1st C)

issuer was to be rated independently. But the bi-directional process and probably iterative tuning of rating by the agencies had made conflict of interest inevitable. This change of 1975 brought conflict of interest between the product issuer and the credit rating agency. This will continue to stay because the objectives of issuer and agency have become interdependent. Till the time that product creation, rating education, rating consulting and product rating are not separated as legal entities, the system will see a glamorous collusion of forces in misguiding investors.

It is not a free market

There are only ten qualified NRSROs in the US and since they all enjoy global domination, the global financial market has only these as the qualified credit rating agency. Of nearly 130 others who had applied for the status of NRSRO, all were refused the status of qualified credit rating agency.

This has resulted in an oligopoly of three agencies that control nearly 95% of the market (Measuring the Measurers, 2007). A look at the credit rating landscape of the global financial market shows an oligopoly of credit rating agencies, each with a similar business model having conflict of interest with the issuer firms.

In the information creation cycle, the oligopoly has complete potential to support misinformation about the product and the rating process. The investment decision depends heavily on the credit rating and structurally the financial information system is bound to fail. Not only does it create an unsafe starting point in the financial product life cycle, but also the compounded effect of these risks affects the stability of the entire market. Investors are obliged to trust the credit ratings because there is no choice. Also, independently, for an investor to work out the credit rating of each product is very tedious and expensive. Therefore, it is a case of imposed trust even if the conditions are apt for sustained trust deficit.

Single-point-of-information-failure

While investigating the reasons for the global financial crisis, it was found that the credit rating agencies had been responsible for providing misleading and highest ratings for products that could have been rated as junk. When questioned, the agencies had contested the validity of

THE GLOBAL FINANCIAL CRISIS IS NOT FINANCIAL

the rating, citing that they were for a particular market condition. One could understand with reasonable intelligence that there has been a failure to issue timely upgrades or downgrades to the ratings with the changing market conditions. Earlier, the credit rating agencies had dodged the accountability of incorrectly grading Enron, claiming that ratings were just "opinions" (Measuring the Measurers, 2007). These misalignments of rating with the appropriate timelines have made the ratings a factor in misinforming the investors.

A rating is the single most important factor for the risk analysis. The CDOs had few (fewer than 10%) sub-prime asset-backed securities (ABS) that were rated at BBB or lower. It meant that the other 90% of the sub-prime ABS were A, or higher. It was also understood that the risk was highest with the lower rated ABS in the CDO and that also was conditional on the housing prices falling by 4% (IMF, Market Developments and Issues, April 2007). By plain reasoning, the 'sub-prime' on its own cannot be 'A' and above, which were part of the bundle assumed to be 'A' and above. In a holistic picture it defies logic in the methodology of credit rating itself.

ORIGINAL RATING	DEFAULT RATE*
AAA	0.53%
AA	0.57%
A	0.87%
BBB	1.26%
BB	4.21%
B	12.80%
CCC	56.90%

*Percentage of defaults by issuers rated by Standard & Poor's

Data: Standard & Poor's (Standard & Poor's, 2009)

A brief analysis of the above table suggests high optimism and complacency of the credit rating agencies. It showed on their unrealistic default rate. Before the crisis, when the going was good, the credit rating and the composition of the sub-prime mortgage into AAA securities were considered to be immune to defaults. The current crisis has proved the default rates to be totally wrong. There cannot be a reason that these ratings have failed to indicate the correct default rate

Information Creation (1st C)

because overall the market conditions were bad. Default rates and therefore credit ratings have to be market neutral.

Where were the Regulators?

The credit rating process in the US had been outside the purview of the regulators, and the investors could not sue the agencies due to protective legislation and case law decisions.

This code creates an ecosystem with natural conflict of interest in play,

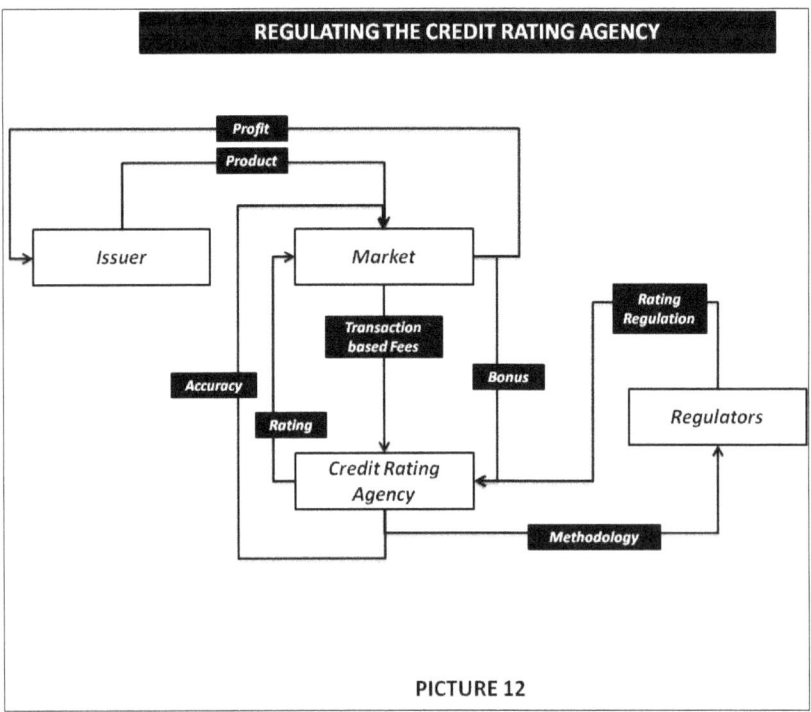

PICTURE 12

between the credit rating agencies and financial institutions without an intensive oversight or with feeble regulation in practice (Gallagher, 2009). It is most contrary to the belief that credit rating agencies are meant to be institutions of sound repute and are facilitators between investors and the money market. In fact the regulators themselves were dependent on the credit rating agencies for the rating of the products and there is no evidence to suggest that the regulators had an independent method of verifying these ratings. **Let's throw the question: who rates these ratings?**

THE GLOBAL FINANCIAL CRISIS IS NOT FINANCIAL

Where is Credit Rating in the Information Life Cycle?

Credit rating is a process of information creation for the investors of financial products. One can argue about the failure of the credit rating process and practice in the global financial system, stating that the process should have complied with certain standards that were to be uniform and regulated across the industry. That was not the case because the process of credit rating had moved from information 'Creation' to information 'Corroboration' in the Information Execution Model. Although, misjudging the authority vested by the government as NRCRO, investors assumed the credit ratings to be as good as a law and the credit rating agencies assumed a pseudo authority role in rating the products.

Since credit rating had been one important factor that investors relied on for decision-making, and will continue to do so, it is suggested that the process of credit rating be regulated as accounting standards are today. An ideal scenario will be if credit rating agencies become part of regulatory authorities and credit rating, a regulatory function. This will insulate the process of credit rating from conflict of interest. Since dismantling the agency business will be difficult, the agencies need to be paid a consolidated fee, with a percentage of market transaction and not on individual issuer basis. It could be somewhat like the British Broadcasting Corporation (BBC) revenue model (British Broadcasting Corporation, 2010) in combination with bonus-correlated with accuracy.

Consequences of Credit Rating

The fact is that credit rating as a process has created dependence for all the investors. Even today no investment is made, not as a law, without referring to credit rating. The dependence on crucial information in this compulsive system creates inherent risk of unchallenged information. Oligopoly creates compulsive dependency and it does not help to secure the system. It corrupts the system with power imbalance and certainly creates a single point of failure. The credit rating process in its current format is still doing just that. In principle, in a system no information created or used must be left unchallenged.

Of course, there is competition which is supposed to naturally check the monopoly (oligopoly) trade practices in credit rating business, but since agencies have no service differentiation in credit rating, actually it created pseudo-competition and brought the ills of oligopoly.

Information Creation (1st C)

Although in 2006 and 2009 there were major reforms in the procedures of credit rating intending to create more transparent and independent ratings, the damage had already been done in the global financial crisis. Trillions of dollars had been invested in 'toxic' assets across the global markets as a result.

Practice Failure

Periodicity of Credit Rating

Investors were let down by the credit ratings for the duration of the mortgages as they invested in products which were not correctly rated for the entire duration of the mortgages. Moreover, the regulators also had relied on the credit rating for their assessment of the market. If the entire market was misled with information about their investments by the agencies, the credit rating became the single point of failure in the process of product credibility assessment.

It is a big event when credit rating agencies rate a sovereign debt, especially when they are important countries from G20 or the Eurozone. Although financial product credit rating is different from sovereign credit rating in the way that it is commercially configured, the periodicity of rating is a very important factor in both cases. The agencies rated Enron in the investment grade right up to four days before its bankruptcy (Borrus, McNamee and Timmons, 2002). While this book was being written, the US long-term rating was lowered due to the rising debt burden. The event sent shock waves across the US and international financial markets.

The point made here is that the size of the US debt burden had been known for a long time and did not reach the magic figure of $14.3 trillion in one single day. But the day when the US was downgraded from AAA to AA+, it itself was marked as an event, provoking the markets to react and deplete the wealth of investors by a trillion dollars across the world. The question that experts need to answer is about the suddenness of declaring the credit rating in these cases, where the figures and conditions have been known for a long time. The US could have been downgraded at $13.3 trillion, much before the debate on the debt ceiling (if) happened at Capitol Hill. Why is the grading (downgrade in this case) not being done gradually to reduce the shock to the system, understanding that the financial system is systemically and highly connected to other sectors of the economy? Here the learning is to understand that the objective of credit rating is also to be timely and periodic, so that the elements of information shock to the system are avoided, as credit rating is a systemic influencing factor on the market.

As the business of credit rating matured, in real practice, the product stopped being designed as a financial product based on rate of return, but as products that will fetch higher credit rating. The focus moved from stamping products from potential rate of return to the tailored grade of higher sales, since the products with higher credit rating would sell faster.

As in the case of CDOs, the credit rating model did not reflect the risk properly. The credit rating of the CDOs is done by mapping valuation methods used for similar products. The mortgage-backed securities (MBS), which were marked as AAA tranche in CDO, were rated using the ABX sub-indices. This meant that the rating of a Credit Default Swap (CDS) was used to rate the MBS, even though it was part of the CDO tranche (IMF, Containing Systemic Risks and Restoring Financial Soundness, April 2008). This is an instance of information asymmetry found in the disclosure by the agencies where issuers were able to take advantage from the credit rating arbitrage, using the credit rating of similar products (Cassa di Risparmio della Repubblica di San Marino SpA v Barclays Bank Ltd, 2011). Also, there is a fundamental flaw in creating the information using a dependent credit rating.

The practice of credit rating needs to differentiate the sameness and similarity (Angell and Demetis, 2010). The CDO and CDS have unique inherent properties even though they may behave in a similar pattern. Creating information based on imported characteristics because they are similar, is fundamentally flawed.

Expectations from Credit Rating

There is a need to create an information system that will address the flaws identified in the credit rating system. These would be as follows:

- A. Disclosure of the methodology and data used for the ratings
- B. Lightning response to upgrades and downgrades
- C. Segregation of investor services and issuer services

Information Creation (1st C)

    D. Prudent regulation by audits of methodology and data used

    E. Including more competition into the credit rating space

    F. Holding agencies liable for wrongful and delayed grading

Credit rating, like any other rating or score, is a convergence of voluminous dataset to divulge information that is required to be most comprehensible to the user. By conventional logic it is a superhuman task of creating just 5–10 ratings acronyms (AAA, A+, BBB etc) based on a few dozen parameters. Those parameters themselves could be dynamic and unpredictable. While considering the process of creating credit rating, it is the complexity of independent variables on one side and consolidation of non-linear multiple variables on the other. It is a crude attempt to assign a quantitative variable to qualitative dataset which changes in time. A fresh look at the position of credit rating agencies in the market and their transparency in methodology, is mandatory and the sooner it is done, the better it will be.

A few important shortcomings have come to the forefront.

First, it is about the credit rating agencies behaving as unsaid 'toll gates' and therefore, being a single point of failure. Second, it is the inability of ratings to reflect the changing grades in real time. Third, oligopoly and zero liability made agencies complacent and unregulated. Fourth, conflict of interest with financial institutions had actually duped investors into flawed investments. Fifth, opaque and flawed disclosures of the methodologies left investors blinded, and issuers took advantage of credit rating arbitrage. Sixth, smudging the role of credit rating agencies, that of being information provider versus information verifiers of the investment grades, created duality of objectives and confused status.

THE GLOBAL FINANCIAL CRISIS IS NOT FINANCIAL

Modelling: It's a Black Box

In this section we will see how the concept of 'risk' played in the creation of the crisis and what does 'risk' signify as a source of information in the financial system.

Risk modeling, ideally, is about predicting the market future using mathematical or statistical formulas (Q world and P world). There are best brains, including those of noble laureates, being applied to get it right. With whatever accuracy the mathematics have been used for engineering results, in the financial market the mathematics are based on probability of an event, such as the Markov Chain. Taming the unknown is the art and science in risk modelling and it is a long way from being perfected in capturing not only market behaviour but also the underlying influencing factors. It is not only a trick to be performed in a specific country but in all countries where modern financial activities exist. Based on the performance of risk modelling techniques with respect to the crisis, the realistic assumption would be to regulate the use and dependence of these risk modelling techniques and make them more transparent to the users.

> All models are wrong, but some are useful ~ George E. P. Box

There is Risk in Risk modelling ....

Risk is defined as a measure of probability of occurrence of an event, mathematically multiplied by its magnitude of damage. The risk is subjective, though derived numerically to arrive at an objective value. There is no measure and verification of the objective value of risk, up to the time when the accident actually occurs. This is because there is a known constraint of measuring the time of a future event. The only option available to mankind is to record the past and the present, not the future. This is a logical statement reflecting the constraint and the sole reason why so many experts and analysts are indulging in the complexities of mathematical risk modelling. ***It is to get hold of the future.*** Necessarily, the risk model depends on historical records for calculations to predict the future and even with all the sophisticated computing abilities available today to predict, risk is still not perfected, especially the impact of tail-risk.

In the case of the current crisis, the tail-risk was ignored as insignificant because it represented a risk in 8% of the mortgage market business. It

Information Creation (1st C)

was considered too small to be a threat. It is learning. Though the tail-risk appears as the tail, this does not mean it needs to be treated insignificantly. This further enhances our learning that although the tail-risk is represented in risk modelling as visible and recognizable, it is the treatment and response to the tail-risk that needs to be perfected.

In this section, risk modelling is discussed as a case for building information asymmetry in the financial system as it reveals less and hides more, while its impact on the global financial crisis has been in question. Since risk modelling is a complex mathematical process, it is understood by few experts even though it influences many across the financial system and its systemic chain. This makes a blind dependence on the final result of the modeling process and everything else in the process becomes a 'black box'. Since, little was known about what went into the modelling, and there was no compulsion by the firms to disclose the assumptions that were considered in the calculation of the 'unknown', to arrive at the objective risk value, **there is a risk in risk modelling**.

While risk-modelling techniques have improved over the years, at the same time financial intermediaries have increased their demand for risk hedging using complex instruments. Due to techniques and supporting information technologies, the increase in the financial risk-taking abilities has expanded the financial market manifold, but it has built-in risk, as the key ingredient (Crockett, 2001). As times have revealed, the complexity of these instruments and their models is not understood well which has increased the leverage and ultimately promoted high risk-taking. Over the last decade, ever since investment banking and commercial banking have been allowed to merge in the US market, financial instruments have only become complex and have added risk to the financial system. The complexity in the financial market came to unsustainable limits when the risk modelling became widespread unregulated practice. There was no regulation to counter check the validity of the model in use.

According to the Association of Financial Engineers, there is a differentiation between operational risk and market risk. Operational risks are potential losses due to people, process, technology or events. Mostly, operational risk is internal to the organization and arises due to failure in internal operational control and compliance. A failure of compliance with the accounting system and internal audits or failure of

THE GLOBAL FINANCIAL CRISIS IS <u>NOT</u> FINANCIAL

employee oversight for fraud and misconduct, are examples of operational risk.

The market risk on the other hand, is due to long-term capital management and credit exposure. This is a risk that is the focus of strategic management of the firm and requires detailed analysis of the economic, social and political environment. The relevance of identifying the risk here is to understand the very nature of the risk that was being modeled in the case of the current crisis.

In order to objectively find the root cause of the failure in risk modeling it is important to identify the risk that the analysts were focusing on. It can be a matter for debate whether the current crisis is due to failure of handling operational risk, market risk or both in combination. By the very nomenclature of the current crisis (housing market crash), all fingers point to the failure of the housing market as the root cause of this crisis. Therefore, it is termed as a failure due to market risk.

The author is convinced that the financial crisis is an operational crisis based on the argument that inherent operational risk exists in financial firms who engaged in disbursement of loans and also those who managed the loan securitization, respectively. During the period prior to the crisis this risk got exponentially magnified because it travelled from one firm to another and then from one industry sector to another, due to the systemic nature of the financial sector.

It is worthwhile knowing that the operational risk was inherent in the process of credit checks for home loan borrowers. A loan to an individual home loan borrower with a poor rating stands out as an operational failure and it was not just one case of poor credit rating being disbursed, but also a few million disbursements to borrowers with poor credit ratings. This is how the operational risk merged into the practice, got rationalized because it was widespread and became an acceptable norm in the business. It magnified the potential risk and subsequently culminated into a failure of one firm, then another and finally domino(ed) to a crisis. While the financial engineers and analysts were using the most complex techniques and technologies to manage and monitor the market risks, the operational risk which was part of the operations and considered insignificant, failed the entire financial system. If the risk analyst were to study the risk profile before, during and after the crisis, they needed to investigate the transition of

Information Creation (1st C)

operational risk to market failure to seek answers if the transition was due to the missing information.

As it is evident from the crisis, risk modelling has been one step behind predicting the failure and had been unable to provide a correct assessment of the magnitude of global market failure. There are two things that are missing from the current form of risk assessment; one is the type of event and the other, the impact of the event.

It may have been acceptable to overlook the inability of a modelling practice to detect an event with a small loss, but risk modelling as a science failed to detect risk and predict events of global proportions. This has raised serious doubt on the applicability of mathematical methods to such a subjective environment, as the financial market. Moreover, if the accuracy in detecting numbers of events were to be considered, then an excuse of missing even a one-off failure is not justified because the impact of this one missed prediction has hampered the global financial system and their dependent national economies. As a consequence of the current crisis, the process of risk modelling and the practice of its dependence on financial decision-making require a critical review.

Modelling is a method of simulating the known conditions for calculating the unknown results. Since the simulating conditions are considered to be known, therefore it is logically assumed that the results would be accurate. With the financial environment ever-expanding and more dynamic than ever before, there will always be some factors missing in the simulation of mathematically 'known' equations. Hence there will be mismatch between simulated results with the reality on the ground.

How does modelling address that part of the risk, which is the risk of risk modeling itself? It is also about factoring risk, the tail-risk, which is usually considered as the remote scenario by the analysts. In some cases, using stochastic methods, the analysts have been found to filter the element of volatility (the spikes) from the historical data. The argument in favour of this practice is to ignore spikes because those are the moments when the markets gain or lose high volumes and is not to be considered as consistent market behaviour. It is the same as how the concept of 'moving average' works. So if the practice is to filter out volatility, the resulting forecast will also be without volatility and that is where the predictability fails. This would mean that predictions trend towards smooth market behaviour, consistent with what seems to be theoretically derived, even though it is different from the ground reality.

The result of the risk modelling is as good as its timing. If it is able to inform the market about the failure, well in advance of the event, only then does it makes sense. It is like you falling from a building and the risk analysts calling it 'good going', because the distance covered accurately matches the mathematically calculated equation with predictive speed and acceleration, until you hit the ground. We know the result of falling from the height because there had been umpteen numbers of cases so the result is tied to experience rather than risk modelling. What if falling from a height was an event happening for the first time, such as the moon landing, and there was no experience to substantiate the outcome?

In this rudimentary example of falling from a height, the link between risk modelling and available information of the consequences is making different sense of the situation. It is the case argued for risk modelling and the financial crisis. Experts never understood the sense of the market until the financial firms and banks started to go under. Had sense prevailed differently from risk modeling, then corrective action would have been taken much before 2008.

What does risk modelling ultimately do?

Financial risk modelling is like pulling the future out of history, using statistical methods without considering the effects of current and independent variables. For the analysis of any event it is a consequence of a variable that is dependent on either a previous condition and/or an unknown condition called an independent variable. That event has either occurred in the past or is being predicted in the future. The author has categorized the possibility of this event in a 2 X 2 grid, in the combinations of past and present and characterized by dependent and independent variables. The grid would look as follows:

EVENTS	DEPENDENT	INDEPENDENT
PAST	Chronology	Accident
FUTURE	Statistics	Black Swan

Information Creation (1st C)

The current science of risk management is about taking account of **chronology**, correlating the **accidents**, converting into a **statistical** formula, to predict the **Black Swan**, may be similar to what Nostradamus did. It is this art of correlation where the mathematical translations to predict the future are failing to create an accurate picture of causality. In the case of the current crisis, the failure to mathematically risk model the 'Black Swan' had demonstrated the difference between correlation and causality. Simultaneously, it has questioned the dependability of risk-modelling techniques for real world events.

The charts are not patients!

The author is not undermining the ability of statistical methods but questioning the mismatch of human instinct in applying these theoretical methods. As seen in the current crisis, these modelling techniques, their application, disclosure, incomprehensibility and complexity have become a single point of failure in the process of sense-making by the market players.

Understanding that risk modelling is about developing a pattern from statistical chaos and transforming it into a prediction, may be good for complex engineering computation but in a social environment, there has to be more room for human expertise in the interpretation of the models to provide fundamental insight and sense-making (Angell and Demetis, 2010). To derive human insight from mathematical equations for an environment that has multiple uncontrolled variables, which may or may not have a history, is a recipe for being caught ignorant.

Risk modelling for Japanese power reactors was done for an eventuality similar to what had been seen as an extreme before, like the earthquake of intensity 8.0. Since an earthquake of magnitude 9.0 had never happened before in that region, risk modelling had its limit. As seen from the Japanese tsunami tragedy of 2011, the events that followed the earthquake, including the failure of their nuclear power reactors and the options available to manage the crisis, were different from what the risk modelling suggested. Rather it will not be wrong to suggest that there was no contingency plan to handle the crisis of that proportion because the risk of an earthquake of magnitude 9.0 and its aftermath was never modeled. It is easier to say on reflection and with hindsight that risk modelling could have included the scenario with a quake of magnitude 9.0 but when the entire modelling is based on history, it is very difficult to cross the limiting boundaries when simulating the worst-case scenarios.

It is the case of events in the space of tail-risk where the analyst fails to interpret beyond the mathematical equations. This could mean more data set and human interaction is required to create information that would enhance the system's intelligence. A risk model on its own is without intelligence. It cannot sense the environment around it and therefore has to be accompanied by necessary feeds and controls derived from human interventions, such as more data, conditions, rules, approvals, authorizations, verifications, reconciliation and abstraction. Any deficit in these inputs to the model would skew the risk profile, and even if all the inputs are suitably applied to the mathematical and statistical equations, there is still a factor that will always be in short supply. This is what differentiates the human mind and the mathematics.

Using these techniques only creates artificial intelligence whose ability has not yet surpassed the ability of organic intelligence, and therefore the sole dependence and widespread use of the modelling techniques require regulation. As humans, we are hard-wired to think and predict linearly, therefore any model that will be used to extend the past will by-pass the human's ability of linear comprehension. That may be an interesting scenario to look forward to, but for now we have to wait for that convergence to ***singularity***, when artificial intelligence equals or surpasses organic intelligence in sense-making (Kurzwei, 2005). Till then it is appropriate to seek regulation for making the modelling simpler and comprehensible to the average investor on the street.

| Information Creation (1st C)

Risk-return profile tends to finally fail

It is found that investors, individual and institutional, are encouraged to take more risks if there are long periods of economic stability because they get trapped in a positive feedback loop of ever-growing asset prices, incomes and therefore, confidence. It is little understood that in the process of growth there is an underlying risk that is getting built into each cycle of that positive feedback. It makes investors borrow more and pay more for the same set of asset class than they would have normally done. They fail to understand that asset prices are a function of both the bull and the bear market forces (Tucker, 2010) which are cyclic in nature. The risk appetite grows with the economic stability which potentially increases the risk in the system. There is a

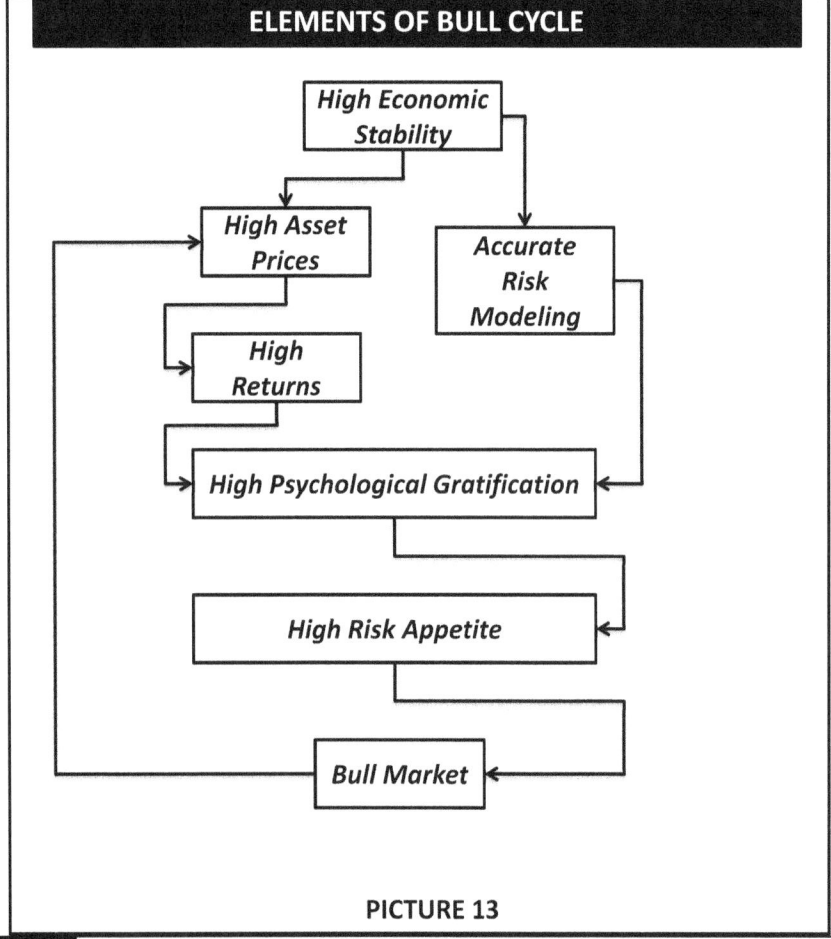

PICTURE 13

sense of psychological gratification in the precision and accuracy that the mathematical modelling simulates during the time of economic stability and which becomes enhanced as users enter into every cycle of risk-taking. It further creates positive feedback for enhanced risk-taking in the future. After a certain point the entrepreneurial risk crosses into betting behaviour.

There is nothing that is a safe risk.

If there was a way to visualize the risk and make that constituent information more symmetrical, then the investors would be more rational on the risk-return curve especially when the breakpoint was approaching. As the capital asset pricing model suggests about the risk-return trade off, both risk and return are not unlimited and the boundaries are not defined for the system but by the prevailing environment. Therefore, exceeding the limits, which is only theoretically calculated, tends to make the financial system finally fail.

The financial market had used mathematical modelling for various indicators, such as indices, yield curves, default probability for CDS and

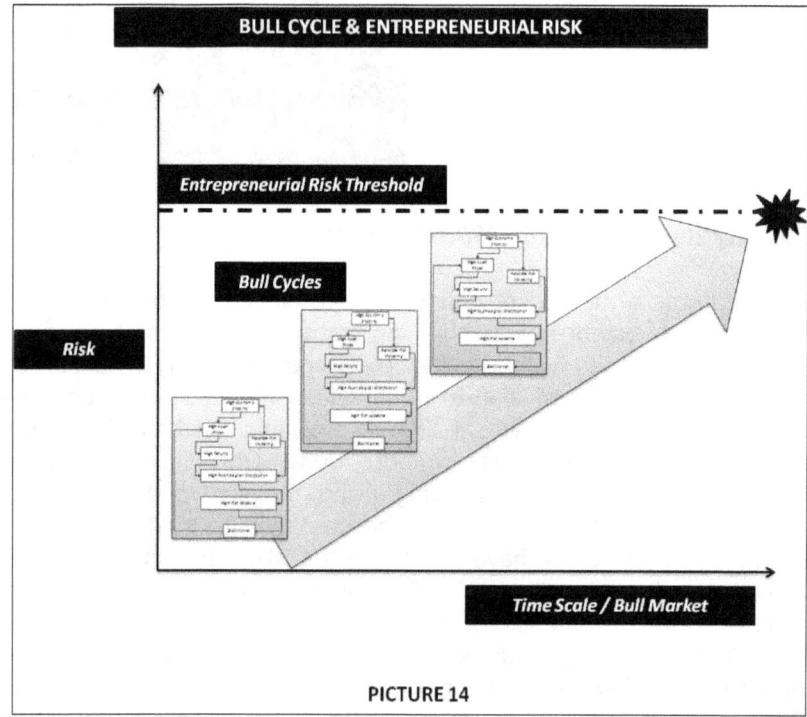

PICTURE 14

Information Creation (1st C)

default risk, to name a few. Basically, financial engineering is the term used by financial product developers to incorporate risk into the products. With reference to the global financial crisis, financial engineering created weapons of mass destruction (WMDs) such as CDS (Credit Default Swaps) and CDOs (Collateral Debt Obligations) among others as described by Warren Buffett (Berkshire Hathaway, 2002). According to research (Nijsken & Wagner, 2010) a securitized asset is more likely to default than a similar characteristic asset that is not securitized. By this argument the purpose of CDOs is lost because in the long run, the risk of an individual component gets lost in securitization and the effect of risk that gets transferred from these individual components to the whole product actually returns to the system.

Learning from the current crisis includes approaches to the risk, which needs to bridge the quantitative methods including technical analysis with qualitative human assessments to arrive at points of risk-taking. It may sound like an anti-mathematical argument undermining the abilities of mathematical techniques, but it is the author's argument that mathematics are to be treated as only a hygiene factor and any usage or dependence beyond that will bring irrationality to the system.

> All that glisters is not gold;
> Often have you heard that told:
> Many a man his life hath sold
> But my outside to behold:
> ~ *William Shakespeare*
> (Prince of Morocco, Merchant of Venice - Act II - Scene VII -)

Risk Layering and Risk Management

Risk layering is a method of defining the saleability of the product. It refers to the practice whereby mortgage lenders combine non-traditional mortgages with weaker credit controls, for instance, by accepting high combined loan-to-value ratios, reduced documentation with little or no down payment (IMF, Containing Systemic Risks and Restoring Financial Soundness, April 2008). Only if the financial intermediaries followed risk layering using the simple 4Cs of credit analysis at every stage of their originate-to-distribute model, could the housing mortgage crisis have been averted. The 4Cs are Character (Reputation), Capacity (Volatility of earnings), Capital (Leverage) and Collateral (Altman and Saunders, 1998). Though, this method of following the 4Cs is considered subjective and does not fit into the functional template of assigning risk to each borrower, the combinational outlook is very objective and probably would have been more authentic than the sophisticated risk management by these quantitative methods. There is a reason for it. At any point in time, if the individual borrower or a securitized product deviates from being a focused cash flow instrument to quantitatively assigned risk-based product for cash flow, the system starts to truncate the 'real' information; in other words, build information asymmetry into the practice. The process starts to accept negatives in the form of risk management.

In the build-up to the crisis, in risk layering there was a tendency to accumulate high-risk credit factors, such as a low FICO score, no income documentation, no asset documentation, no down payment or second mortgage collateral in lieu of the down payment and the entire mortgage itself. This model of risk layering was used by all the mortgage agencies, and was getting passed on to the investment banks. As the investment banks securitized these mortgages further up the product chain, investors failed to trace back the risk layering because of the originate-to-distribute model. With the originate-to-distribute model the CDO and CDO^2 products lost the traceability of the individual components because the process of securitization remixed the components (individual mortgages). As a process, the information of these individual components got lost in the up chain while the credit ratings were hard-wired to reflect the best, as seen in the chapter on credit rating. There were no guidelines for risk layering from the regulators either, so it was solely dependent on the individual financial institutions to internally construct, operate and validate the models of risk layering. With this flexibility, it was convenient for all the financial entities in the chain of mortgage securitization to continue using this flawed practice of risk layering.

Initially for many years it showed positive financial results and the housing market was booming (like the good going of the falling object) until the crash actually happened in 2008.

CDOs are a modern-day example of how complexity in risk modelling had created information asymmetry. Unverified objective risk is still used as product information and passed on to the next stage of product remix and formulation as CDO^2. The component risk gets hidden in the composite risk and the sum total of composition risk is not labeled as 'risky'. Is it a failure of risk management as a practice or the information system that provides information to the players, or both? It is being

Information Creation (1st C)

questioned because together they are unable to reveal the 'real' risk associated in the CDOs and its components.

So far it was about the measurement of risk in risk management, and now the other part is about the use of risk for the formulation of financial products. Risk forms a significant part of the description of a financial product. The rate of return in the modeled risk attached to each product reflects its corresponding tranche. One may call it incomplete information if these two are taken discretely, but in combination they create a third piece of information; the investor's 'perception'. Further, this perceived risk changes with time and therefore the time dimension is as important as the other two core components. The time factor of risk is not included in any description of the product as it is the greatest unknown factor.

If a financial product description is to be reconstructed using the components identified, in future it will be called as a rate of return with a probability of not meeting the expected returns, which may change depending on the prevailing conditions. In a sense, the financial product is a combination of three uncontrolled variables; risk, rate of return and time, which's combined success rate is assumed with reference to historic data.

If the time factor was assumed to be part of the rated risk label (AAA, B+ etc) attached to each CDO then these rating labels should have been sliding (upgrade or downgrade) between the tranches over a period of time, more frequently than they currently are, with the changing market conditions. As it looks, prior to the crisis, these risk labels were insensitive to market conditions and therefore, were approximately stationary. It was also the complaint from investors. Tracking the changing value of these components with time introduces **'sensitivity'** into the investor's 'perception' of risk. This means that investors will never know enough about the product if the information is not 'real time'. That is information asymmetry due to risk labels, known as 'credit rating' in the financial system. Although information asymmetry has been discussed in the previous chapter, it is important to appreciate early on, the concept of sensitivity in the investor's perception of risk in the financial system.

In Section 945 of the Dodd-Frank Act it requires asset-backed issuers to perform a risk review of the assets underlying the asset-backed securities (ABS) and to disclose the methodology of that review to investors. After all, the pharmaceutical companies declare the formulation on every pack of their products, even though few of the consumers understand their complete significance. What the Dodd-Frank Act does not lay out is the periodicity of these risk reviews. The risk at the time of initial issue will be different than at the time of subsequent trades. Therefore, the product could be insufficiently labeled with risk information, something that investors must be aware of, at the time of the transaction.

This challenge of bringing sensitivity into the system is still not addressed and information asymmetry will still remain unaddressed in the financial system.

Further, the system is devoid of the holistic 'impact' analysis. Though the risk modelling takes into consideration the default of the instrument, the holistic impact of the default is missing from the information disclosed in the public domain of the financial system. This is because it is neither in the scope of any authority nor are there any tools or methodology available to map the systemic risk. If the exercise of systemic impact analysis was part of the risk model followed by the regulatory and supervisory authorities, it would have limited the effect on the solvency of individuals, firms and nations. Today this assessment is not being done by anyone who could establish the impact on the global systems if 'Too-Big-to-Fail, fails, or for that matter the impact of default of a particular CDO.

Building a robust and crisis-proof financial system, all players must be required to have a visible and transparent disclosure of impact due to any default. The spectrum of impact needs to include small products, such as individual mortgages and large products such as CDOs and derivatives to very large entities such as Too-Big-To-Fail.

Derivatives: Worth Abandoning

Credit derivatives such as CDOs and other complex products are based on quantitative risk modelling for their value assessment, investment decisions and pricing. According to the IMF, the underlying risk model for all these complex products is similar and therefore, there is a risk of 'herd behaviour' by the investors to exit at the same time. This was stated in 2005 when the financial crisis was not in anybody's wildest dream. Considering the statement in hindsight, not only did it pose a problem of 'herd behaviour' on the market but these risk models became a single point of failure for the entire global market.

Derivatives, like all other products, are subject to both market and operational risk. Accounting these risks is the most significant challenge because it changes the composition of the derivatives altogether. Derivatives are priced based on many assumptions which can change according to market conditions. In the likely event, the derivative contract has to be revalued and priced again. This is a methodology and it is the way derivatives work. The arguments against the presence of derivatives in the market are twofold; first, its gigantic value held in the market surpasses many times the GDP of the richest countries, and second, it is based on many assumptions. As feared by Warren Buffett in 2002, derivatives were potentially lethal much before the crisis point was reached. One of the reasons cited, was the inability of even experienced investors to understand and analyze the derivative contracts (Berkshire Hathaway, 2002). While the argument for not having an oversized tree near the house is easily understood, similarly the risk of holding gigantic finances in instruments that are based on assumptions, using quantitative techniques, is potentially catastrophic. The safety of these derivatives is misunderstood. Often there were arguments before the crisis in favour of derivatives, as driving growth of rich economies, but that argument fails to hold ground now because emerging economies, which are registering double-digit growth, were very low in the derivatives market.

Derivatives have been the core of the financial crisis, because it has been the least regulated practice in the financial system. The determinants of the derivatives are vague and more instinctive, based on a combination of quantitative calculations and speculation (Sanio, 2010). This is very close to gambling by social definition and therefore, one view is to ban derivatives. In turn, let the markets play whatever is measurable and have an element of entrepreneurial risk rather than rely on speculative and gambling risk. It is found that investors with entrepreneurial risk often succeed while gambling has made players broke. Also, those who are into gambling are never called investors. So the market really needs to redefine and differentiate its parlance for those in the market with an objective of investment or gambling.

Many financial predictions are based on a financial time series analysis, as modelling and forecasting of the financial series have become mainstays of financial operations. It is not a guess that these series are influenced by numerous factors including financial, political, economic, business and social conditions. The practicality of using this model for decision-making needs to be reconsidered based on the findings from this study. A study of the S&P 500 and the Hang Seng Index (HSI) data for 80 and 35 years respectively, using the Artificial Neural Networks (ANN) and Auto Regressive Integrating Moving Average (ARIMA) models, suggests that analysts are far from predicting the market accurately using statistical models. One of the reasons for the shortcoming is the problem of sampling in terms of size. The prediction accuracy of both the S&P 500 and the Hang Seng Index using these two models had never exceeded a hit ratio of 80% and it seems to hover around 40–60% (Kumar, 2009). With this kind of prediction accuracy, one would like to be leaning the least on these models. But the visibility of these indices and being frequently quoted for market trends adds risk to the sentiments. This is just another case of misled methodology in modelling being used in the creation of financial market information. Hence, it supports the author's previous argument of the risk of using risk modelling, and the creation of information imbalances in the financial system.

The information afloat in the financial system generated from these modelling techniques is a hygiene factor. It is important to understand that there is a difference between relevance of these numbers and the wholesome dependence on them. The information prevalent in the system has to reflect the reality of the financial environment which includes the results from the risk models and their accuracy at that time. The market will be more symmetric if the players are aware of the assumptions, which these modelling techniques use to arrive at the proposed risk. That will bring more human judgment and sense-making into the system. The **'black box'** of risk modelling used for a financial product that creates information symmetry has to reconfigure as an **'open book'** to bring more transparency and reliability.

Chapter 5
Information Corroboration (2nd C)

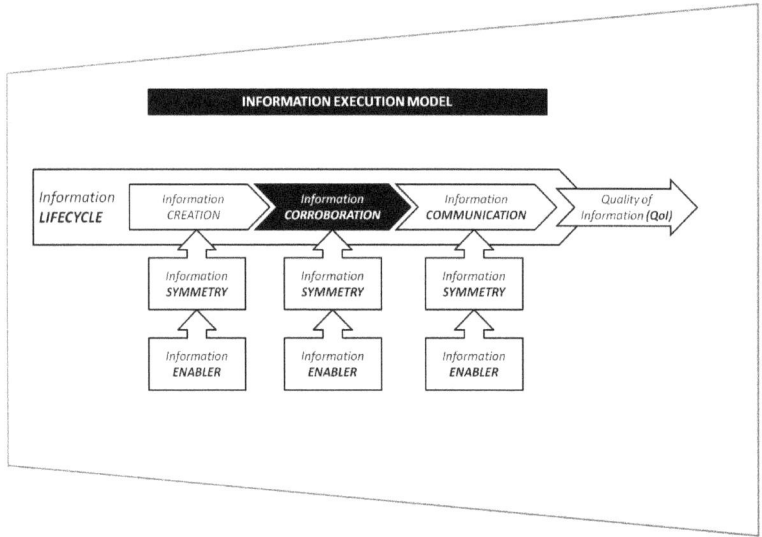

THE GLOBAL FINANCIAL CRISIS IS <u>NOT</u> FINANCIAL

Audit: responsible, this time again !

Audit Standards

There has been no direct and established connection between the current financial crisis and the practice of audit or their underlying audit standards, but when the current financial crisis is seen from a systems point of view, the audits seem to be at the centre of its root cause. All this while, the author had been basing his argument on; if high QoI is created in the system, the system would not fail and one of the ways to ensure this was corroborating the information created in the system. As in the case of the current crisis, not only the information created was asymmetric, but also the methods to corroborate the information failed to detect and prevent it. Audit, along with regulation, is one of the methods that had been used to corroborate the information created in the financial system. Audit quality refers to the probability of detecting and reporting a breach in the financial processes followed by a firm (DeAngelo, 1981). By that definition, failure to detect or failure to report the detection, reflects poor quality audits and therefore, have contributed to this financial crisis. According to experts, there are multiple factors responsible for the quality of audits.

The bottom line to the argument is the inability of the auditors to detect breaches in clients' account books and report them back to the standard's organization, especially for these Too-Big-to-Fail firms, who had significant systemic impact. Although the cases of clear breaches are few, it is more of a practice in the grey area that is required to be questioned by these auditors.

It is also understood that these Too-Big-to-Fail firms had hired the big five audit firms for both audit and non-audit services and together the bigwigs of the global financial sector have failed to prevent the crisis.

The role of the auditor vis-à-vis their client firms had been in question every time there was a financial crisis, large or small, because of which SOX legislation was enacted and the Public Company Accounting Oversight Board (PCAOB) formed. They were to bring more quality to the audit profession and resolve the issue of conflict of interest impeding the intended relationship between the auditors and their client firms. The core challenge in the audit profession is the independence of the auditors in providing a balanced judgment to the firm's accounting treatments.

Information Corroboration (2nd C)

The two benchmarks for the accounting judgment are the concepts of fairness and materiality. The practice of audit as a profession, need to present the balanced judgment about the materiality of the client firm with fairness to the investors. Any artificial deviation in that judgment will bring conflict of interest to the system. The role of the auditor is somewhat semi-judicial with responsibility and accountability for upholding the truth of the financial statement beyond the pleasure of the firm's management and profit-seeking investors. The ground reality had proved otherwise.

The current crisis finds auditing responsible too

It is a known problem; there had been important legislations in the US and other countries to avoid the conflict of interest in business, especially those arising due to the auditor-client relationship. Although the current crisis is not considered directly related to the conflict of interest between the financial institutions (too-big-to-fail) and their auditors, there is a very important correlation with the quality of corroborated information released by these Too-Big-to-Fail firms and the information asymmetry created thereof, for the investors across the global markets.

After the Enron crisis, the SOX Act of 2002 had a positive impact on the practice of audit and the processes followed by the auditors. A lot more needs to be done. At least the first level risk, where large corporations had directly manipulated financial statements, has been addressed. Still there continues to be a secondary risk, such as deliberately overlooking the provisions of auditing and accounting standards for the ambiguous use of accounting rules such as the Repo 105 to manage the daily balance sheet, or overlooking the non-disclosure of OBSEs to have vibrant results. Auditors were not able to question directly the use of Repo 105 with the client's firm nor were they able to report to the audit standard board for clarification or feedback. This is what had gone fundamentally wrong with the process and practice of audit.

The information corroboration failed as a process in the making of the current financial crisis. The financial information remained hidden by the management and only partial or selfish information went out to the investors. Since the auditors authorized the disclosures, they contributed in that process of creating information asymmetry between the firm and the other players, including the regulators. The disclosure was partial at its best. For a long time, auditing standards had been following a boilerplate process of disclosures and declarations in the financial reports. These declarations have been overly generic, more customary; hence it revealed all that is necessary from an advantage point of view of the management. This is how auditors pose a secondary risk to the system.

Generally accepted accounting principles (GAAP) are really 'generic'. There are few discrete areas with clarity on the accounting treatment but many grey areas, from where the accounts get their window dressing. The assets on the balance sheet have a 'reserve' supporting it, which is an open area in the accounts to be used to manage earnings. The inventory has a reserve for obsolescence and shrinkage, capital assets have reserves for impairment and depreciation even though there are rules to account them, and finally receivables have provisions for bad debts. The ways to create these reserves are made during divestures, write-downs and acquisitions (Damman, 2003). As a concept these are placeholders to be judiciously used by accountants to capture the financial reality, and auditors are required to make fair judgment of this accounting treatment. So, in the build-up to the current crisis, when mortgage borrowers were falling behind with their repayments and the accounts reflected the defaults, these reserves were used to manage the earnings.

The auditors were toothless. They were neither able to challenge the financial results nor their risky financial model, as long as the accounting standards were being followed. The practice of audit is to just assure that financial transactions are recorded as per standards even though it meant recording (colossal) losses. It was not their responsibility to get underneath the skin of the business.

Questioning the independence of audit services

As a system, there are multiple entities involved in the process of audit and each has an objective to fulfill. From the client firm's side, whose accounts have to be audited, there is the powerful audit committee which includes the Chief Executive Officer (CEO) and Chief Financial Officer (CFO). Both these positions have the ability to influence the decision to order and reorder the audit and non-audit services from the favourable audit firm (Damman, 2003). On the other side there is this market, consisting of investors, who perceive the firm's earning and auditor's independence in a typical manner. This had created interest in researchers to conduct various studies about the perception of the

Information Corroboration (2nd C)

investor regarding the financial results, the auditor's independence and the size of the firm. But it really does not matter, according to the author, because the investors have no direct method of challenging the financial results except to decide against investing in that firm.

The audit firm's revenue is based on audit and non-audit services, rendered to the client. The services are just not restricted to one area of account audits; the performance of one area of service tends to influence the potential business opportunity in the other area, for that client. Hence the conflict of interest is bound to crop up in the business dealings.

Based on a long history of business dealing with their auditors and the kind of influence one wield on the other, the auditors have been profiled in three ways by the researchers of accounting standards. They are Principle Oriented, Rule Oriented and Client Oriented. It is done to compare their objectivity in auditing their client. As the name suggests, the Principle Oriented auditors are oriented towards principles underlying the rules in accounting standards. They are process driven and capture well, the essence of the standards. The Rule Oriented auditors abide strictly by the rules as set by the accounting standard with little consideration for the underlying principles. They focus more on the practice of audit. Finally, Client Oriented auditors are soft in their approach to the client, in order to seek business gain from a sustained client service. But in all three profiles, the auditors by the very nature of their profession are supposed to maintain the true value relevance of the firm (Jamal and Tan, 2010). The auditors can be a mix and match of these profiles but the third profile; the Client Oriented auditors are considered to be of concern to the author, for the success of the financial system.

> There is a conflict of interest between the audit firms and the financial firms. It is because the audit firms in pursuit of business usually makes inroad into consulting projects of the same firm (Johnson. 1999).

There are both advantages and disadvantages in having these types of auditor profiles prevalent in the market. While Principle Oriented auditors are considered to be ideal for both the regulators and the clients, there could be instances where aggressive reporting may not find its way with this profile of auditors. In the end, within the legal ambit, it is not just the auditors but it is the desire of the management and the stakeholders who endorse the aggressive approach in reporting the earnings. The disadvantage with the Rule Oriented auditors can be the element of conservatism that creeps into the system and it could be that resources are unallocated (Jamal and Tan, 2010). The stakeholders may not like it if the earnings are affected, and therefore it really depends on how conservatism is taken in the market. The Client Oriented auditors are the most vulnerable of all as observed earlier. They bring about an element of conflict-of-interest to the system. In the accounting system, because all parts are not governed by rules, probably there never will be a complete set of rules, these profiles of auditors tend to help clients play with the ambiguity of the rules to report higher (rather suitable) earnings. With that ability due to their unique position with reference to the client firm, the auditors attempt to get more business and service fee from the client in return for favours of handling managed earnings. The SEC had recognized this profile of auditors for a time, much before the bankruptcy of the genre of Enron and the current crisis, but the law to restrict this profile to prevail is still not in sight.

If history is the record all major corporate frauds and manipulations, then the presence of auditors with the third kind of profile, appears common. While there is no incentive for auditors to be principle-based or rule-based, there are discrete incentives to be a client-oriented auditor.

Moreover, if one reviews the business model of the auditing firms and the fee relationship in the financial system as a whole, conflict-of-interest is natural. It is like paying the policeman directly to get an official character certificate. It is too easy to influence and manipulate the situation, if the policeman wishes for repeat business and especially if his livelihood depends on that fee.

There are many reasons cited for the inability of auditors to support the financial system to prevent the crisis. At the top of the list is the auditor's independence. As discussed earlier, it is the ability to detect and report a breach in the accounting system without the consequence of losing the client's business opportunity. The auditor's independence holds the key to the success of the profession of audit and therefore, the business model in which the auditors survive as a profitable profession must ensure that priority. Although auditors' independence is dependent on the business opportunity derived from their clients, in a

Information Corroboration (2nd C)

way, the independence is negatively associated with client importance, which is in line with the economic theory of auditing (Ghosh, Kallapur and Moon, 2009). This is where the system gets caught in the conflict-of-interest, as discussed before. In the pursuit of the business opportunity, the audit firms have to manage their customers with 'importance' which is measured by the total (audit and non-audit) fee earned from that client, as a ratio of total revenue earned in that year. The higher the percentage of this ratio, the higher is the 'importance' the audit firm attaches to that client.

The services rendered to the client have the potential to grow only if that part of the client's management who is responsible for ordering, enhancing and re-ordering the services is able to meet their objectives.

The fulfilling of objectives, also known as management wishes, is therefore directly linked to the business growth of the audit firms (not limited to hire or fire or fee determination) and if the wishes are required to play with the grey areas in the standards, the auditor's independence is compromised (Krishnan, Sami and Zhang, 2005). The influence of getting the management wishes fulfilled can also result in non-audit services and a separate revenue stream for the audit firms. On the sides, there are practices that require the reinvention or redesign of the structure and function of the audit committee, their authority, member nominations and individual career paths. They have been adding complications to management wishes and the power structure in the client's audit organization.

The audit firms are in competition and therefore would like to be part of the client operations for as long as possible and as much entrenched as possible. In the UK, the select committee has found that the FTSE 100 companies have not changed their auditors for decades and 99% of the FTSE 100 companies had only those big four audit firms (Select Committee on Economic Affairs, 2011). So, there is a combination of oligopoly mixed with conflict of interest in the profession of audit.

On the other hand, it has to be also understood that audit and non-audit services offered are typical services which require not only deep knowledge of the business domain but also specific knowledge of the client's operations, and therefore longevity of the business relationship between the two would help in getting competitive business solutions. Also, the investors perceive the non-audit services by the audit firms as a sign of stability, growth and profitability.

THE GLOBAL FINANCIAL CRISIS IS NOT FINANCIAL

One cannot audit everything in the account books and the rules cannot be watertight in this dynamic world of financial complexities. Judgements have to be applied and that is the responsibility of the auditor, fulfilling its role as an independent semi-judicial entity.

Preventing the fox guarding the chicken...Who's Accountable for the accounts

As a client firm, to have a differentiation between the accounting and financial functions is important; presently both are part of the common chief financial officer (CFO) function. Differentiating the two functions will hold two separate authorities accountable and there will be no conflict of interest. Management wishes and objectives would be clearly demarcated by objectives of audit and commerce. While the chief accounting officer (CAO) will be responsible for recording the transaction and getting the accounts audited, the responsibility for getting the profit and earnings right, will be the responsibility of the CFO in the role of fund manager using financial management techniques and tools. Extending this model, why not have chief audit officers who will be responsible for the audits only? In a reconfigured business model, this role can also be a liaison with the regulators or the government.

One can suggest that the audit practice as a function, be completely scrapped as a business profession itself. Instead, it should be part of the regulatory authority's portfolio which will provide an independent and neutral service to the financial system. This would eliminate the conflict of interest and continue to maintain the sanctity of the audit. That may look like the role of financial police, but the author would like to keep the model more like the graduate course examiner who assesses independently the individual firm's ability to bring materiality to the financial market. Like the previous change proposed, this transformation also would require gigantic effort and shift in mindset, but one is convinced that it would still save the public at large from the pain of an economic debacle like the current crisis.

The third model could be the complete outsourcing of accounting to the firms responsible for recording the transactions as and when they happen, who will be audited for accounting practices. In real time, the investors will see the accurate accounts (at least the unaudited) without a delay of months or quarters. The accounting services and their audit service can belong to a separate outside firm and that will serve the

| Information Corroboration (2nd C)

lasting objective of the auditor's independence. According to this model, auditing firms will have to be paid by the pool of funds contributed by the firms in proportion to their respective earnings or revenues in case it is making a loss. Since the disclosure of audit and non-audit fees, as mandated by the SEC, is found to affect the market's perception of the auditor's independence and earning quality (Francis and Ke, 2006), the proposed model will facilitate that finding. While the client firms cannot decide upon the choice of the auditors, the proposed model has an advantage in preventing the auditing fraud. The audit firm will have to bear the expenses and the loss to the investors.

Of course, these ideas have to be expanded for finer details to hold footing with the financial community.

Global financial architecture is suggested as a solution that includes high-quality auditing standards, strong international audit firms, effective quality controls, profession-wide quality assurance and meaningful regulatory oversight (Levitt, 1999). The results of effective audit standards will show directly on the quality of reporting and disclosures which is the source of symmetric information to the investors. Assuming that the firms do their best to report the financial numbers to the investors, stakeholders, regulators and other players, the effect of high quality audit services will ensure that whatever has been said is correct, dependable and trusted for future reference, in short high QoI. So one would know who is accountable for the accounts.

There are many factors in play in the system, which has both negative and positive influence on the auditor's independence, audit quality, conflict-of-interest and ultimately, the trust displayed by them. In the new financial architecture, these factors will be positively configured in the system such that they address the objective of the audit functions. Some crises in the past have created a direct dent in the reputation of the auditors and that needs to be reinstated to an unquestionable status. As the SEC had been insisting, auditors have to be independent in practice, as well as in appearance. It may require some painstaking and radical changes, including redefinition of the business model, if the financial system is to produce and corroborate robust information for the investors. The feedback loop from the auditor to the regulators (including standards) has to strengthen in order to seamlessly move news of abnormal practices from the client firms to the regulatory system. With that feedback loop, the audit and regulatory system will

THE GLOBAL FINANCIAL CRISIS IS NOT FINANCIAL

create a more sensitive environment to information corroboration providing just-in-time updates of any exceptional practices in the financial system.

| Information Corroboration (2nd C)

BASEL Framework: Responsibility sans Power

Objective of the BASEL Accord

In perspective, regulatory frameworks are the key to the smooth running of the financial system by ensuring that investors have trust and confidence in the market against any malpractices that could affect their wealth creation. It will be very difficult for an individual investor to go all out by himself and assess the risk in the market; also it will be difficult and a waste of resources for the banks to reinvent the wheel of best practice. Rather, it would like to follow, in trust, whatever standards and guidelines are laid down by the authorities. Over the last two decades the structure of regulation has changed because of the blurring national and legal boundaries in this globalized economy. This has also made banking and capital markets high speed while making its very nature as complex.

The international regulatory bodies had attempted to establish a sound regulatory framework with BASEL-I, II and III versions to make capital allocation more sensitive to risk in the financial landscape across international borders. It attempts to quantify and separate market risk, operational risk and credit risk to reduce the scope of regulatory arbitrage, while being generic and universal in approach. On the face of it, BASEL I, II and III had been primarily involved in defining the capital adequacy ratio. For an organization with the calibre of BASEL, that objective to be pursued as primary objective, there are arguments both in favour and against it. For reference, here is the list of some important guidelines released by BASEL.

Year	Release	Objective
1992	A framework for measuring and managing liquidity	Consolidation of liquidity practices followed by major international banks.
2000	Sound practices for managing liquidity in banking organizations	Liquidity Management and Risk Management
2006	Core Principles for Effective Banking Supervision	Banking Supervision
2006	Management of Liquidity Risk in Financial Groups	Liquidity risk management
2008	Liquidity Risk: Management and Supervisory Challenges	Global standards for liquidity regulation, supervision and risk management

THE GLOBAL FINANCIAL CRISIS IS <u>NOT</u> FINANCIAL

Why Capital Adequacy Ratio?

There is a reason why capital adequacy ratio came to be the primary objective more than ever, especially after the crisis. The current crisis, like all other crises, raised important questions and because the Too-Big-to-Fail firms were not able to meet their obligations, it became the analytical reason and the most talked about cause for the current crisis. Hence, capital adequacy came into prominence. Although, the focus of the BASEL framework had been capital adequacy to prevent systemic liquidity crisis, operational risk had additional attention because of the comfortable liquidity environment that prevailed in the decade before the crisis of 2008 (IMF, April 2008). It is logical to cite the regulatory capital as the root cause of the crisis but the author argues that it is being reactive. After the crisis, the BASEL recommendations had come to light as the proponent of regulatory capital, renewing the importance of global capital adequacy standards and supervision. The current crisis, which was also called liquidity crisis, along with other names, started to point towards the capital adequacy ratios of the banks in failure mode. Naturally, it became the 'reactive' source of solution to the current crisis. *The focus on capital adequacy still remains, even though the primary reason had been the undetected poor quality of the collaterals.*

Capital Adequacy Ratio in Arguments

One side of the argument is that capital adequacy ratio helps banks stabilize the financial system and avoids any catastrophic bank runs due to 'information effect' as banks are more prepared with the buffer capital to support the liquidity squeeze. The argument against the BASEL framework suggests that it amplifies the business pro-cyclicity in the market which adds adverse effect to the markets already in the downturn. Also, during the crisis the capital adequacy ratio holds more assets than is required. This actually dries up the market of the much-needed resources to revive the market from the

> "The instruments of banking regulation can be described by the following basic categories: the government safety net, restrictions on bank asset holdings, capital requirements, chartering and bank examination, disclosure requirements, consumer protection, and restrictions of competition (Summer, 2003)".

Information Corroboration (2nd C)

downturn. If capital adequacy ratio was important enough, then there is no justified reason why Northern Rock failed when it had one of the highest capital ratios in the UK (Walter, 2010). Therefore, some do argue that the 'one-size-fits-all' BASEL framework for all the banks will not work because of the heterogeneous nature of the geography, demography, business and local legal requirements.

For the sake of discussion, ignoring the role of the BASEL framework as argued in the previous section, the framework separately allowed a fundamental error in its guidance when it lowered the capital reserve for the structured finance products, compared to asset growth in the underlying structured products. As the IMF (April 2008) indicates, the ten largest banks from Europe and the US doubled their underlying assets to nearly 15 trillion Euros during the period before the crisis. According to conservative banking methods, the regulatory capital requirements should also have doubled, but in reality, the risk-weighted assets, which drive the capital reserve, increased only moderately. This leads to another argument against the BASEL framework, which had embedded the inability of supporting the risky assets in the securitized products that the market players used extensively to arbitrage regulatory capital. Was it the failure of the BASEL framework or the smartness of the financial intermediaries to arbitrage the regulatory capital?

Whenever the BASEL framework laid down the guidelines, it had been focusing on the capital adequacy of the financial institution. This leads us to debate between regulation using risk-weighted capital adequacy and regulation using market surveillance. Both methods have their own constraints; hence the debate is justified.

It will always be difficult in defining capital adequacy based on a universal value, as each financial institution, bank or investment firm is systemic in nature. This is because they have different risk- weighted assets and the calculation of these risk-weighted assets is based on their in-house and propriety risk management system. Therefore, choosing a universal value will lead to comparing oranges with apples. Segregation of information on each asset may not be important for applying principles of capital adequacy because the risks are combined and cumulative. On the other hand, if the regulation used market surveillance suggesting unique capital adequacy requirements, the regulators need to be in control of comprehensive financial information of all the assets in the system. It could be tedious and voluminous beyond the current capacity of the regulators.

In both cases, the financial risk-based information is the key to the BASEL guidelines for the market. This needs to be harnessed with efficiency and effectiveness for determining the accurate and precise capital adequacy ratio. With reference to information created in the system, having a universal value for capital adequacy will truncate information about risky assets and generalize the calculation. As argued earlier also, categorization creates information asymmetry because it tends to hide information. The effectiveness of the framework is lost here. If each asset is tracked to determine the underlying risk, though the method is going to be very effective, it may lose its efficiency due to the data volume. This may not be true in the future. The future belongs to harnessing big data. However, the current generation of computational power can support the changing value of the risk associated with each asset over a period of time, say on a weekly basis. Capital adequacy can be treated more like a variable.

As a proponent of system effectiveness, the author recommends that the new financial system tracks the risk associated with each of its assets in determining the capital adequacy for the firm holding them. The ***individuality of the assets*** has to be maintained. How much information is appropriate, considering the data volume that needs to be processed to arrive at the variable capital adequacy ratio? The answer is - 'All'.

In short, all information is appropriate even if it contributes minutely to the larger picture of the system. No information is insignificant.

On a purely financial consideration, applying standard capital adequacy across the financial plane would mean an inadequate level playing field for the market players. Banks might end up blocking its resources more than required even though the risk-weighted assets are less than the guidelines requirement or vice versa. In order to avoid creating uniform calculations in heterogeneity of business (Bowe et al., 1998), it would require tailoring capital adequacy for each and every institution in the financial market. In turn, it would require a standard method of calculating the risk across the industry sector rather than depending on the in-house and propriety risk management systems. More so, the information that is locked in these propriety risk management systems is adding to the information asymmetry in the system, as the content is

Information Corroboration (2nd C)

not shared for the sake of protecting copyright. It is yet another 'black box'. This information will be freed up for a more symmetric information flow in the system.

Here is a brief description of how the banks and non-banks will have different capital adequacy ratios. On the asset side of the balance sheet, the banks have long-term loans that are illiquid which only mature at the end of the term. On the liability side, the retail deposit is the chunk of non-capital liabilities, which is vulnerable to 'information effect' and may result in bank run. For the non-banking firms the asset profile is dynamic and changes with the change in the market situation. The non-capital liabilities of these firms are mostly long-term secured borrowings and therefore, any rapid changes are not resilient (Bowe et al., 1998). These differences in the composition of the balance sheet make the design of universal value of capital adequacy, tricky. Further, if the BASEL framework focuses on capital adequacy as a risk management method then it is repeating the same mistake that the Gramm-Leach-Bliley Act of 1999 did then. It unified the already segregated banking and non-banking capital adequacy. Not only will the capital adequacy be different for banking and non-banking institutions but also it will be different for regional, emerging and developing markets of the world, that are signed up for the BASEL accord. When the business cycle changes, it is a matter of further research, more for the financial experts, to analyze and understand, how during the last decade of high liquidity and low volatility, the financial system performed in the mandatory stress tests, which the BASEL framework had recommended. The analysis, whether the capital adequacy ratios provided enough support during that stress test, will provide answers to many questions.

The position of the BASEL accord in the international regulatory framework

The position of the BASEL accord has grown in significance over the decades, as the world of commerce had changed its shape and form which is closely linked to the process of globalization. First, it was the unification of Europe under the Eurozone, and now the ever-expanding trade regime with freer borders having necessitated the role of one common way of regulating the global financial system. Is the BASEL framework positioned to provide that unified regulatory system and if not, where is it positioned with respect to the other regulatory bodies in their respective countries? Is it a think tank providing guidelines for the countries looking for a modern financial system (as described in its charter) or is it assuming a consensus on its role of **unified global regulatory authority**? Can there be accountability to what the BASEL framework is trying to achieve?

Based on the list of advisory releases, whose scope is system-wide, it is inappropriate to classify the BASEL Committee as only an advisory body because member countries tend to follow them as strict guidelines, citing themselves as 'BASEL Compliant' making it a pseudo-regulatory or pseudo-supervisory body. The reason it is pseudo is, because it is an important ability of 'bargaining power' that a regulator must possess (Armstrong, 1995), and as is evident, the BASEL committee wields some undefined powers over member countries and hence, the financial firms operating in those countries. The undefined power is confusing because of the presence and role of other bodies such as the European Central bank, European Commission and country-specific financial regulatory authorities. So where does BASEL really fit in the global regulatory structure?

An argument against putting all the regulatory powers under one authority (if) would again create a monolithic structure that would enhance the risk of being a single point of failure. It will be a colossal loss if it failed next time. Moreover, politically it will not suit the countries to follow the extra-national body on a day-to-day basis that will regulate the national financial institutions. All these go against the argument of a monolithic structure, which would be too much regulatory convergence. Therefore, the risk had to be mitigated with additional diversity in the model and have a global body of regulation. Whether it is the BASEL framework or something else in future, global financial architecture will be incomplete without having a body that will work in the interest of participating countries; especially where the centre of financial gravity lies elsewhere and the poles of developed and emerging markets exist significantly.

The way forward for the BASEL Accord

One can argue about the inability of the BASEL framework for overlooking the implications of lowered risk-weighted assets and hence reducing the safety capital requirements. So what the financial market knew was different from the reality. The framework did not create information asymmetry directly but failed to detect information asymmetry as a consequence. Meanwhile, during the build-up to the crisis, the lag in adopting the BASEL framework by the member countries also remained inconsistent. The non-conformance to the BASEL framework by various countries was because it is not binding and hence the status of BASEL will continue to be pseudo because it is just an accord and not an international law.

As an outcome of the financial systems failure, it is suggested that the BASEL framework moves on from being just an accord to being an international law. It will seek better compliance by the member countries. Even before doing that, it needs to clarify its position in the international financial regulatory and functionary framework, so as not to overlap with other bodies. Instead, it needs to fill the lacuna in the international regulatory segment. In order to do this, the experts in the financial system need to reposition the BASEL accord to a more powerful role with accountability, something like a *'regulator of regulators',* and it would be appropriate because more than before, it now influences the regulatory authorities of many countries.

As seen in the past, the BASEL framework had been arguing for a universal value of capital adequacy. In the times when computing abilities were limited it was convenient to have a generic 'one size fits all' formula. But in the current situation, when the financial market is in chaos and the economic environment requires detailed information with respect to transparency and building trust, the adequacy capital should be dynamically calculated based on individual risk-weighted assets in the financial firm's balance sheets. Today's technology allows the bandwidth for running these kinds of rigorous calculations, which will only improve in the future. It is well known that the value will be different for different financial institutions and can vary multiple times over a short period. It would only reflect that the *system is sensitive* to the changing conditions on the ground. According to the author, the future must see the capital adequacy ratios for the individual firms fluctuate like the daily currency exchange rates.

THE GLOBAL FINANCIAL CRISIS IS <u>NOT</u> FINANCIAL

Moral Hazard: Hazard continues...

Defining moral hazard

Defining **moral code** will be as difficult as holding water in the hands forever, because it is very subjective, especially for people in the business of financial products where the product is 'virtual' and the objective is only profit. Whatever has been understood of moral codes in society, they are still not substantial because in simplistic terms, the ills in society are a result of the failure of the moral codes. One reason for failure of compliance is the lack of clear definition. Several laws exist which govern the broad behaviour of society either by statutory law, religious beliefs or individual values, yet they are never able to cover the entire moral guidelines for ideal behaviour. There is a reason for this – most of the laws are based on the religious beliefs of the majority community of the country, practiced and redefined over a long period of time. The basic code of conduct matches across the nations, but then there are variations in the severity with which they are treated by the specific law of the land. As in the case of financial sources of income, they are treated with varying severity across all the nations. For example, in some countries ownership can remain anonymous paving the way for money laundering and stashing black money.

If you include in society, a kind of community that is handsomely rewarded for making profits out of speculative risk taking, then it is easier to hold water in the hands than to define a code of conduct for the community that is guided by this objective. If the financial sector is to be governed by a code of ethics that prevents moral hazard, then corporate governance is the nearest and most influencing factor that can control moral hazard.

The financial system does not work in isolation. It has functional connections with other sectors of the economy and therefore it needs thorough corporate governance practices in line with the societal ethics imbibed into the business system, lest other sectors become affected by their shortcomings. In terms of practical morality, because corporate governance is an important source of moral behaviour in the business, which is an integral part of the society, it needs to be counted as other tangible components, such as assets, infrastructure, legal and accounting systems (Crockett, 2001). The prudent corporate governance can put a check on moral hazard; it has been proved time and again that there is a thin line between profit and ethics that the corporate have to walk.

There is grey area in between the moral and immoral that belongs to neither of them; legally it is neither wrong nor right to operate in that space. It is more a case of judgment. Amoral is that ambiguous space which provides advantage and flexibility to the operators to use the law for their own benefit. The law of the land may find it difficult to prove or punish, mostly debatable, but from an instinctive view it certainly looks immoral. Since the status of being ambiguous makes the law work hard to reach a suitable conclusion, the amoral practice meanwhile continues to make a profit, damaging the interests of at least one party. Moreover, the law enforcement is initiated only when there is significant visibility of a debatable practice. This complex mix of ethics and practice that sounds unethical, yet is not clearly illegal, is infamously called '**moral hazard**'. It is different from fraud because fraud is a practice that is already known to be illegal and participants know it, right from the start. In the act of fraud, the participants focus on avoiding detection, but in moral hazard the participants focus on misinterpretation of the law in their favour. Like the corporate executives hide facts behind percentage figures and statistics for the analysts, so do credit agencies and large investors, by overrating securities with conditional clauses, or in another example mortgage lender, conspire to artificially inflate loan documents.

Moral hazard has been included in the corroboration phase of the information life cycle because it had to be undertaken as a continuous process since this problem cannot be completely eradicated from the system.

Conflict of interest

Conflict of interest is one reason that fuels moral hazard. One of the operational risks in the firm is conflict of interest. This goes unnoticed most of the time and become so inherent to the system that it becomes part of the formal organizational practices. So moral hazard is not only prevalent at the highest decision-making rung of the organizational hierarchy but even the individuals in the remote corners of the organization are vulnerable. Conflict of interest provides an opportunity to the guarding fox to enter the chicken farm at will and make gains at the cost of others' productive resources.

THE GLOBAL FINANCIAL CRISIS IS NOT FINANCIAL

It is difficult to identify conflict of interest in a running system when the going is in green. This is because no one in a 'going concern' wants to question the profits. Only when the amber and red lights start to flash will the conflict of interest come to the fore. As a system, it is important to map the constituent entities with respect to each other to identify the connections that encourage conflict of interest.

The financial system has seen conflict of interest prevalent with audit firms and credit rating agencies, while interaction with their fee-paying client firms. While this was the design for day-to-day working, when moral hazard crept into the system and became an endemic, it went unnoticed. Had the mortgage crisis not happened, the practice would have continued unabated and no authority would have questioned it. Now, as a consequence of the crisis, the moral hazard due to conflict of interest is being talked about as a root cause and soon we may see a change in the working of audit and credit rating agencies.

Policy Assurance and Overconfidence

Moral hazard is a natural outcome from the sense of confidence given by policy assurances in the system. To keep the system stable and free from moral hazard, it requires an act of tightrope walking, providing balance between the right kinds of confidence, using policy assurances for the safety of the players and overly regulated regime, with the least risky market conditions. In the current crisis, on one hand, a sense of high assurance by policy, like deposit insurance or operating spirit of too-big-to-fail, made the system a potential case of excessive risk taking, where the players deliberately overlooked the potential risks and by-passed the required research for information processing. On the other hand, too little confidence would have increased the effort of the market players to be risk averse or to fear market participation altogether. On one extreme the market had perils due to moral hazard arising out of high confidence, while on the other extreme, low confidence could have shrunk the market even for normal business activities. In a way, it may be a case of limiting the sentiments in the market.

The current crisis is like a modern-day video game where the missing fear of physically crashing the flight makes children irresponsible in their flight simulation games. Certainly, the caution would have been higher and the actions more responsible, if the same simulation were real life and accompanied with the fear of hurting or killing oneself.

Information Corroboration (2nd C)

Confidence and assurance go hand in hand and together they make another composite factor of moral hazard. As humans have the propensity to take risks if handsomely rewarded and in the process of achieving high rewards, they suppress information which they think will negatively affect the transaction. Information asymmetry then becomes part of the transaction and in many cases may cross into the zone of moral hazard because using the new age financial innovation the fund manager is able to 'socialize' the costs of risk taking (Bair, 2011). It suggests that the longer the chain of participants in the originate-to-distribute model, the broader is the scope of information asymmetry and the higher the number of losers in case of a default.

As a conclusive statement it can be said that information asymmetry is one of the tools of moral hazard. As more asymmetry increases in the system due to various reasons, moral hazard becomes prevalent till the time the system finally gives way. In fact the IMF (IMF, Global Financial Stability Report, 2005), much before the crisis had begun to take catastrophic shape, generally alerted of the scenario where the government could be supporting the sustained market downturn as being the 'insurer of last resort', the advantage of that position could be leveraged. This was the card that had been played by many as 'too-big-to-fail' and consigned the nations to bailout at the expense of the taxpayer's money.

Moral Hazard and Regulation

The regulation comes with its pros and cons. From the seller's point of view, regulation and information symmetry reduce the 'information arbitrage' and therefore, the seller fears tougher competition, higher sales effort and lower margins. Too many regulations make investors drop their guard, and if they feel assured with concepts such as deposit insurance and Too-Big-to-Fail, as a safe system, then the players can be reckless. The sense of not losing anything even in the worst-case scenario can lead to non-pursuit of information or market intelligence (wisdom). This can be treated as a moral hazard in a way, where the fear of failing is absent and the sense of security makes players invest irresponsibly.

For millions of investors in the global market, the dwindling confidence in financial institutions can be improved and enhanced through supervisory oversight. Not only is the oversight required for the guidance, they can examine the risks players are taking, its affect on

THE GLOBAL FINANCIAL CRISIS IS NOT FINANCIAL

moral hazard and coordinating among supervisors, to monitor international, cross-border transactions and exposures (IMF, Containing Systemic Risks and Restoring Financial Soundness, April 2008). It has been a lesson learnt from the current Euro crisis where the interlinking exposure of one country's bank in another country with economic crisis is affecting the financial survival of the entire region.

The overpowering finance

Too much money was being handled by too few. Combine this with natural human behaviour to mix power and money to suit self-interest. Moral hazard is a natural outcome of this combination. The system failed to recognize that the global financial system rests on a very risky pivot, which has all the reasons to be affected by moral hazard. In this example, the naked Credit Default Swaps (CDS) have been playing the fireman and arsonist at the same time. While they insure the default on one hand, they also provide premium to those who bet in favour of a default, on the other. This is certainly contradictory to the basic philosophy of morality. How can an entity make a profit when there is a credit event (loss) in another part of the same system? The CDS market operates unlike the insurance market where the buyer of the protection has to compulsorily own the exposure. The CDS market allows speculation and profit on the credit event (loss) of an entity and since the volumes in CDS had bet up to five times the global GDP, it cannot be called a financial process, with high morals. There is a differentiation between the 'protection' and 'profit on failure'.

The other overpowering finance is the compensation of the employees that is linked to the profit. The performance criterion in determination of compensation had multiple criteria, but as of 2006, the return on equity became the sole criterion for the compensation of senior executives. It is a matter for debate whether the return on equity may or may not be a true reflection of the

> In the area of financial crisis-related cases, we filed charges against nearly 100 individuals and entities – actions against Goldman Sachs, Citigroup, J.P. Morgan and top executives at Countrywide, Fannie Mae and Freddie Mac. And more than half of the individuals charged were CEOs, CFOs or other senior officers.
>
> Chairman Mary L. Schapiro
> U.S. Securities and Exchange Commission, 2012

robustness of the firm. The books can be cooked for managed earnings, knowing the issues of moral hazard, become visible only after some time and sometimes, only if an incident is investigated. There are factors such as overwhelming compensation, power concentration and flexibility in disclosure, which make it easier to tread this path with moral hazard. With icing of media limelight, on the cake of superlative compensation, also featuring in the salary league table, to achieve this, any 'ordinary' human will risk walking the path of moral hazard. Of course, there is a factor of talent and skill required in attaining the pinnacle of compensation, but the criterion of bonus based compensation makes compulsion of moral hazard an option, especially when the corporate profits are under pressure.

For some time now, we have been discussing information asymmetry as being a natural part of the financial system leading to moral hazard and adverse selection. In the case of Greece we are witnessing a case of **synthetic information asymmetry.** This means that information asymmetry was deliberately built into the system in order to mislead the investor into the adverse selection of Greek bonds. The Greek government was found to be window dressing their books in order to mask their budget deficits, following the global financial crisis. The moral hazard is significant, as a cooked disclosure covering up the public debt would create wrongful investment decisions in the Greek bonds (Faiola, 2010). Since the financial market is highly interconnected, Greece has prolonged the duration of the global financial crisis because the investments are spread across the banks with toxic exposure in Greece. The contagion is causing a serious effect on the stability of the Euro and its union.

What is the moral landscape of the system?

Moral hazard is a widespread phenomenon, easily contagious, and has been an issue throughout the history of mankind. Great philosophers have provided insight into the issues of morality, including moral hazard, and it is beyond the author's capability to write a commentary on their work in the limited scope of this book. But ironically, it seems that moral hazard appears to not only exist but also is more prevalent than ever before, like the virus that is more resistant to laws and regulations. Does this indicate that the laws and regulations are only tackling the variations of moral hazard and missing out on its root cause? The moral landscape of the sector is to be screened, not by law or regulation but by practice, by one and all. **There is nothing in the**

THE GLOBAL FINANCIAL CRISIS IS NOT FINANCIAL

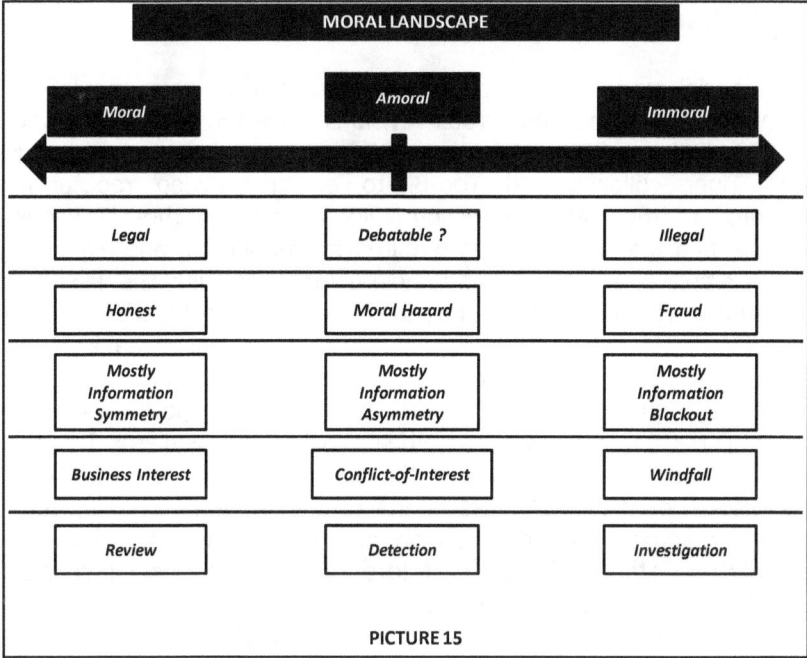

PICTURE 15

firm, if there are no people. It is the people who compose the firms and their individual ethics govern the spread or containment of moral hazard. It cannot be taught in academics along with financial engineering and innovation techniques since it is built over a long period of time, as an individual's character. It is a way of living one's life and collectively conducting the business in the global financial system.

Curtailing practices in the system that are supporting moral hazard is important as a process of detecting fraudulent practices. These are two different approaches to it: detecting fraudulent practices which require constant policing of entities in the system, and identifying moral hazard with a holistic view. A systems approach would provide that holistic view, connecting the involved entities with their objectives and then judging their activities for deviations due to moral hazard.

Information Corroboration (2nd C)

Regulation: Laggard in the system

The financial market has come through time and so have regulations, which have undergone numerous revisions since the Great Depression of 1933. Still the financial crises, such as the Savings & Loan crisis, Asian Tiger collapse and Too-Big-to-Fail crisis keep reoccurring. According to the role and responsibility defined by the US Federal Reserve, banking supervision is required for monitoring and examining the condition of the banks and their compliance with the laws and regulations. The regulatory authorities are required to issue specific guidelines to govern operations and activities related to banking and non-banking activities. This can be considered as a generic charter for all banking regulatory authorities across the globe. Specifically in the US, the Federal Reserve acts as both supervisor and regulator. It is true for many countries also where the central banks act both as a supervisor (Board of Governors of the Federal Reserve System, 2009) and a regulator, with an exception of the UK where the FSA is a separate regulatory authority. Therefore for all discussions, we consider regulators to provide a combination of supervision and regulatory services to their respective financial markets. Whether or not to have a split agency for the role of supervisor and regulator is not debated much in this book. Rather the point of grave importance is the ability of the system to view the systemic risk by itself and proactively act to prevent a crisis. A quick look into the pros and cons of having a split role or a single body will do no harm.

There can be an argument against the merging of these two roles because unifying the responsibilities in one body and the merging of the two could create a conflict of interest within the governance of the financial system. The argument is that segregating the information on which the supervision and regulation works, is difficult, as there is a greater chance that positive feedback of 'self-satisfying' supervision or regulation may result in failure of their individual objectives. It could also be that the convergence of the objective as a body, may override the objectives of regulation and supervision. Further, in the current scenario of the complex nature of the financial market combined with overly complex unification of financial institutions, as was done after the Gramm-Leach-Bliley Act of 1999, it is easy for any governing body to become lost in the complexity, to the extent of ineffectiveness.

This leads us to the knowledge that when the macro forces are overwhelming, micro regulation will have to be equally insightful. This

THE GLOBAL FINANCIAL CRISIS IS NOT FINANCIAL

was not taken into consideration at any time before, and that itself became the primary reason for failure of the financial system. The information generated and shared in the system is similar to a deep and dark sea, with unknown and unpredictable terrain of information with high variation in the contents. This is why the information was tedious to manage. This makes regulation difficult, and with the one-size-fits-all generic approach, regulatory governance is vulnerable to mismanagement.

The market has become more complex in the last two decades using models and instruments about which few understand the underlying engineering. Therefore the challenge is even more severe. Setting guidelines alone does not solve the problem if the macro and micro working is not monitored. Too much regulation makes financial engineering playful and looks for ways and means for regulatory arbitrage. Firms innovates models that go around the regulation which also becomes an individual innovator's incentive. Regulators, on the other hand, are under-equipped, therefore less proactive to upfront trap the flaw or the arbitrage. It is a wrong expectation to find them ahead of the financial innovation curve. Maybe it is this reason that over the years many countries have unified the supervisory and regulatory authorities in order to get everyone under an umbrella and reduce the gap in understanding the financial innovation curve.

As seen from the structure of regulators in various countries, there is a debate about having multiple agencies regulating the sections of the market. It could be a fragmented structure as in the US administration, semi-fragmented as in the UK or unified as in Sweden, Germany and France (Barth, Nolle, Phumiwasana and Yago, 2003).

The current system of regulation in the US is complex while it looks much simpler in other countries. Here is the snapshot of the most complex regulatory structure, found in the US financial system.

Federal level:
- Office of the Comptroller of the Currency (OCC)
- The Federal Reserve System (Federal Reserve)
- The Federal Deposit Insurance Corporation (FDIC)

Thrifts:
- Office of Thrift Supervision (OTS)

Credit Unions:
- National Credit Union Administration (NCUA)

Information Corroboration (2nd C)

Securities:
- Securities and Exchange Commission (SEC)
- Commodities and Futures Trading Commission (CFTC)
- Freddie Mac and Fannie Mae
- Office of Federal Housing Enterprise Oversight (OFHEO)
- Federal Home Loan Banks (FHLB)
- Federal Housing Finance Board
- Farm Credit System
- Farm Credit Administration
- Pension Funds
- Employee Benefits Security Administration
- Department of Labor
- Pension Benefit Guaranty Corporation

Along with these authorities, the Department of Treasury, Department of Justice, Housing and Urban Development (HUD) and Federal Trade Commission (FTC) play ancillary roles in the overall regulation. The insurance sector is regulated at state level and not at federal level, which also regulates the financial service providers, who are licensed in their jurisdiction. Such is the distributed organization of the US regulatory framework that it becomes more complex with the presence of financial service providers with operations in multiple states and countries who have a portfolio of services cutting across the different regulators. How regulation happens in the US is of great interest because they say that if the US sneezes, Europe catches a cold. It holds true, as demonstrated by the current crisis.

The future of regulatory challenges in other countries is an important cue when viewed from the US regulatory system point of view.

As the financial system complexities are growing in other countries also, they could start to reorganize their regulatory structure like that of the US, assuming it is a natural structure of the future, due to its sheer size of operations. Then the future will see many more complexities in content and regulatory activities. As the market continues to add complexities in structure and contents, the financial system has to cope with growing information asymmetry. The system can overcome the effects of these complexities with prudential micro and macro regulation readjusting in tandem with the complexities.

THE GLOBAL FINANCIAL CRISIS IS NOT FINANCIAL

It is better to start preparing to handle the nature of complexities earlier than agreed, either by planned reduction or some other option, lest the market have more blind spots. This is what is visible with hindsight.

A bible is yet to be scribed that can show ways of regulating a financial system; till then let the system be based on the basic principle of prudent governance for the safety of the market players, and since the financial system is emergent it has to continuously be redefining itself. It is important to note here that the structure of the financial institutions has changed in the last decade. Prior to 1999, commercial banking and investment banking in the US were different while in the current situation, large financial institutions have merged all the functions of the financial market.

So back to the discussion regarding the structure of regulatory and supervisory authorities; the global financial landscape does have many variations. In some countries, central banks have both supervisory and regulatory roles, and in others, they have only a supervisory role as the regulatory function is segregated. In the case of the US, regulatory authorities are split further into areas such as securities, commodities, currency and others. There is a trend here: the larger the market, the more complex the regulatory structure has become.

Together, all these structures have both, done well and failed. Therefore, the crisis cannot be considered as governance 'structure centric'. But one thing is clear: that whatever the structure of the monitoring authorities, there has to be timelier sharing of information between the financial institutions, supervisory authorities and the monetary authorities to match the fundamental changes in the market (Crockett, 2001).

For most practical purposes, the US financial market has been leading the way for both developed and emerging market economies. It is not only true for the financial processes followed but also in terms of regulatory structure because of its sheer size of the financial market. Moreover, the cross-border financial transaction from the US influences global economy in a significant way and this has been demonstrated by the earlier boom and bust cycles in US economics. Therefore, it will be apt to consider that the centre of gravity of global financial activities lies in the US. It is a reference point in this book, and many arguments are based on this outlook. Today many have forgotten that the US is the financial centre of gravity considering the fallout of crisis in the Greek banking system and the Euro crisis. In actual fact, the crisis in Greece and many other European countries is the fallout of the meltdown in the US. Moreover, the financial crisis has now crossed over from debt crisis to economic crisis, then political crisis and now culminating again in another banking crisis. All these crises are underlined by continuous social unrest and protests. There have been changes in governments in the UK, Greece and Italy along with social protests such as the 'Occupy Movement'. Even if the US recovers, there is a good chance that others may take much longer to recover because from now on, the path to recovery is different for different countries. In the author's view the continued global financial crisis is more a crisis of fundamental principles than financial or economic. **The argument is that a country can have a slow economy with sound financial system but the reverse is not true.**

Regulation in a tight spot

Many commentators have observed that the banking regulators were complacent, and for this crisis in particular, their response was slow, reactive and untimely, rather than rapid, proactive and just-in-time. While investors and bankers interplayed to derive gains, consenting on risk taking, it was the inability of regulators to keep the marketplace safe and stable. The US financial system had converged at the top with four mega-banks and institutions holding 40% of the banking assets. According to the chairman of the FDIC, the concentration of financial activity had outstripped the capacity of the regulators to impose market discipline and regulate these mega-banks (Bair, 2011). One reason for this overloading of regulators could be the intensive regulation that the financial sector generally attracts, which is the hygiene factor for this sector.

This overload is overwhelming even after the regulatory function has been eased out to facilitate the trade during the period of expansionary globalization in different countries. Prior to this era, there was heavy regulation in the system, to the extent that there were controls for prices, competition, restrictions to a particular industry sector, mergers and acquisitions and so on (Crockett, 2001). Further, there seems to be an assumption that tighter regulation would mean higher cost of loans and higher deposit insurance premiums (IMF, October 2009). These are the principles shown in simplistic terms that rule the market. The objective of higher yields is met with complex products and hence the nature of regulation, cost and risk involved.

THE GLOBAL FINANCIAL CRISIS IS NOT FINANCIAL

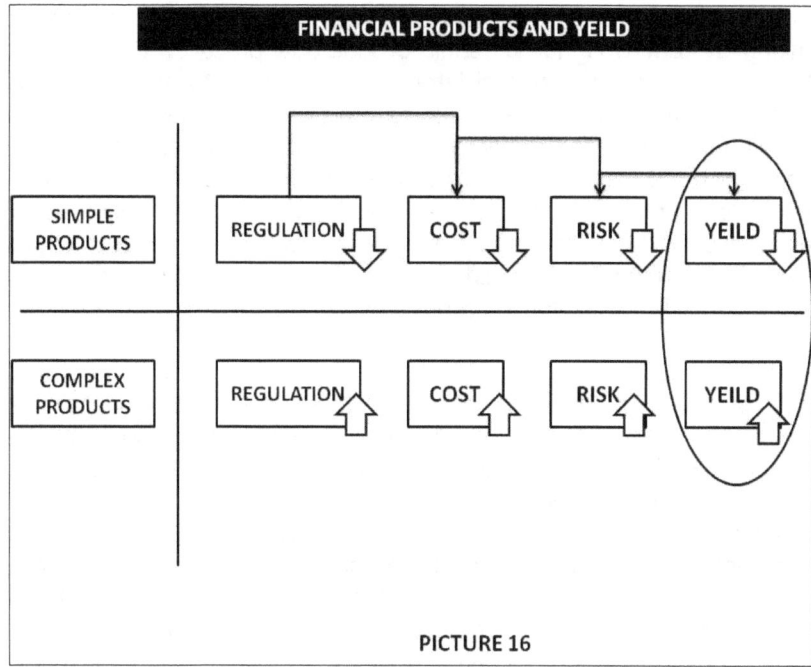

PICTURE 16

The reason cited is that the banks would need to hold more and higher quality capital, and yields are lower due to simpler products. Also, the IMF views the correlation between tighter regulation and lower profitability. While the simpler products will bring lower risks, the banks would subsequently have to reduce their deposit insurance premium. Complex products may give high yields because of the high risk. In return the regulation may ask for higher deposit insurance premiums and hence the cost. This perspective may be supportive of the prevailing practice of bringing financially engineered complex products, which are detrimental to the practice of bringing simpler products. As discussed before, the financial systems are emergent so the regulation needs to be ahead of the curve.

In future, if correction is to be based on learning from this crisis then the face of regulation will be very different, something that will respond just-in-time with the financial innovation curve, at least.

The Shadow of Shadow Banking

The shadow banking system interacting with the large financial firms had been evading prudential regulation and supervision. This meant that they lacked capital standards increasing the risk of failure with

Information Corroboration (2nd C)

uninsured investments (Bair, 2011). The development of the shadow banking system was not a result of one-day practice. It had been allowed under the nose of legislators and regulators for years together and the volume of trade grew multi-fold in the last decade. The answer to be sought is how the regulators allowed the shadow banking system to grow with no warning of the growing risk, in the sector. The shadow banking system was seen as part of the bigger financial model, which was an accepted way of working and therefore, no fingers were pointed at the risk, it inherently imbibed. Even though, it has been the source of information asymmetry for the regulators.

The US Federal Reserve computes the hedge fund in the household sector by calculating the assets of the fund as the residual of the total assets minus the addition of all other assets. The reason for this calculation is that the Federal Reserve does not have a record of the funds operating in the system, as they are mostly unregulated and are a private pool of funds. Moreover, the funds are not required to report their asset values to any official authorities (Council of Economic Advisors, 2010). In principle, the status of being unregulated hedge funds brings information shadow into the system. Considering the $1.7 trillion (2008 calculation) as the size of the funds altogether, it makes the fund one big monster in the regulated market. Just to gauge what $1.7 trillion means, it is equivalent to the nominal GDP of Canada.

Based on the above discussion, there are a few reasons that come to the forefront for the failure of the regulation in preventing information asymmetry across the board. Information asymmetry needs to be avoided not only at transaction level, but also at institutional and market level. There is no doubt that the current crisis emanated from the housing mortgage sector and was contagious to other types of financial institutions, which were providing liquidity. But even today regulations have not been able to reach the depth of the financial institutions, such as hedge funds, mortgage pools and asset-backed mortgage issuers, which would remove the blind spots of shadow banking. This is how information asymmetry got built into the system due to the prevailing market's structure and practices. It will only get worse with the asymmetry that gets braided due to complex financial products. It will continue to completely dodge the radar of regulators, as it has done in the past.

THE GLOBAL FINANCIAL CRISIS IS NOT FINANCIAL

Information strategy, a key to the process of regulation

The solution lies in making the market more transparent and (accountable) to the market players, such as investors, bankers, regulators and governments. The trust deficit that has crept into the social outlook is required to be rebuilt. Since the primary motive of being in a financial market is to make profits, there is a good chance that the players can deploy legal, illegal and half-legal methods. It makes the regulator's additional objective of trust building, very important. To achieve that, the financial system is to have regulation as a comprehensive oversight process, in order to secure compliance with the legal requirements, simultaneously detecting and preventing half-legal (amoral) opportunities.

Although, the scope of the regulators had been well understood over a long period of time, still the regulations have been lenient or stringent to varying degrees. The 1980–1990 era in financial regulation was considered a period of lenient regulation because of the overwhelming philosophy of free market and self-regulating business interest. But it changed its tone to be stricter after the crisis in order to quell the panic and uncertainty. Hence, when one of the reasons cited for the current crisis is the inadequate role of the regulators, and then there is a need to ask **"Who Regulates the Regulators?"**

The author will seek an answer to this question later in this chapter.

Although there is no theory to substantiate the compulsory role of regulators in the financial system, still history has proved that they are a necessary part of the financial system and for that matter any other system which likes to pursue prudential governance. If the system without regulators is out of the question, then it is the right balance of leniency and controls that decides the prudence of governance.

So how much regulation is necessary such that regulation is a critical factor of success and failure. Let us consider this particular scenario.

It will be an extraordinary approach to completely deregulate the entire system and let the players manage their own business interests. A system without regulation would be a system with intensified Brownian motion without controlling factors. Profit-making will make firms drive markets to compelling practices and the players may operate in an imperfect market. Though the contents would be available to

Information Corroboration (2nd C)

everybody, it would be at the discretion of the users to do the due diligence before taking a decision. Of course, the cost of research, intelligence gathering and surviving the unknown risk would be enormous. Often, people have given Internet content as an example of an unregulated market where the contents in the World Wide Web (www) are made available and it is up to the users to use it or ignore it. For the moment it is working well and more players are added each day with innovative content to suit the different needs of users. Although, there are shady areas too, as far as civil society is considered, it is working well. This example is relevant because of the scale and size of its influence, which cuts across international boundaries. It is similar to the influence that is wielded by the financial market. Like the World Wide Web, if the financial market were unregulated, the respective players would do their own due diligence before making the decision, rather than assuming the content as safe. Information seeking would be more important than it is today. The virtual accountability that resides with the regulators today will vanish and the players will feel more in charge of the situation. This is contrary to today's belief about the role of regulators, which creates a false sense of security with the players, as they enter the market with an inherent understanding that the market is a safe place to be in.

There are valid arguments on both sides. It really remains to be evaluated, after the Internet would have been in existence for at least 25 years, whether the same model of unregulated content, can work in the financial system or not. For now, to the author, it seems that financial transactions need extensive regulation because the financial market is all about profits, and players do undertake actions that are not appropriate.

Information Symmetry as answer to: 'Who Regulates the Regulator?'

To understand the key responsibility of the regulation, it must be understood that whether it is a stringent regulation or an unregulated market, the players, will naturally do their best to bring information symmetry, before conducting their transactions. It is a separate topic about their ability or inability to achieve the symmetry, but the process of seeking information symmetry invariably exists as part of the business transaction. This understanding of inherent process of acquiring symmetry actually neutralizes the intensity of all functions of the regulators and makes the function of securing information symmetry as primary responsibility. Thereafter, the remaining functions of regulation will become enabled with enhanced efficiency and effectiveness, as they would derive transparency and accountability from the symmetry. Even for regulators to monitor the moral conduct of the businesses, their effectiveness depends on the information symmetry. This implies that regulators become the natural custodians of information symmetry in the system. In a way, the level of information symmetry in the system is one of the measures of effective regulation.

Another logical way of looking at the primary role of regulators is the history of the financial system. It is found that overall the markets had created information asymmetry, irrespective of the nature of regulation. Knowing the tendency of market behaviour, removing information asymmetry or facilitating information symmetry becomes the important and primary function of the regulators.

The main argument of the author does not lie with a magical regulation or legislation that will put an end to the crisis but in a pursuit of a 'symmetric information system', which will run the financial system with perfect information symmetry. It will be an advantage to the genuine entrepreneurial market players and the regulators themselves. In order to meet this objective successfully, the regulators need to ensure that information flows in the systems without an element of opaqueness.

To have a system that is transparent not only requires more information but also an open access to the information. This translates that in a highly regulated market, the market players should have shared, both accessible and homogenous information, especially when they are transacting.

The author considers information asymmetry as a primary result of information system failure leading to the failure of effective regulation. Therefore, to judge the performance of the regulators, it is the degree of information symmetry that needs to be measured and there lies the answer to – *Who Regulates the Regulators?*

| Information Corroboration (2nd C)

Legislation and Regulation: Twin reactions

There is a strong correlation between legislation and regulation in terms of their content and timing. During the transition between legislation becoming regulation, there is a significant time lag. There is time required to pass the legislation, time to create the regulation corresponding to the legislation and time to implement the regulation. Each of the stages has a corresponding lag which adds up to the final time lapse when the scope of legislation actually touches the intended issue. Since it will be a long drawn-out exercise to explore legislation from their cycle time of tabling the legislation, to implementing the regulations for all important events in the financial sector, for the sake of our discussion, readers can certainly assume that it is a lengthy and tedious process. For the financial sector, legislation has played an important part in changing the history of the financial sector across the world, and in a generic sense has changed the face of the communities, countries and continents, both for good and bad. We will briefly discuss a few legislations and their relationship with the consequence of the crisis, at different points in history.

How is banking legislation and regulation different?

If history is to be followed, most legislation came at a time when the crisis had already occurred and correction is required. Thus the legislations are found to be only a reactive method to fix the problem and they operated in a paradigm of contingency. Now that the Dodd-Frank legislation has been passed, the regulators are writing the rules, adding strength to the legislative truss. The process of writing and rewriting the regulatory rules will continue for some time and the market will keep adjusting to those changes. If one follows the timelines, the peak of the crisis was in September 2008, while the (corrective) legislation was passed mid-2010. Thereafter, the regulatory authorities are following up with the nuts and bolts. The implementation is not yet complete at the end of three years. This reaction time is of concern, when global markets are in crisis and the final fix is still not in place. It would have been acceptable a century ago, but in today's market of high-frequency trading and trade values of more than nominal global GDP, the current time required to fix can be considered no more than glacial pace. For two long years, after the peak of the crisis and the passing of the legislation, the financial markets had continued to operate in the same conditions which actually brewed the crisis. What needs to be challenged here, is the allowed duration of the continued practices (responsible for the crisis), knowing that a crisis is in play. This is not accounting for the time that regulators in the US will take to adopt the new regulations, and subsequently other governments and companies would change their regulations because they are part of the international and interconnected financial operations. **The principle of timeliness in fire fighting is being defied here.** Regulations, on the other hand, are a real-time method to fix the issues which the regulators foresee. So, it is argued that the regulation will be able to proactively resolve the reoccurrence of the crisis more rapidly than the legislation, and therefore, the regulators need to be empowered more to undertake the fire-fighting role before legislators actually react to pass the corrective law.

In the current crisis, a typical situation has risen. While the Dodd-Frank legislation was being legislated, there was an exclusive inquiry – the Financial Crisis Inquiry Commission (FCIC) – was in progress. This inquiry included interrogating the top executives of the Too-Big-to-Fail firms, academicians, financial experts and also those who were responsible for risky financial instruments. The inquiry submitted the report six months after the Dodd-Frank Act of 2010 was actually passed. Since the legislation came into being earlier, it is either assumed to have proactively and instinctively incorporated the findings of the FCIC or is in shortfall of incorporating the findings of the inquiry commission. In both cases, there is a mismatch between the 'intended' and the 'fact'. It will be an interesting fact to know sometime in the future why all the learning from the FCIC had been omitted in the Dodd-Frank legislation.

Do Legislations and Regulations have same risks?

Although today, in practice, legislation is considered a method of regulating the regulators, this is not true. With respect to the facts referred to, the legislators and the regulators are in the same pool of information. So it is the recirculation of the same information (asymmetric) in the system that creates laws and regulations. According to (Pelaez 2009), if the market fails because of imperfect information, government intervention will also fail for the same reason, as there is no superiority of information by the government during intervention. One argues here that a prudent information system is required to ensure that verified information is consolidated in the system to avoid the recirculation of flawed information.

Information Corroboration (2nd C)

The legislators and the regulators across the international environment have the same risk as the financial market. It is because there are soverign governments that promulgate the laws, specific to their countries. Similarly, the regulators have jurisdiction in their respective countries only. In a typical case, in the Eurozone, although there are central banks in their respective countries, the European Central bank, still influences the regulations, legislations and the market risk. The BASEL accord further adds to the complexity of international organizations operating between countries across the continents and markets. This complexity is the risk to the regulatory and legislative processes and provides a confused state of governance. Although each country would like to go its own way in resolving the effects of the crisis, which is emergent to the situation, yet they cannot do so because it has to be in agreement with the Eurozone or the BASEL accord. All have to agree on the type of road to recovery, making it, none or all. At this moment, across the global financial system, there is a regional currency union, individual currency status and global financial unison, but no political unification (which there can never be). This imbalance brings the most severe risk to the global financial system. With a holistic view it is observed in the system that discrete is only partial and homogeneity is incomplete. Hence, for the global financial market, regulation and legislation are in a mixed-up state.

Primarily, this chapter suggests the segregation of the role of supervisor and regulator, leaving the choice of having a single agency or fragmented agency to the governance of the country's financial market. The primary objective of both, the legislation and regulation, is to continuously maintain a transparent functioning while making changes to facilitate a higher degree of information symmetry in the system. If it is information asymmetry that failed the regulators then it is the failure of the underlying information system to facilitate the information symmetry. We will see how a symmetric information system can be achieved with the proposed financial information architecture, later in the book.

As a post mortem to the crisis, one finds the ladder of regulators on a wrong wall. It is apparent that if the regulators had the necessary information that could have scanned the internal accounts (like the balance sheets of the market makers), the build-up of the crisis would have been proactively dealt with. But the irony is that the regulators themselves were also the victims of information asymmetry. They had asymmetric information that was also showcased to them.

THE GLOBAL FINANCIAL CRISIS IS NOT FINANCIAL

In the real world, regulations are followed if it is easy to comply and entities comply with regulations, if the benefits are realized. It is an argument against a complex regulatory structure and policing because the propensity of seeking only the profits leads to regulatory arbitrage. For better regulation and compliance, it is important to demonstrate their benefits, in theory and practice, and the disadvantages of non-compliance reiterated with penalties and punishments. If firms make provision for the penalties in their profit and loss accounts, then there is something seriously wrong with the messaging of the regulation.

Simplification is the need of the hour. Too many layers and authorities bring confusion and regulatory arbitrage which brings uncertainty. It reduces the confidence level in the system. This is a process of transformation in itself; a matter of cultural change for the financial community, where the inertia to adopt changes in regulations is heavy. Therefore, the author anticipates that it will take a very long time to change and will be accompanied by enormous effort and willpower.

Chapter 6
Information Communication (3rd C)

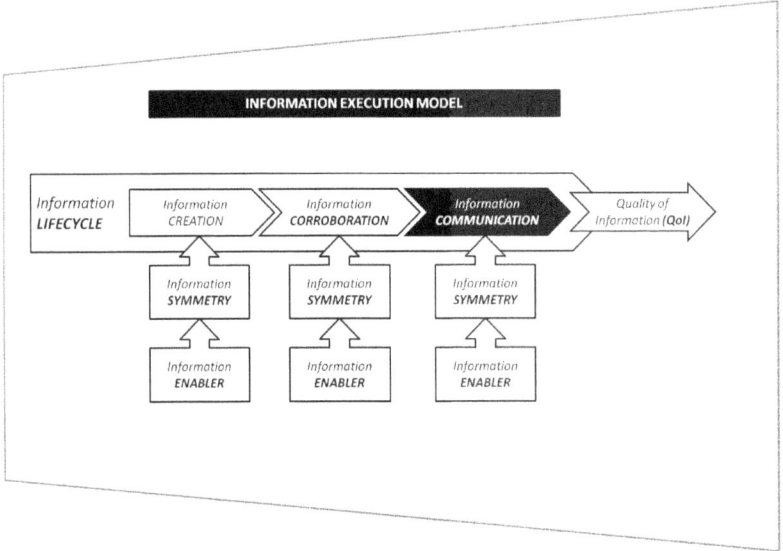

Disclosure: Need for more

The Meaning of Disclosure

This chapter on disclosure is based on the author's argument in the previous chapter on accounting standards and reporting. The argument there was related to the inability of accounting initially and financial reporting to provide complete information to the market players. Overall, the accounting and reporting standards are inept in providing information that can provide, at best, the information required for decision-making. Extending this argument, the greater the difference between the information provided by the standards with the ground reality, the more is financial disclosure required to cover the gap. This gap questions transparency, information asymmetry and ultimately the QoI as a measure of the standard's capabilities.

Disclosure is the sharing of business information in addition to the accounting and reporting standards. Financial disclosure is required by the firms for the shareholders with limited liability so that a view of creditworthiness is available. The disclosure process is important because it is a formal instrument and the first step in attempting to enhance comprehensibility and transparency in the system. Thereafter, it is the effectiveness of the process and the compliance which defines the extent to which it brings transparency.

Provisions in the Investment Advisers Act of 1940

The US had the Investment Advisers Act of 1940 that protects the rights of the investor with mandatory disclosure requirements. As of 2006, fund managers are required to fill in form ADV, which provides disclosures on conflict of interest – both internal and external, history of regulatory and legal problems, problems of any investment advisors and operational risks, that investors are required to know before they make an investment decision. Prior to 2006, while the small investors were deprived of this vital information, the large investors already have known these risks because of their indigenous due diligence. There was a potential disadvantage to the small investors for whom the cost of due diligence was not affordable.

In its current form, are the disclosure instruments good enough? There is no formal test to indicate the intensity of the disclosure, especially when the disclosure is made in the director's report which is subjective.

The figures in the disclosure may signify the situation but this only reverts to the same debate about the strength of revelations by statistics and numbers. As intangible assets, such as derivatives and risk allocation like Credit Default Swaps (CDS), continue to grow both in size and scope, the current crisis has questioned if the true value is being reflected timely in publicly available disclosures (Levitt, 1999).

The disclosure of more information is required in accordance with the accounting standards as laid down by the US GAAP, IFRS and other national accounting bodies. These disclosures create an important source of information for investors, creditors, regulators and the government to make their respective decisions. While the institutions internally do follow a guided practice in transacting business, there are guidelines to make disclosures to the external world. The very fact that they are called disclosures is because normally they are not known in the public domain. All that is officially disclosed is the source of information symmetry in the system, and the extent of the symmetric information lies in the comprehensiveness of the standards and disclosures.

So what stops the firms from making comprehensive disclosures? There are risks to the firms in making disclosures. Too much information may frighten away the investors and too little may bring overconfidence. The definition of balanced narrative disclosure is still to be benchmarked. There has been effort by trade associations to garner support for enhanced disclosures, especially after the fingers have pointed to **informational insufficiency** as one of the reason for the current financial crisis (British Bankers Association, 2010).

At the core of the current crisis lie the structured instruments. The reason is a significant uncertainty about the valuations and disclosures attached to these structured instruments. An important question is whether or not structured finance products are worthwhile, even with the intended benefits, compared to the extent these products increase the risk of a crisis in the system. (IMF, Containing Systemic Risks and Restoring Financial Soundness, April 2008). Following a particular accounting standard for the structured products brings an element of judgment in their valuation and hence, the disclosure is incomprehensible. It does not happen effectively because the disclosures are periodic and the interim revaluation disclosure is not mandatory either. Moreover, it is less prescriptive in the accounting standards (IMF, April 2008). The transaction of these structured instruments happens without proper disclosure and brings information asymmetry into the system.

While the disclosure leads to information compliance and symmetry, non-disclosure adds risk to the system by way of creating uncertainty. With higher QoI in disclosure comes lighter regulation, as the market players are more aware of the real performance of the firms. With increased non-disclosure the information asymmetry increases in the system and leads to practices of moral hazard. In a bid to still keep the marketplace safe, the authorities have to indulge more into regulations

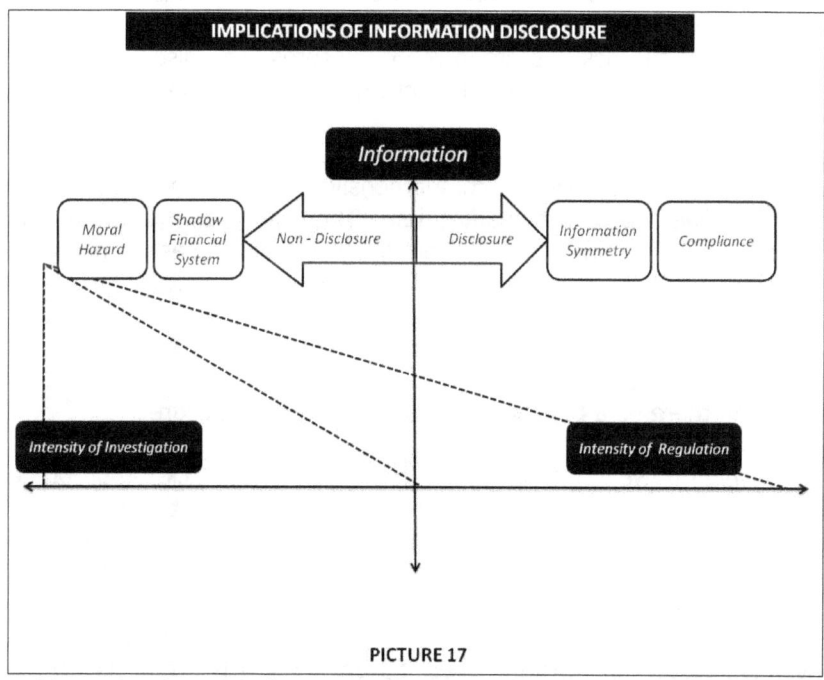

PICTURE 17

and investigations. Disclosure is a function of QoI and the consequences are direct and substantial. An improper disclosure, as in the case of interim valuation and director's report, does lead to risk exposure and creates avenues for moral hazard. As the IMF stability report suggests, the current crisis is a result of non-disclosure of structured financial products in a shadow financial system of OBSEs (IMF, April 2008).

One can argue about the periodicity of disclosure as having a direct relationship with the business cycle. In the case of manufacturing, the value is assessed once a quarter; the same periodicity seems to be out of place for financial institutions whose transaction cycles are measured in seconds. Although, the periodicity of disclosure for financial instruments requires another round of research, one can safely conclude that it cannot be quarterly, which would be the same as that of manufacturing.

Like mandatory disclosures 'Disclaimers and Warnings' also help investors to be aware of the impeding risks in a product. In the case of CDOs the products were built on statistical modelling without verifying the risk of underlying assets, as they actually existed on the ground. While these structured financial products transitioned from one generation to another, from CDO to CDO^2, there seemed to be no traceability of the risky assets in the disclosures. The disclosures were out of tune with the real risk encapsulated in those structured instruments.

Disclosure in itself, however comprehensive in its current boilerplate, cannot define the exact market risk. There will always be a gap between the disclosure and the ground realities. It has to be more subjective and emergent. The question is how the financial system as a whole looks forward in closing the gap between the disclosure and the reality. What should be the format that is best-suited for the market players with respect to accuracy, timeliness and comprehensiveness? In future can there be a benchmark to the quality of disclosure?

The sovereign wealth fund is another area which lacks appropriate disclosure mechanisms. Governments have control over the investment decisions, but are found to be poorly regulated. Moreover, since it is cumulative tax wealth that the government intends to invest in foreign assets, the disclosure is mandatory to an extent of informing the citizens about the risks. It is an indirect risk that the citizens of the sovereign behold by virtue of their citizenship and hence makes them obliged to exercise their rights as stakeholders. The Euro crisis has shown the vulnerability of one European state over another and all EU citizens are affected significantly. It is the reason, the citizens of each EU country and collectively as EU citizens; need to know more about their sovereign exposure. It is of paramount importance to have a clear understanding of the big picture of the global financial system, not only by the experts in the Too-Big-to-Fail firms, but also by the retail investors, and as a case, each EU citizen also.

THE GLOBAL FINANCIAL CRISIS IS NOT FINANCIAL

Interconnectedness: Inevitable source of contagion

Interconnectedness has consequences in the financial system and is a proportionate factor for appropriate response by the connected entities. By the very nature of human development, wherever humankind interacts, interconnectedness is inevitable. When a system like the global financial system is based on interactions, the nature and characteristics of interconnectedness as a process has a completely new meaning.

> Look at how our American colleagues are extremely concerned about the events in the Euro area, 3,000 miles away, we are just across the channel
> ~ (King 2012)

In these superfast, interdependent, highly digital modern-day global systems, including the financial system, a resultant of highly responsive interconnectedness called contagion becomes an important parameter to be kept under control for overall stability of the system. Interconnectedness had played an important part at all times of the financial and economic cycle, during the bubbles as well as troubles, especially, when the financial system is volatile. As the author sees it, there are two parts to the process of interconnectedness, **the connectivity and the interdependence**. The variation in these two variables marks the responsiveness of the market. Interconnectedness had strengthened the process of globalization irrespective of the consequences; rather they are looped together. Interconnectedness had deepened the process of globalization, irrespective of the consequences of globalization. In fact, both are looped. This brings interconnectedness as a prevailing factor in the current financial crisis and the negative consequences are observed in the phenomenon like bank runs, capital flight, and fragility of the Euro with other derivatives of contagion.

Globalization has been in existence since the times of Marco Polo and the Chinese silk route. Colonization was one form of globalization but today's version is very different. Globalization would have been different if the interconnectedness, as a process, was not as refined and sophisticated, as it is today. Connectivity has enhanced the interdependence and with the factor of sustained stability, globalization in its current version is increasing in complexity and dynamism. It has moved from globalized business to globalized business processes. The globalization of a financial business process has added a complex dimension to the financial system which was unheard of, in the last century. This means that a business transaction crosses multiple international boundaries to complete one business transaction.

As a process, interconnectedness has brought down barriers between countries, and the capital flows across boundaries are factored where the rewards are the best. The integration of the markets is the process in play where the exchange of information between two parts of the system tries to bring equilibrium to the known factors, much in line with the Ricardian theory of comparative advantage and

> The effect of interconnectedness is in broadcast of asset prices and risk allocation in the economies and the information effect due to chain reaction in the interdependent institutions handling a scenario of default (Summer 2003).

the Adam Smith theory of absolute advantage. The propensity of the system to achieve this equilibrium firms up the process of interconnectedness, and therefore it is an important determinant in the stability of the global financial system. Apart from the economic gains, the system's effectiveness and efficiency are related to the interconnectedness, as a process of creating financial and sentimental equilibrium. As time progresses, even though efficiency is getting better, the effectiveness of the interconnectedness is debatable, considering the current crisis and its consequences.

Affects of crisis due to interconnectedness

The financial market and sovereign economics are tightly interlinked by an intricate global web of financial relationships and interdependencies with the highest correlation. For instance, small Norwegian towns above the Arctic Circle had invested in sub-prime mortgage securities related to California, for its municipal payrolls and school budgets. Although, the daily operations of both the entities were loosely connected, the effects of the market in the US led to a significant impact and budget slashes in these remote towns of Norway. Similarly, the Eurozone crisis – a fallout crisis to the global financial crisis of 2008 – is a living example of the dangers of unsafe interconnectedness. Is the Eurozone crisis limited to countries of Europe? If the Eurozone breaks up, it could have a negative global financial contagion, further adding to the chaos in the already depressed economic environment. There will be bank runs, and investors will try to find safe havens for their money. Already, we are seeing the effects of economic slowdown in the Eurozone, China and other emerging markets due to slowdown in the US. Cross-border interaction benefits during boom and is equally detrimental during bust; it is at all times when controls have to be ascertained. This only suggests the intensity of the interconnectedness in the global financial system which has all the variations of business scale, economic cycle and geographical distances. All these factors converge on a singular plane leaving no one in the system as a standalone entity. In the singularity or flatness of the global market, fencing the interconnectedness seems to be the logical answer.

Another lesson taught by the crisis is the neutrality of interconnectedness. It is both a curse and a boon, depending on the time of the cycle; therefore its consequences need to be considered more meticulously than ever before. The interdependence had reached deep into the remoteness of the global economies, and a ripple in one corner makes waves on the other side. A credit squeeze can bring about a revaluation in the risk allocations leading to consequential slowdown in the system. So an increased credit in one part of the system can justifiably increase the value of an asset in another part of the system. Similarly, in a positive sense, the monetary transmission created as a result of interconnectedness makes it a facilitator for an efficient risk allocation across national boundaries. Banks have used credit risk transfer (CRT) as a mainstay of its risk reallocations objective. Even though an individual institution will shed its risk to another one by way of securitization of loans, overall the system accumulates risk, elsewhere. Hence, the overall systemic risk increases every time a unit CRT takes place which further increases the correlation between those systemic risky entities in the system (Nijsken & Wagner, 2010). In a way, even though buying CDS protection or selling loan securities increases the activities due to interconnectedness, still they are transferring amplified systemic risk back and forth in the system. The shifting of risks between different sectors, across borders, is an objective of global asset allocation, which in turn has consequences for global financial stability, as the reallocation of risks and excessive funds leads to only partial uniformity (IMF, Global Financial Stability Report, 2005). The cycle of interconnectedness is just not complete by achieving partial uniformity or total equilibrium in the system; there is more to its operations and safety.

As discussed previously, interconnectedness has blurred the national boundaries but standards still vary. Regulatory arbitrage has become a methodology which takes advantage of these national variations in accounting, auditing, market practices and government interventions. One example of the effects of interconnectedness is the vulnerability of markets by the firm trading across the borders that follows different standards, laid down by the International Accounting Standards Board (IASB) and the Financial Accounting Standards Boards (FASB). Both boards represent the poles of the global financial system, and the differences between the two systems provide a ground for convenient

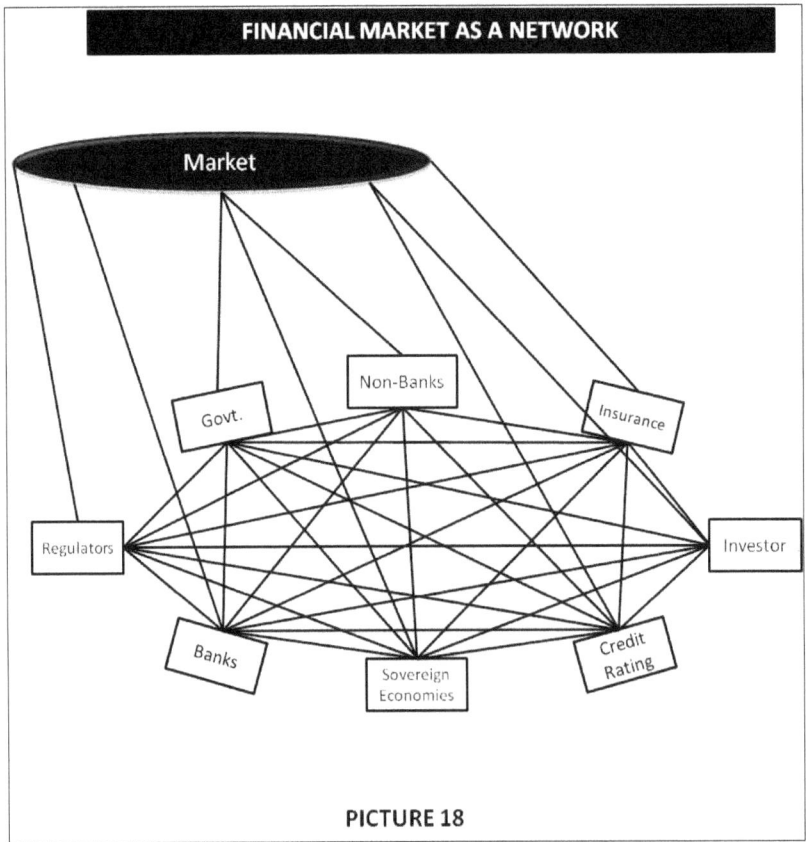

PICTURE 18

arbitrage. Firms that overlap the two standards undertake the jugglery of financial reporting in compliance to the respective countries. The slice and dice of financial information to be used in one standard and ignored in another makes it a good recipe for both regulatory arbitrage and information asymmetry. Since interconnectedness brings arbitrage to the global systems due to the divergence in standards, it can be viewed as a logical outcome of interconnectedness; hence arbitrage has been provisioned in business-as-usual by the firms. The global market is

THE GLOBAL FINANCIAL CRISIS IS NOT FINANCIAL

represented in a network of at least eight important forces. For each there are variations due to local and national factors. Based on this snapshot, one argues that though the markets are interconnected globally, yet they are not homogenous in terms of regulations, accounting standards, currencies, government interventions and banking practices. While interconnectedness had been problematic in the case of the current financial crisis because of imbalances rocking the ship, the author agrees that well regulated and symmetric interconnectedness will enhance the stability of the financial market by the reallocation of risks of the national markets which will also be a measure of an integrated market.

Today the interconnected financial system at best can be monitored for basic and financial processes and practices that are standard across the system, but much of the heterogeneity still remains a formidable risk. The Euro crisis is a reflection of the heterogeneity in the system that was being attempted to be bound by the homogeneity of currency and regulation. With some insight into the factors of interconnectedness, European leaders have started to call for fiscal union, which is another route to challenge the heterogeneity in Europe. It looks like an unrealistic goal, but that direction of thought suggests the validity of the author's argument. It can be described like a ball, freely rolling through the unlevelled turf of national standards, making random impacts on the globalized financial system. The challenge in this case, like the current crisis, is to manage those impacts. Like creating a level playing field for business transactions, the interconnectedness also requires a level field of regulations and standards. This differentiates the concept of interconnectedness with connectivity. Following are a few examples of impact due to differences.

The economic cycle is different in different parts of the globe. While loss recognition is faster in US banks, it is slower in European banks (IMF, October 2009). This difference leads to an extended heterogeneity in a banking system even though they are interconnected and might belong to the same business group. These imbalances in the banking system will take a longer time to reach a unified working standard, but that would mean a global monolithic block of banking regulation. In the author's argument, it increases further the risk of banking regulation as a single point of failure. Even though this topic of interconnectedness is more to do with the principles of economics and business, it is worthwhile to note that even though a standardized information system can bring consistency in processes, globalization does highlight

Information Communication (3rd C)

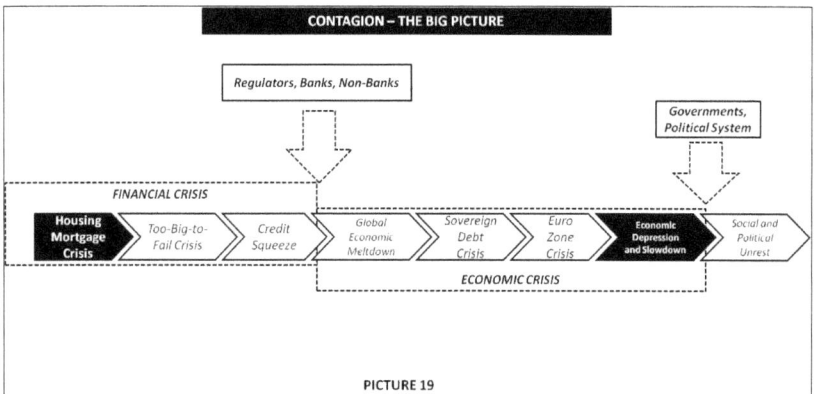

PICTURE 19

imbalances in economic cycles. Therefore, the author suggests that for the time being, it is appropriate to take the heterogeneity as a reality. This is to seek a solution by way of a managed heterogeneous financial system which is grappling the crisis of 2008 and the Euro crisis, as its off-shoot. This opens up a whole new field of studying the interconnectedness where connectivity and dependence coexist with heterogeneity in economic cycles of boom and bust.

The interconnectedness is just not limited to the financial system; it integrates and affects the other systems too. As this crisis has shown, the effects of the financial system engulfed the global economic system and now had enhanced further the scope of the crisis into the Euro currency and Eurozone. In a late reaction, emerging markets also have been affected to a proportion of a varying degree of interconnectedness with the US and Euro markets. As a consequence, the imbalance in the liquidity market aggravated the weakness in a number of emerging markets that relied heavily on foreign bank credit to finance their domestic credit. This is NOT to say that interconnectedness was the villain during the crisis, but it was the inability to foresee and control (fence) the affects of the interconnectedness that is being emphasized. Needless to mention that the uncontrolled interconnectedness had elevated the impact of the crisis on the other connected markets.

There is a crossover boundary between the financial system and the economic system which needs to be identified. Suppose the banking system was smart, the government quick and regulators wise enough, to handle the crisis, then the effect of the current crisis would have been much smaller. The contagion from the US housing market would not have been as severe, in other connected global economic, social and political systems, as has happened with the current crisis. It is important that along with managing individual connected systems, in the big picture the points of crossover between the systems, especially those systemically connected, need special treatment.

This is the big picture of **contagion** due to interconnectedness. The crossover entities between the financial system and economic system are the financial intermediaries, regulators and banking and non-banking firms. These crossover entities are to be managed with transparency and morals in order to minimize the effect on the wider population. The next boundary is the political system which lies between the economic and social system. If interconnection between the economic systems starts to hamper the social system, then the political system, as a crossover entity will come under strain, therefore the transition of crisis into the social system can only be managed using the political system. The author has indicated the political system because different countries have political systems with varied flexibility and agility. It depends really on how the government reacts to the situation and thereafter, how the political system backs the response of the government. This is the most difficult of all the entities to manage. The learned and the experts have already written volumes on this subject.

In what manner are these crossover entities managed? Or do they manage the crisis? These are two key questions. Certainly, they are also the affected parties. According to the author, these affected parties are first the responsible entities themselves. Therefore, if the contagion was to be prevented, these responsible entities are to be proactive in detecting the signs of the crisis, and failure to do so make them the affected entities. This starts the discussion of figuring out the required resources and the ability to detect signs of the crisis and the contagion. The author argues that symmetric information sharing is the key to visualize the signs of crisis, as much as an ingredient of the interconnectedness. If there is an imbalance between the information shared to maintain the interconnectedness (connectivity and dependence) and the information available for detecting signs of crisis, then the crossover entities will be laggards. The system cannot be called as 'well integrated'. In a measure of system integration, information available for regulation and supervision compared with the information available for business-as-usual needs to be equal.

Information Communication (3rd C)

Reporting: Informational risk

Financial reporting is required for monitoring and making decisions by the investors, creditors, regulators and other market players. Hence, it is assumed that the reports are:

- Comprehensible
- Timely
- Objective
- Free from bias.

These characteristics are defined to make financial reporting a toll of high QoI and utility. As a case, all known incidences of fraud and bankruptcy have remained undetected because of the inability of reporting standards to bring transparency, much before it actually hits the market.

Financial reports are the face of a firm's solvency. It is an important source of information to the creditors, investors, regulators and lending banks. Any deviation in financial reporting amounts to information system failure for the dependent entities and a loss of confidence in the system (Kroeker, 2010). Hence, financial reporting is sacrosanct and needs to be protected by means of standards, audits and regulations. As an analogy, financial reporting is like a language that communicates to millions of investors every day whose future depends on it (Levitt, 1999). If financial reports do not reveal enough information then the system sits on ***informational risk***. Even though accounting principles have the ability to record business transactions and fund flow, it is the characteristic of reporting that is a key to the transmission of the content to the intended destination. This determines the requirements and features of the reporting, as listed above. Reporting is an integral part of the financial system architecture because in its broadcast, lies the degree of information symmetry. This is the reason why reporting had been included as another crucial part of the information life cycle and execution model. Accounting and reporting standards need to reflect the roots of the business and economics. As seen from the crisis, the firms took advantage of the financial accounting and reporting standards which masked the real economic status of the business. The debate provoked here is about the match between the financial and economic accounting and reporting. One can also argue about the fundamental flaw in the representation of the financial information.

Accounting standards have been in play for a long time and are able to standardize accounting and reporting practices to a great extent. There is a future that needs to be addressed. The financial system is getting more complex and transactions are no longer posted in the same old way of the nineteenth and twentieth century's. Since the system has become layered and overly complex, the changes need to bring more transparency, flexibility and timeliness to the system. One of the efforts by the international accounting bodies is the convergence of ISAB and FASB in order to bring standardization to both accounting and reporting practices. The author had argued earlier that the divergence needs to be leveraged in order to provide a more varied perspective of the accounting and financial performance. Even if this means displaying financial reporting in multiple standards it would make a lot of difference in bringing information symmetry into the system.

Why financial results are once a quarter

Currently, the firm's annual report, which includes the income statements, balance sheet and disclosures, as a form of financial reporting, has been used by the investors more reliably and habitually for taking key decisions. The challenge is with the periodicity of publication for these kinds of official reports, as various market players can rely on the figures, only when it is published. The reason that financial results are reported every quarter is because in olden days it took time for the accountants to consolidate the manual and handwritten accounts into the statements. In today's world of high-frequency transactions, real-time recording of transactions and business being conducted at the speed of thought, **one wonders why financial results are still being reported every quarter.** Of course, for the non-banking sectors there could be large variations in the daily inventory figures or seasonal sales due to the nature of business. But for the banks and financial institutions, it makes complete sense to do a public balance sheet every day. Though the results will be unaudited, it will still be of more benefit than harm to analyze and make the decisions based on the financial numbers that are as fresh as real time.

There is another significant factor that needs to be considered. The quarterly financial results do bring in speculation in the market and the speculation brings an element of uncertainty, therefore any mechanism that will prevent uncertainty will be of advantage to the system. It is important to reduce the element of surprise in the financial results because the comparison is with the previous quarter or the year. On a timescale, if the two markers of comparison are brought closer, from a quarter to a day, the element of speculation will be completely eliminated. A trend line of the daily financial results will enhance the quality of information (QoI) and the quality of investment decisions. Considering the result of daily reporting of the financial product, it will enhance the quality of the credit rating also.

Reporting for the layman

The process of investment is the engine of the financial market and includes all shapes and sizes of investments. Large institutional investors are a consolidation point somewhere in the chain of small retail investments, whether in the form of pension funds or securitized home loans or other similar products. This chain of investment transformation can be elongated or short, depending on the financial product, but that should not decide the depth of financial reporting. The reporting needs to be standard, irrespective of the size of investment or the type of investor.

The benchmark of quality reporting is the ability of retail investors with an average level of education to assess and comprehend the complexity of the financial reporting. In other words, the financial reports need to be comprehensible to the smallest investors in the transformational chain, as they are the least resilient link in the case of a financial loss.

Then why can't the reporting be as standardized as traffic lights, whichever country it is, red always means stop and green always means go? This question is not meant to be answered with singularity of format but the comprehensible nature of the financial reports. In the global financial system, the players, including national and international investors, would find the financial information symmetrically displayed. **It will be a case of one standard understood by all.**

Most of the issues of financial reporting are due to accounting standards and its representation. There is a direct dependency of the reporting standards with the accounting principles. For example, if the accounting framework supports transaction-based accounting, the financial reports will not represent the fair value of the asset. There will be misrepresented information in the absence of assets being traded in the liquid market (Ohlson, 2010). Independently, the financial reporting will report the figures with the mention of transaction-based accounting or fair value accounting, as the case may be. Whether the figures provide the true picture of ground reality has to be understood by the accounting standard board and the regulators.

Chapter 7

Information Enabler

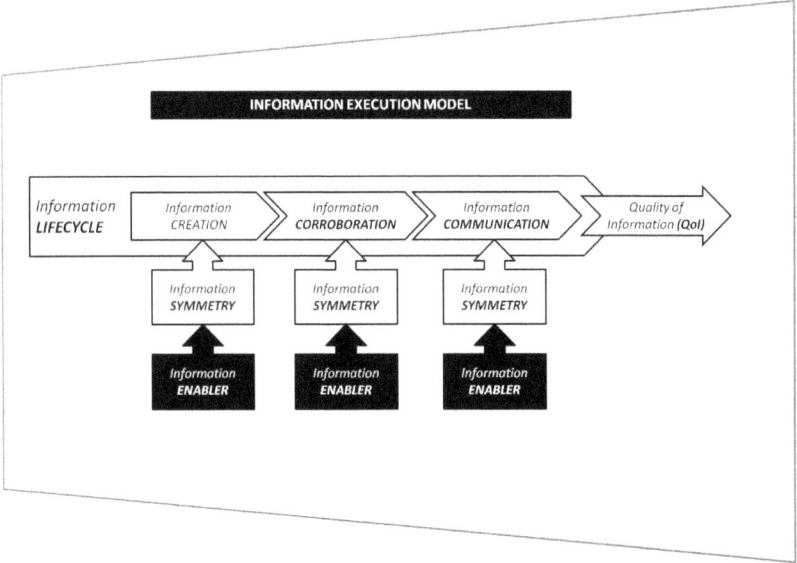

THE GLOBAL FINANCIAL CRISIS IS NOT FINANCIAL

Foresight, is more than Forecast

There are many chapters in this book that the author considered important in reconstructing the outlook of the global financial system. But this chapter seems to hold the underlying philosophy of the entire exercise. Foresight is to **visualize** an event in future and starts with a process of proactively identifying a relevant event in the future.

The design of the information system running the financial system needs to fulfil this function in order to avert a crisis like the current one.

Systems' thinking predicts that individuals will not change their mode of thinking or operation until their existing modes are proved beyond doubt, through direct experience, to be failing, and there will be change in thinking only when their previous thinking has been demonstrated to be inadequate (Chapman, 2004). The current crisis still defies this argument because a similar crisis, though not of the same magnitude, had been part of the global financial history. If the worldly learning is based mostly on convincing experience then the practice of creating foresight is left with limited use. Probably the change is a function of more vivid foresight of both good and bad times. Assuming vivid foresight will bring both proactive actions, the challenge lies in creating that foresight in the system.

It will require no special intelligence to understand that the nature of foresight lies in the quality of constituent information. Considering high quality of information is available, it then remains to be structured and presented in order to create foresight. The author's favourite example is the driving map. Maps are a good source of information in the case of driving. It provides accurate information of the direction and the nature of roads. Over a period of time, the same information on the maps has been enhanced with GPS services. Now the user is updated in real time with the current position, while showing the way ahead in the journey. With GPS, the QoI has been enhanced from being facts on the map to real-time information with automatic information about the next miles. Still further, GPS services have enhanced the information with real-time updates of traffic conditions. The updated information is supported by a statistical forecast of journey time. These two pieces of information create foresight to the user which prompts a response. It is then left to the user to take a detour or stay on the chosen route.

Information Enabler

In this whole example, enhanced information on the map, which is a representation of the fact on the ground, is suitably structured to create foresight. With reference to the current crisis the author argues that the current crisis could have been averted if the facts on the ground were enhanced with high QoI to create foresight. It is in this pursuit that this book has been written.

The US financial system, including the regulators, Federal Reserve, government and of course the smart investors, was not able to comprehend the impact of failure of the housing market or the downturn of the asset-backed securities on global investors. The investors in Europe also were not able to see through the possibility of downturn in the US housing market and the impact on its own financial system and the sovereign economy.

This is how the IMF in its global financial stability report of April 2007 interpreted the stress test. Conducted prior to the crisis, the stress test forecasted that 'A' rated products would not face losses until the housing market fell by 4% every year for the next five years. Further, the report showed confidence in the stability because the products had 90% sub-prime deals which were grade A or higher, therefore the risk was assumed to be limited. The IMF did acknowledge the weakness in the sub-prime market but suggested that it does not pose a serious systemic risk. It further quotes the results of the stress test conducted by the investment banks and predicts that investors will not face any losses due to the securitized sub-prime mortgages contained in the financial products. The IMF report also cited the safety limit of investors beyond the 'historically unprecedented' scenario of the downturn in the housing market (IMF, Market Developments and Issues, April 2007). The IMF was nearly there in effectively creating foresight. The report does indicate a possible serious systemic risk, but they moved away from the probability of the crisis. In the author's argument, the IMF missed the effectiveness of foresight because they failed to apply human judgment and were stuck with the statistical forecast.

Hence, Foresight is not same as Forecast.

Foresight is a result of the combination of multiple methods of processing the information of the past and the present. Creating an early warning system would include improvements in alert measurements, evaluation of contingency plans and interpretation of stress tests. It is certainly different from being a fortune-teller. On one hand, the system has to keep learning from the failures in history as indicated by Chapman (2004), and on the other hand the system will have to create wiser and prompt early warning alerts, using a methodology of collating information.

There is a conceptual difference between foresight and forecast. It seems that the mathematics has taken over human judgement and the world of 'money systems' has tripped over the forecast and lost its ability to create foresight. As the previous chapters in the book discussed the mathematical modelling techniques and the robotic program trading, it comes to light again that the information created by these methods has failed to provide foresight. Few scholars in academia

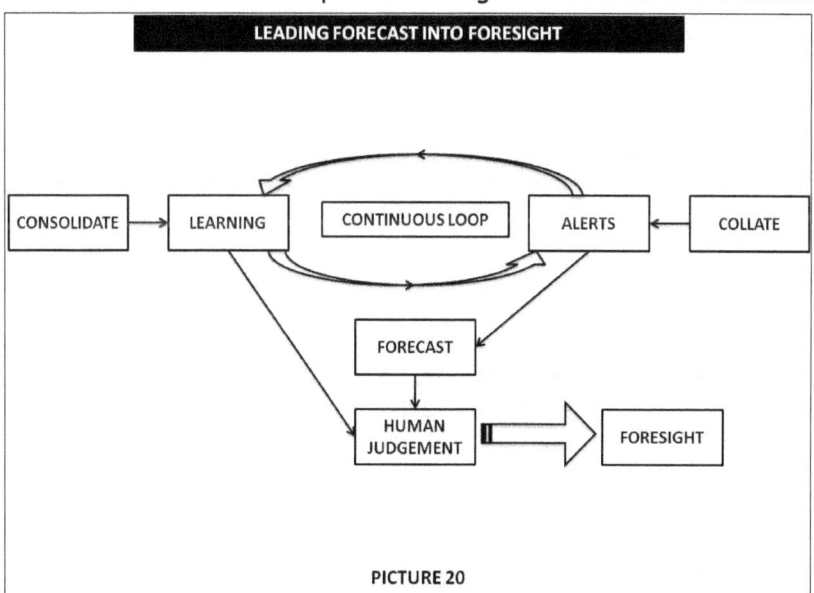

PICTURE 20

and experts in the financial sector have spoken at length about the construction of foresight or the supporting information system to create high QoI for it. Rather, truckloads of readings are available to discuss, enhance and glorify the forecasting techniques. The information system running the financial systems has to redefine itself and strike a balance between the forecast and foresight.

Based on this premise, one finds that there had been no learning from the Savings and Loan crisis of 1989 which led to the failure of more than 700 US-based thrifts firms. There is a direct parallel in the roles played by thrift firms in the S&L crisis with the role played by the Too-Big-to-Fail firms of 2008. In both instances, the loan equity and

Information Enabler

mortgages were securitized and traded in the market using the originate-to-distribute model. In both cases, the market was moving towards an artificial boom of real estate with retail investors on the lowest rung of financial transformation. In both cases the regulators were late to respond to the growing malfunction (not malpractices) of the system and the moral hazard. Nearly twenty years apart, the financial crisis of a similar nature reoccurred but this time was global in impact. The only difference between these two events of 1989 and 2008 lies in the severity and the global consequences. While this book is being written, the crisis still continues and all those nations who were once rich and powerful are grappling to contain the aftermath of the crisis of 2008. **The question is: where did the learning from 1989 go?**

Learning is important; it is to be recorded as part of business-as-usual as it creates the right information to **create alerts**. If the learning were well recorded from 1989, the alerts during the period of build-up of the crisis would have definitely warned of, in a loud and clear tone, the impending crisis of 2008.

As understood by now, the crisis is not the failure of the financial system, but the failure of having foresight in the system. It is worthwhile to mention that any information is as good as its ability to create foresight. There could be tonnes of data and information circulating in a system that would have created an accurate weather forecast, but it takes one piece of missing information in the space of foresight that renders a crisis such as a tsunami.

The fundamental concept in which the financial system is set up to function has to change. Its inadequacy to fulfil the demands of consistent stability for a long period of time is a concern. There is no doubt about its performance if viewed in the short term of ten or so years, but in the long run the resurfacing of the crisis makes the system look vulnerable. Since the crisis is a repeated phenomenon in the history of the financial system across countries, some fundamental changes in the business-as-usual are urgently required. The focus should be to restructure the information system to create foresight and visualize the interrelatedness of events as a possibility of a crisis.

In whichever part of the financial system they work, if the community of experts JUST recognize that the path to averting crises lies in the ability of foresight, half the battle is already won. Then it would be only to

THE GLOBAL FINANCIAL CRISIS IS <u>NOT</u> FINANCIAL

construct or restructure the financial system to bring about the information that will provide the necessary foresight to the players in the system.

To end this section, after finding similar examples of crises, and with reference to the Chapman quote, an important question remains unanswered and will require further deliberation. Has the system thinking proven correct by showing the inability of the players to change course, even when the information available was assertively indicating a failure ahead?

| Information Enabler

Real-Time View – Just in Time

Ideally, a view of the event that has a zero time lag between the occurrence of the event, recording of the event and the broadcast of the event can be termed as real-time view. An event could be as small as a significant transaction and as large as filing for bankruptcy. It was impossible in the earlier days of hard-copy media to achieve real-time view, but today the advancement of information technology has reduced the number of excuses for not having a real-time view of any event. Information technology has played an important role in bringing the concept of 'real time' into the business and more importantly, into the financial system. There are two parts to the system where information technology has contributed in realizing the concept of 'real time' – the actual business transaction and broadcast of the results including the analytics. As said, information technology is the medium that has to perform the role of an enabler to provide real-time view to the intended recipients.

Information technology in the financial system moves markets at lightning speed. At least the sentiments of the market are reflected instantaneously. This creates a need to capture effectively the emergent and momentous change in the economy also (Levitt, 1999). Economy, as a bigger picture of the underlying financial system, reflects sentiments from many interconnected systems. Any change in the financial market condition has to reflect in the economic spirit instantaneously, in representative form that is comprehensible to all kinds of market players. Any lag in information communication among the players in the environment may create information asymmetry of dangerous proportions. It makes two dimensions to the real-time view: one, the content of the view, and the other is the time. The content as a representative form is discussed in the chapter relating to the systemic view. Earlier to the crisis, the SEC had confirmed the changes in the computing environment and warned that the financial reporting view has to change its shape and form, from being an industrial age tool to an information age practice (Elliott, 2001).

There are factors for setting up a real-time view for the players, which includes the cost of setting up and the cost of chasing the technology curve, which itself is accompanied by its own complexities of managing technology set-up. These can be considered as side issues when the objective of the global financial architecture should be to bring the proceedings in real time for the entire set of market players. The SEC chairman revealed that from FY 2005 until FY 2009, the investments in information technology had reduced by half (Schapiro, 2010). It is a surprise that the experts did not favour more information agility using newer and efficient technology, even when the market volumes were growing and required more supervision and regulations. At this point, one finds a reiteration of systems thinking that people do not change till they experience failure (Chapman, 2004). Now that the crisis had affected one and all, the focus on the information system is expected to intensify, if the root cause is understood to be the system-wide failure of 'knowing'.

There is hardly any argument that will be against the concept of real-time view, though in some quarters there are reservations about the unnecessary panic or overwhelming sentiments that can result from the instantaneous nature of information symmetry. The author understands that as the markets mature with daily, weekly, yearly and seasonal cycles of business and economic variations, the sudden rush due to overwhelming sentiments do smoothen out over a period of time.

Spikes are a function of market maturity. One example is quoted in the IMF's Containing Systemic Risks and Restoring Financial Soundness (April 2008), where the slippages in the timeliness of confirmations and affirmations in the trading at the OTC market had led to CDS exposures. This was because market participants were not able to assess the market conditions in real time due to weakness in the information system infrastructure. Though the information system infrastructure is not restricted to technology infrastructure, it also includes back-office processing delays. Therefore, in the chain of information if there is a delay in one of the links it leads to the overall defeat of ***real-time information symmetry***.

Another example that comes to the forefront is the lag in reporting losses during 2008. European banks had a longer reporting time than their counterparts in the US. The non-banking financial institutions took even longer to report losses. Thus the seriousness of a global crisis unfolded over an extended period of time and it took the governments even longer to respond. Consider the scenario of financial crisis seen in a real-time view. If the market players had a simple view, they would have responded differently, some two years prior when asset prices were reaching a plateau or the structured instruments with sub-prime or not were rated as 'AAA', irrespective of their composition. At least the red flag would have been raised with the regulators much earlier or 'just in time' before the outbreak of the bankruptcy contagion. Experts would have found it easier to translate the financial and economic condition of the market for remedial action. Today, based on hindsight, when we look for an answer to what could have been done differently, among other resolutions proposed, the simplest of them is the availability of a financial architecture with a ***real-time view*** for all the market players. Real-time view is necessary to track emergent changes in the financial position of the market and the firms which will bring the real responsiveness into the market conditions.

Path to achieving Wisdom

In the pursuit of high-quality accounting standards which will report the true relevance of the firm, it is not only restricted to un-editable recording of the transactions to reduce the scope of earning management but also it is to respond to reporting timely gains and losses to the stakeholders and other market players (Barth, Landsman and Lang, 2008). This would require an agile analytical system that builds wisdom-oriented data set for recording and decision-making. Wisdom is certainly a function of timeliness which is further a function of an agile information system. Wisdom is both time-oriented and action-oriented and so is informed decision-making. It only means that the process of decision-making does require an element of wisdom based on real-time information symmetry.

The information system has to capture an event, record a transaction, create analytics and include an element of wisdom out of experiential and historical learning, which does add a change to the current formats of financial reporting and disclosures. Since technology makes it possible, one can argue that there exists no reason in failing to create a comprehensive real-time view of the financial system. It would mean, collating and consolidating information to create ***a pinnacle of information called wisdom.*** The author understands that it is a far-fetched idea today, but once it catches the imagination of financial architects, it will soon see the light of day.

THE GLOBAL FINANCIAL CRISIS IS <u>NOT</u> FINANCIAL

Systemic View – the real BIG picture

The Effects of Systemic Risk impacts 2015

There is no formal definition of systemic risk, but the term is generally used to define the risk in the financial market due to contagion effect (Canedo and Jaramillo, 2009). By that characterization, the systemic risk is just not restricted to the financial market but can be extrapolated to the non-financial sectors too. The reverse can also be true. According to the working definition by the 2001 'Group of Ten', the factor of significance and adverse effect on the real economy is considered the core of systemic risk. It is no surprise, that new countries in the Eurozone are being added to the list of those with a debt crisis while on the other side there are symptoms of slowdown in the BRIC economies. All those sovereign nations who are remotely connected with the US economy are feeling the heat of the meltdown, and the worrying perspective is its duration which is going to last more years than anticipated. The author suggests that ***if the global economy returns to its pre-crisis levels by 2015, it will be a pleasant surprise.*** That is the kind of effect and seriousness of untamed systemic risk, which both the financial and the economic experts have failed to understand over these decades.

In the report by the Group of Ten (2001), it was understood and thereafter warned by the members that consolidation of banking and non-banking institutions will lead to systemic risk because they will open channels of problems for each other. Also, cross-border consolidation, defined previously as interconnectedness, will further enhance the systemic risk from one financial system to another. The report does provide some remedial measures in the wake of this anticipation and recommends that the risk should be evaluated not only at the level of an individual financial institution but also from the 'systems' perspective. Although, it is very difficult to derive an empirical formula for calculating the systemic risk, the closest we can get is the improvised rich picture from soft-system methodologies, depicting probabilities of failures and exposures associated with each player.

The 'systems' approach is the way, to the analysis of the financial crisis or for that matter any other crisis. This approach prevents compartmentalization of the system into issue-based resolutions. It is being done currently, which had truncated the big picture of faulty financial interconnectedness (Connectivity + Dependence) into separate

Information Enabler

issues such as debt, inflation, growth and unemployment. Since the holistic solution is not targeted, the crisis therefore, is likely to relapse in one form or another. It is found that a crisis of a similar kind, when resurfacing the next time, has greater severity and heavier impact. **This is because the system has already learnt to deal with the symptoms from previous experiences.** It happened with the S&L crisis, Asian Tigers collapse and now the global financial crisis.

Systemic Risk to Systemic Failure

The systemic failure is made of two components, occurring separately or together: first, an independent event and second a number of interconnected events that trigger varied risk zones, translating into

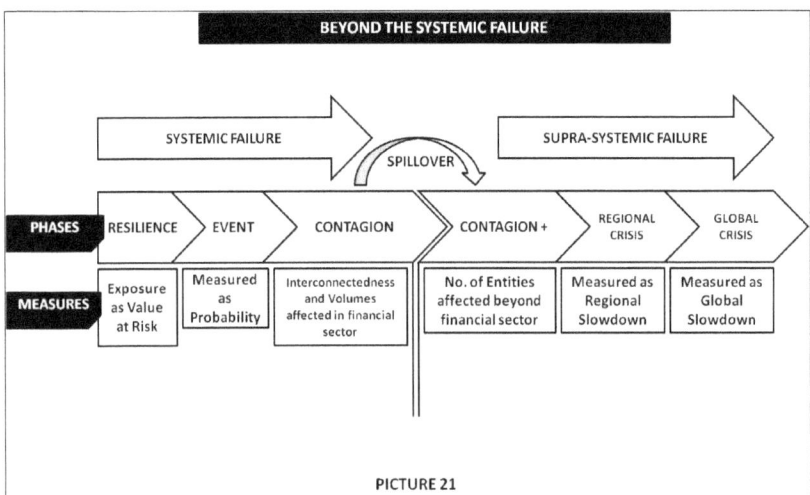

PICTURE 21

multiple failures in the sub-system. This creates contagion in the system which culminates in a classic systemic failure. If the definition of systemic failure, as earlier defined by Canedo and Jaramillo (2009), is to be followed, then the boundary conditions of systemic failure, is defined purely as a financial system boundaries, which also has other connected systems. The effect of spill over to other systems will have greater consequences as failures percolates to the various sub-systems and beyond. The author is calling the spill over the 'Supra-Systemic' failure.

The process of contagion as an after-effect of systemic risk has two parts. It is the behaviour of the constituent entities in the system and effect of their behaviour. The 'herding behaviour' or 'follow others' lead to the contagion effect and that spills over the boundaries. The

THE GLOBAL FINANCIAL CRISIS IS <u>NOT</u> FINANCIAL

important thing to identify in the contagion is the reason for the herding behaviour and the boundaries (Canedo and Jaramillo, 2009). The thresholds limits of these boundaries, define the resilience and thereafter the spill-over in the making of a 'supra-systemic' failure.

While we are talking about systemic risks, the factor that defines the threshold value is the resilience of the entity. The interconnectedness of these entities defines the resilience of the entire financial system. A view of the resilience of a single entity and the composite view of entities would provide a holistic view of the system's resilience. Of course, the resilience threshold would change every time the entity indulges in a transaction, risky or safe, with an increased or decreased level of exposure. The resilience of the system in some way is currently being measured by the stress test, which the banks conduct periodically, but the author is not sure if the bank stress test also includes the measure of it as a function of interconnectedness (interdependence and connectivity).

The global financial crisis, as a systemic failure, is a change of system status in phases. The initial resilience withholds day-to-day shocks, until a major event happens, which had very low probability of occurrence. In risk studies, they call it tail-risk. The interconnectedness plays a crucial role in affecting the connected entities. The factor of volume makes interconnectedness a phenomenon of contagion, from financial sector initially to other sectors. There is a stage where the contagion in one sector actually started to spread to other sectors and is depicted as contagion+.

An 'event' in discussion here, is a shock to the entity that takes it away from the transactions, which it normally conducts while in status of 'business-as-usual'. It stresses the exposures of the entity and challenges the entity to survive the losses. An event can influence one or more entities, and if the entity is fragile it may buckle under the pressure of losses and may default. If a group of entities are fragile for an event, the affect of the event is likely to be more severe. The entities needs to be prepared for any likely event and for the sake of governance, it is preferred to assign a **probability** to well-known events.

The most important learning comes from the history. The current crisis had risen from the most unlikely event, for example the collapse of the US mortgage market, which was only 8% of the total mortgage market, leading to this global financial crisis. Similarly, an earthquake of 8.0 on the Richter scale resulted in a 30-metre tsunami that brought catastrophe to the Japanese nuclear power plants on the shores of the Pacific Ocean. Therefore, the author's outlook to any event, though easily termed as conservative, is the assignment of probability, only for the purpose of reference. If the system experts are relying on the probability of an event for its preparedness, then they are committing the same mistake that has led us all, to this crisis. In both these iconic examples, the system was fragile (not resilient).

Since the probability of occurrence was very small, it overrode the preparedness for sustained and unconditional resilience. **Probabilistic resilience** is a thing of the past and new ways have to be evolved to address this situation, if the system has to be managed with a preventative and proactive outlook.

Contagion is a behaviour, which is influenced by the action of the others in proximity, and collectively they become widespread with unified behaviour. It could have both positive and negative effects, and in both cases is a deviation from the business-as-usual. Analyzing the contagion, it is important to consider the boundary conditions and recognize the spill-over as a function of threshold levels. Beyond the threshold, the initial reaction culminates into a critical mass before being termed as contagion. Therefore, indicating the measures of thresholds while they get crossed in the build-up to the crisis is vital to the system monitoring. It was certainly not the method that the monitoring and regulatory authorities followed. With contagion, the element of probability is to overcome by certainty. Probably, this is the reason why there were no published and agreed thresholds in the systems that were being monitored by the regulators and the experts.

The essence of time to respond to an event is critical otherwise the change in behaviour to accommodate the event, adopted by the entities, becomes business-as-usual. Bailout was a change due to an event, which has now become business-as-usual. Entities, whether banks, non-banking institutions or countries in themselves, are working on the model of bailouts, which was least heard of, in the past. Contagion has a constant and overwhelming influence on change, even though friction appears in the system to adjust to the changes, while deviation from business-as-usual is also the fight for survival.

THE GLOBAL FINANCIAL CRISIS IS NOT FINANCIAL

The next parameter is to be watched is the 'fragility' of the entity, as a measure of resilience. If the contagion spills over to the other sectors, for example the effects of credit crunch on the manufacturing industry or automobile industry, the author calls it 'supra-contagion' and it is systemic risk involving multiple sectors, including the financial sector. Volumes would get added in supra-systemic failure and would result in the crisis of regional or global proportions. The impact of the crisis due to supra-systemic failure would be like the recession in the 'Asian Tigers' economies in the 90s or the current recession in the US or the Euro debt crisis.

There had been a number of theories for the financial network model but the author comes back to the same argument, questioning the ability of these networks in determining the systemic risk before the situation gets into a system-wide failure mode, like this global financial crisis.

One reason could be the difference between these models as a theory and the realities on the ground. Considering, these theories do hold well, it is the inability of the industry to use these models effectively as a routine and determine the systemic risk on a continuous basis. To whatever sources one refers for analysis of this financial crisis, experts have been talking about all other possible causes of failure, except for systems failure.

Experts in the market did see the dangers of escalating home prices along with the inability of borrowers to keep up with the repayments. But the missing thresholds in the system did not create any alarms hence no corrective actions were sought. Those financial intermediaries, who were lending sub-prime mortgage, also had an idea of the risk associated with the classification of 'sub-prime'. Further, the effect of transforming cash-flow based mortgage underwriting on repackaged speculative financing, left experts without a trace of the dangers creeping into the system. Regulators were not able to detect the growing systemic risk as commercial paper and the repo market were tools for CDOs without the thresholds and measure of the system's resilience.

The component of the sub-prime market was only 8% of the US housing lending market, but it was very difficult to comprehend the contagion of the sub-prime market failure on the overall economy of the US, subsequently on the other interconnected economies of the world.

Information Enabler

To summarize, the systemic view is important because the financial markets are interconnected with different industry sectors and international economies. In the making of the crisis, as the figure shows, there exists an important dependency between the US housing sector, investment banking, the banking sector and ultimately the sovereign economies. Although, each of the sectors seems to be regulated on their own, the systemic risk profile becomes complicated and elevated as more and more sectors gets cascaded. In general terms, the macro-economic stability is maintained by the monetary policy, while the micro-economic stability is a factor of a sound financial system. Uncontained spill over of risk from micro to macro-economic space, as in the case of the current crisis or vice versa, is possible. Moreover, the transformation is not a linear case. There is a complex relation between the two and each determines the other (Crockett, 2001).

THE GLOBAL FINANCIAL CRISIS IS NOT FINANCIAL

Systemic Risk as an appending Risk

The residual systemic risk continuously persists in a system. For those who are unable to perceive the affected connections in case of an unlikely event, the risk can be severe. The nationalization of Northern Rock by the UK government, not only raised the nation's debt to £90 billion but also created a spiralling effect on other parts of the economy, due to national debt recovery and adjustments. The same is the case with the nationalization of Freddie Mac and Fannie Mae, where the US

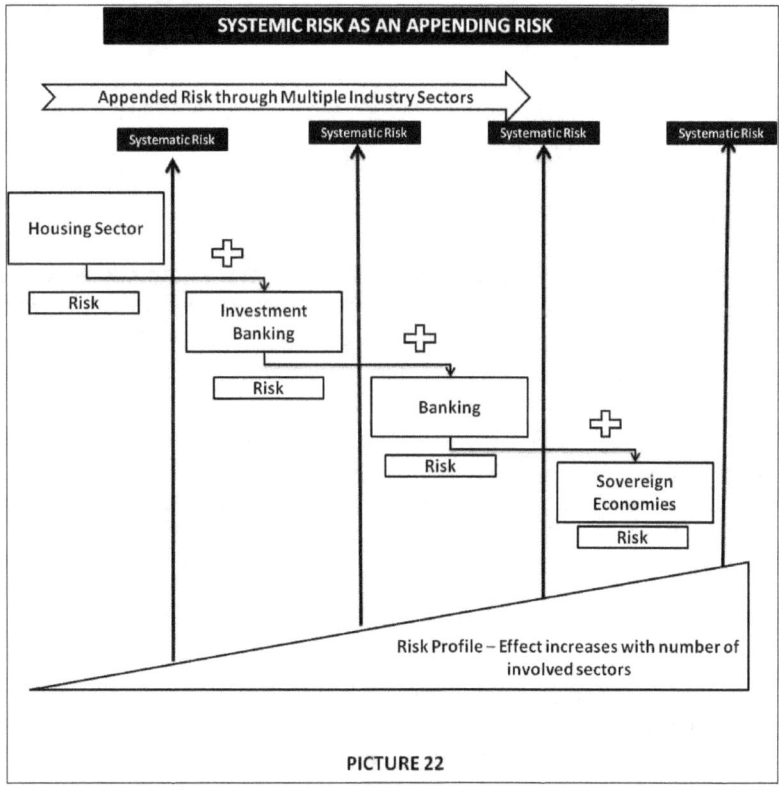

PICTURE 22

governments had to intervene with their nationalization package of $5 trillion. The nationalization was equivalent to half the US mortgage held by the US home lenders and half the national debt. It is no secret about the effects of high national debts. In the case of the US, the country lost its AAA investment grade and has had to compromise with the associated disadvantages. In a well-governed scenario, the government and its agencies should have mapped the effects of failure of these UK and US based firms respectively and simulated the impact on their own economies.

| Information Enabler

According to the IMF, limited data and high interconnectedness have made the systemic risk and macro-financial spill-over difficult to ascertain (IMF, Containing Systemic Risks and Restoring Financial Soundness, April 2008). Some may argue that it is easy to make pointers with hindsight but that argument fails as an excuse when the impact of risk should have been known as 'humungous', worth trillions of dollars, falling credibility of currencies, lost livelihood of billions across countries and survival of sovereign economies themselves. This brings us back to the author's earlier argument that the bigger the impact, the more symmetrical information is a necessity, to create smart alerts and warnings.

Not to have information about the systemic risk in today's world of interconnectedness is perilous.

Systemic Risks as a science of Consequences

Systemic risk, as a characteristic brings consequences into systems after a particular event has occurred, crossing the boundaries of various other systems. If the experts have to look at it differently, from now onwards, they need to treat 'systemic' as a ***science of consequences*** in a highly dynamic interconnected system. It would be a case of utmost precision, where ignoring a factor considered insignificant and unconnected to the big picture could result in a catastrophe. It happened in the case of the US housing mortgage crisis and Japanese nuclear reactors, after the tsunami. Earlier, these factors were termed in the butterfly effect or tail-risk, but they are a significant risk today. That is very much a key lesson learnt from the current crisis.

Here is a list for quick browsing before further discussion:
- Securitization of mortgages
- Overvaluation of debt holding by banks
- Flawed overvaluation of bank assets
- Faulty bank capitalization
- Lower profitability
- Difficulty in refinancing themselves
- Squeeze in short-term liquidity
- Reduction of credit multipliers
- Reduction of consumption
- Fall in GDP levels
- Corporate losses due to low consumption
- Loss of international debt

THE GLOBAL FINANCIAL CRISIS IS NOT FINANCIAL

- Loss of creditworthiness
- Fear of insolvency
- Increase of spread in CDS and interest rates = $58 trillion = global GDP

Country	Variation since 5-Sep-08 (bps)
Germany	+39.3
France	+43.7
UK	+89.8
Italy	+126.2
Austria	+138.4
Belgium	+104.2
Greece	+231.9
Portugal	+104.2
Spain	+108.5

Source: Bloomberg

- Higher cost of borrowing
- Reduced market capitalization
- Loss of shareholders' wealth
- Reduced investment by way of delay or cancellation
- Increase in personal cash reserves and shelter-goods
- Fear and panic

This is the familiar list of topics that are associated with the current crisis though not necessarily sequential. Each of them looks at one of the factors responsible for the current crisis and experts talk about them in isolation. Even media reports these factors as an individual news item. While some of them are subjective, others are clearly quantifiable. According to the IMF's 2008, Triennial Surveillance Review, which focused on bilateral surveillance of Germany, Switzerland, the US and the UK, these listed issues were repeatedly identified as a risk prior to the crisis, but somehow fell short of raising the right kind of warning for preventative action (Initial Lessons of the Crisis for the Global Architecture and the IMF, 2009).

| Information Enabler

There is a reason for this inability. The analytical methods used are based on snapshots with little or no reference to history. This means that whatever is seen at the moment, in a short-time scale, is considered relevant. *The depth of analysis is as good as the public memory.* If there was a systemic map available in the public domain, these items would have thrown alerts in some combination, one being a consequence of the other, the *crisis would have been seen earlier and by many.* Similarly, a closer look at the list will suggest

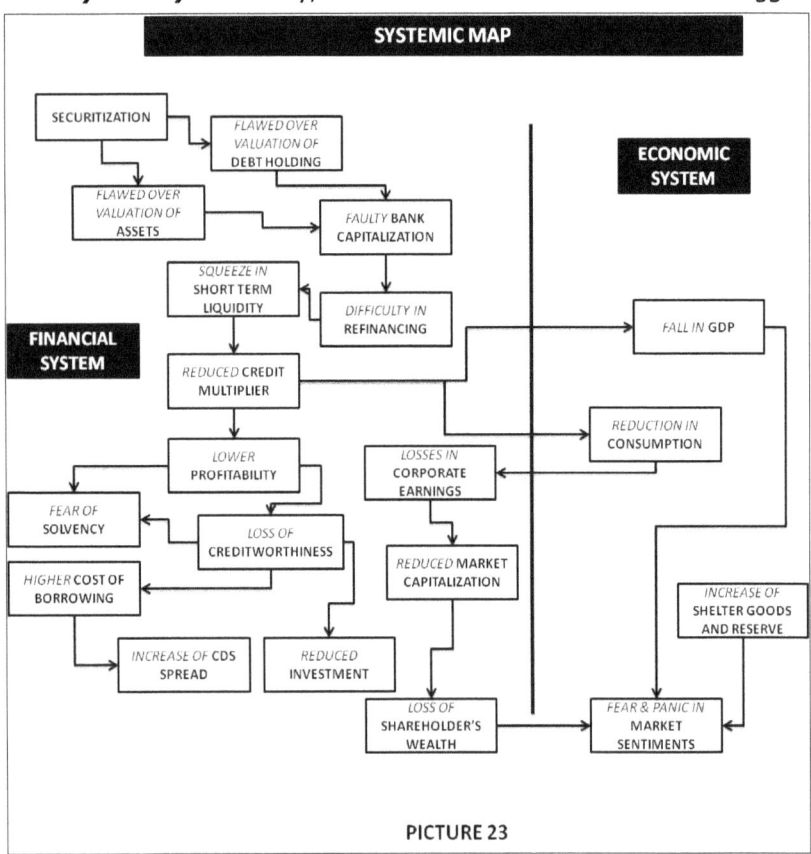

PICTURE 23

interconnection in terms of stimulating factors and their consequences.

The author visualizes the systemic map like a typical road map where every junction represents these systemic factors with a true status of its performance. On a typical day, the economic and financial factors, along with other factors, could have holistically represented the status of these junctions or nodes. It will be easier to trace back to the interdependent factor and extrapolate to reach a 'consequence'. That would make smart alerts in the system and address both the stimulants and the consequences. Below is an example of the envisaged systemic map.

If those topics were to be represented on a systemic map as shown here, certainly the public domain would have captured the essence of crisis much before. This is of course a very simplistic view, but the argument is to state the importance of the systemic map (Picture 23) and a holistic picture of the financial system with its connected systems. Isn't the systemic view of the system adding value to the current state of information symmetry and QoI?

Simulated Systemic View

Stress tests are another important exercise to determine the future strategy for the market players (IMF, Navigating the Financial Challenges Ahead, October 2009). To create a systemic view, systemically important institutions and markets need to be identified with some grading rather than stating just a few as 'too-big-to-fail'. The financial system, during the stress test, can simulate the potential systemic effect, one systemic factor following the other. The effects can be varied using a switch mechanism. This would be more analytical like China, conducting a stress test for its financial system sustainability, simulating a 50% drop in housing prices (Anderlini, 2011), and then publishing the results of the impact to real estate developers, cement companies, steel producers and others who are interconnected. The results need not be limited to only the financial impact but also to the consumer behaviour in other sectors with high correlation to the housing market. What if a similar impact analysis was done for the US mortgage market and the loan loss published in the public domain? Certainly, the global financial crisis would have been averted or the impact minimized with this simple solution of creating en-masse information symmetry. It would be a robust system, if all in the system saw the alerts and warnings simply as traffic road signs.

The objective of the exercise is to make aware the fact that simulated scenarios can demonstrate system resilience using the systemic view and can be beneficial for both current and potential market players.

Failed warning system

| Information Enabler

While most consider that the financial crisis came as a surprise, and even the best in the industry were at loss with the 'unknowns', the fact is actually contrary to this myth. A battery of experts across the financial industry, governments and independent analysts community saw the market trends and had issued alerts and warnings based on their own research. Below is the list that shows the warning as early as the spring of 2002, much before the actual crisis. The list also suggests that the warning was related to the financial sector and also had ramifications across other sectors of the economy. The author has categorized the alerts to indicate if they were specific to the financial sector or systemic in nature, and whether there were any agencies that were bound to take corrective action based on these alerts.

THE GLOBAL FINANCIAL CRISIS IS NOT FINANCIAL

Alerts / Warnings	Sector	Systemic	Binding
World Economic Outlook			
(i) Global imbalances (since Spring 2002);	·	☑	⊗
(ii) Low global interest rates/high risk taking (Spring 2005);	☑	·	⊗
(iii) Elevated global house prices (continuous, notable early warnings in Spring 2003 and Spring 2004) with emphasis on global synchronization/risks (Autumn 2004) and a US-specific warning (e.g. Autumn 2005);	☑	·	⊗
(iv) Excessive reliance on external funding by EU accession countries (from Spring 2004);	☑	·	⊗
(v) Impact of globalization on inflation (Spring 2006);	·	☑	⊗
(vi) Financial system feedback to economic cycles (Autumn2006); and	·	☑	⊗
(vii) European housing market valuations (Autumn2007).	☑	·	⊗
	·	·	·
The Bank of International Settlement: Annual Reports since 2004			
(viii) Global imbalances;	·	☑	⊗
(ix) Liberalized financial systems prone to instability;	·	☑	⊗
(x) Low interest rates distorting behaviour;	☑	·	⊗
(xi) The danger of either "overt inflation ... [or] implications of growing debt levels";	☑	·	⊗
(xii) The need for domestic and international macro-financial stabilization frameworks, notably 'macro-financial stability issues could fall between the cracks'; and, later,	·	☑	⊗
(xiii) The danger of a rapid turn in the credit cycle;	☑	·	⊗
(xiv) The vulnerability of untested structured products;	☑	·	⊗
(xv) Credit ratings not capturing the full distribution, potentially leading debt holders to underestimate loss exposures;	☑	·	⊗
(xvi) Mortgage-backed security investors exposed to unexpected losses; and, further,	☑	·	⊗
(xvii) Medium-term risks increasing;	☑	·	⊗
(xviii) Problems with household balance sheets and US mortgage markets;	☑	·	⊗
(xix) Spillover effects to Credit Default Swap and other derivative markets (before July 2007);	·	☑	⊗
(xx) 'market risk and leverage';	☑	·	⊗
(xxi) Problems with the 'originate to distribute' model; and	☑	·	⊗
(xxii) banks 'intentionally or inadvertently, retain[ing] significant credit risk on their books'.	☑	·	⊗
	·	·	·
Independent commentators:			
(i) Paul Krugman and Robert Shiller - potential for a drop in US house prices (mid-2005);	☑	·	⊗
(ii) Kenneth Rogoff - risks to the global economy, including a danger of house price collapse and weakness in the global financial system (Early 2006);	·	☑	⊗
(iii) Nouriel Roubini - global and US house price bubble would collapse and global growth slow (early 2006);	·	☑	⊗

'Quality of Information' in Question

Information Enabler

The US Office for the Comptroller of the Currency: Annual Credit Underwriting Surveys from 2004 through 2007.			
(i)	Ambitious growth goals foster imprudent credit decisions;	☑ ·	⊗
(ii)	Enhanced credit risk management practices were needed;	☑ ·	⊗
(iii)	Relationship managers needed to be held accountable for both the quality and the quantity of their deals;	☑ ·	⊗
(iv)	'The worst of loans are made in the best of times';	☑ ·	⊗
(v)	Everyone needed to keep pace with new products, changing risk selection practices and underwriting standards, and emerging concentrations;	☑ ·	⊗
(vi)	Rapid appreciation of housing values was raising concerns about price volatility and overvalued markets; such that by 2006	· ☑	⊗
(vii)	Credit risk was increasing with continued weakening of underwriting standards.	☑ ·	⊗
		· ·	·
The Bank of England: Its Financial Stability Reports from 2005		· ·	·
(i)	flagged many of the issues raised by the GFSR,	· ·	·
(ii)	the short-run outlook remained good,	· ·	·
(iii)	"search for yield" and mounting vulnerabilities on borrowers'	☑ ·	⊗
(iv)	financial institutions' balance sheets cause for concern and	· ☑	⊗
(v)	Challenged the GFSR's April 2008 loss estimates as too high.	· ·	·
		· ·	·
The Financial Stability Forum (FSF): In several reports over 2003-06, the FSF highlighted the need for improvements in			
(i)	risk management practices, disclosures, investor due diligence, supervisory approaches, and in credit rating agency management of conflicts of interest.	☑ ·	⊗
(ii)	In September 2006, it highlighted risks associated with household indebtedness, inflated housing prices, rapid growth in leveraged buyouts and debt-financed acquisitions, the growing complexity of financial instruments, and global imbalances.	· ☑	⊗
(iii)	It urged financial market participants to take account of the full implications of a possible reversal of benign conditions, including less liquid markets.	· ☑	⊗
		· ·	·
Bilateral surveillance			
(i)	Institutional weaknesses (especially through **Financial Sector Assessment Program FSAPs**);	☑ ·	⊗
(ii)	Low interest rates;	☑ ·	⊗
(iii)	Wholesale funding risk;	☑ ·	⊗
(iv)	Expansion of credit risk transfer products;	☑ ·	⊗
(v)	Risk of house price corrections;	☑ ·	⊗
(vi)	Mounting international exposures, in particular through interbank markets; and	☑ ·	⊗
(vii)	Lack of information on ultimate holders of risk.	☑ ·	⊗
		· ·	·

THE GLOBAL FINANCIAL CRISIS IS NOT FINANCIAL

	Global Financial Stability Report			
(i)	Market complacency/'search for yield' (e.g. Autumn 2003);	☑	•	⊗
(ii)	Lack of information on holders of risk (e.g. Spring 2004);	☑	•	⊗
(iii)	Increasing leverage and complexity of credit products (Spring 2005);	☑	•	⊗
(iv)	Dependence on continuous liquidity (Spring 2006); and	☑	•	⊗
(v)	Sub-prime lending and housing markets (Autumn2005, Spring 2007).	☑	•	⊗
		•	•	•

Source: IMF, 2010

As seen from the above table, most of the advance warnings and alerts pointed to a particular sector, such as credit risk or housing. While some pointed towards operational issues, for example complexity of financial products, disclosures and credit ratings, very few made reference to the systemic risks arising from the tail-risks in main banking, non-banking firms and shadow banking, pointing towards the global consequences.

The non-responsive behaviour of the authorities validated that part of the behaviour as studied in the system's thinking where the players do not respond, till they actually find demonstrable evidence (Crockett, Banking Supervision and Regulation: International Trends, 2001). It will be an area of further investigative research, to understand why these organizations failed to respond to these advance warnings of the financial crisis. One observable reason is the nature of the alerts; which were not binding for any action for any of the governmental or regulatory authorities.

The alerts can be classified as an alert, if and only if there is a binding action as a follow through to this exception information, even if the action is to ignore the alert as a 'false positive'. As seen from the table, there is no alert that was binding, leaving the interpretation of the alert to the individual players. This brings up the argument in favour of bringing in a *sole regulatory authority*, to effectively address the alerts. This regulatory authority can be a body of regulators working synchronously for international supervision or an open system in the public domain with widespread information symmetry. This arrangement would result in a self-governing and self-regulating systems.

> Major dislocation still appears to be a low-probability event, but the risks would be heightened if many subprime credit events were to take place simultaneously (IMF, Market Developments and Issues April,2007).

Overall, the reports missed or underestimated the risk of systemic failure arising from the housing market.

It is evident that although these reports had identified the problems in bits and pieces, there still exists the inability to connect the dots. In a holistic picture these pieces could have been translated into a potential problem statement to analyze the likely impact and prepare for remedial actions. One reason for this inability is the inappropriateness of the system to integrate the problem dots into a holistic outlook and simulate the likelihood of an event. Since the integrated outlook was missing, the right alert and advance warning went missing from the actionable layer of the system.

It leads us to multiple inferences. Could a superlative regulatory authority overseeing the financial system, with the systemic view, be able to detect the crisis in the making? Are there too many authorities, and therefore the disintegrated warning fell through the cracks of the seriousness and actionable policies?

So the argument is in favour of one regulatory authority that would oversee the financial system and prevent a systemic failure. In the integrated global financial architecture, the author attempts to create space for this missing regulatory authority.

Systemic Liquidity Risk: Identification and Measurement

It has been the markets' understanding that mitigating liquidity risk is complicated because it is not easily measurable, as the fund market is diverse and heterogeneous. In more specific terms, the systemic risk is linked to systemic liquidity. There are reasons that can be thought of, for this understanding. In the current practice, the institutions do not make public the consolidated accounts on a periodic (daily) basis to bring about a systemic view of the liquidity position. This is because the financial statement, though available for internal management, is not available to the public or regulators on a daily basis, neither on demand nor by law. The financial statement though, is available only on a quarterly basis, and there exists no mechanism to monitor the systemic risk based on the quarterly results until something dramatic happens in that quarter and the media puts it in focus.

The measure of systemic risk is by monitoring the CDS spreads, probability distribution and equity prices of the banks and financial institutions (Huang, Zhou and Zhu, 2009). This method may continue to work and show results, but when we are in pursuit of finding a more reliable method based on primary data, CDS spread and probability distribution won't work. All these methods are a combination of subjectivity put into mathematical formula and therefore, more susceptible to error due to human judgment.

The transaction-based data available via financial statements needs to be used more frequently. This would mean that updated financial statements be available with the same frequency, as the CDS spreads. We have already discussed the frequency and availability of the financial statement as the primary source of information.

The systemic view provides a balance of view of all the interconnected players and their affect on each other. There comes a situation where a sector of the economy is heavily dependent on the financial market or manufacturing sector for a country. To what proportion the sector becomes affected, needs to be visible to all the players, in order to anticipate and react to the trends. So when the proportions change, so the systemic view changes its shape. Like the main losses for the US banks were driven by the residential sectors, in the UK and other European banks the foreign loans were the contributor to the losses (IMF, Navigating the Financial Challenges Ahead, October 2009). Therefore, each economic region is seen to have a different systemic effect, even though they are connected by the same business transactions.

There are fundamental changes to the nature of business. Over the period the funds market have changed in profile also. Instead of interbank markets, other intermediaries, such as in money market mutual funds with secured lending together with repurchase options, provided funds while traditional and more stable depositors are falling behind (IMF, Global Financial Stability Report - Oct 2010). Hence, changes in the landscape of the funds market have to further integrate the micro aspect, deeper into the systemic view of the market. A systemic view of heterogeneous economies for a homogeneous business then becomes a priority.

Information Reduction and Simplification

There are thousands of financial products for investments, available to institutional investors as well as to retail investors. These products are

Information Enabler

complex within themselves. The complexity increases manifold as the input to the product may be dependent on activity, in remote geographical regions. The investors, especially retail or small investors, in most likelihood, would know in simplistic terms about the operations and their dependencies. The primary factor of this phenomenon is initially the cost associated with the research involved in assimilating the information and then updating with current trends. It is certainly prohibitive for small or retail investors. Further, if an investor has many products in the portfolio which change frequently, the investment will be based on reduced information and simplified outlook. Therefore, the risk of loss of vital information in the reduction and simplification of information aggravates with every step of the investment process and sustained updates. The aggregation of information reduction and simplification builds risks of information asymmetry and hence creates an opportunity for moral hazard.

It is a fact that not all players, including the regulators, are well versed with the technicalities of the business in which they are dealing. It is about the dynamics of the information creation and communication that has the problem of information reduction and simplification. As one of the solutions, a view that allows the user to drill-down to the last known crucial information will benefit all the market players in creating a level playing field. In principle, if the investor, irrespective of size, were to be empowered to limit the effects of information reduction and simplification, more information-symmetric enabling methods, have to be evolved.

Information Reduction and Systemic View

The new architecture will provide a market for more structured information, simplifying the facts on one side without losing relevance, and on other side leaving it to the choice of the user to go into as much detail. The challenge is about making an informed decision without getting deep into the technicalities of financial engineering, but taking their risk factors into consideration, communicating in a universal comprehensible language. This is where the credit rating process and portfolio manager were to facilitate the players. Thus a CDO, with municipal bond from a remote town of Arizona can be visible to an investor in Singapore, trading in the financial product or the range of assets that can be part of the CDO. The investor would be able to track the listed assets, even when it moves from CDO to CDO^2. This kind of visibility to interconnectedness is not visible today in the public domain.

THE GLOBAL FINANCIAL CRISIS IS NOT FINANCIAL

There is a long way to go on the track of providing visibility into structured products. As an example, according to the Euromoney handbook of 2003, the diversity by types of asset repackaged under the CDO structure can be as follows:

- High yield bonds
- Leveraged loans
- Investment grade bonds and loans
- Revolving credits
- Mezzanine debt
- Middle market corporate debt
- Emerging markets sovereign and corporate debt
- Project finance debt
- Structured finance securities (Asset-Backed Securities and Mortgage-Backed Securities)
- Distressed debt
- Municipal debt
- REIT debt
- Trust preferred securities
- Forfeiting debt
- Credit default swaps
- Hedge funds
- Private equity
- Financial derivatives exposures
- Stripped securities (I/Os and P/Os)
- Synthetic securities

Each of these asset types are themselves complex instruments and their combination is certainly going to add complexity in tracking both the composite and individual performances. It is humanly not possible, to tame this complexity and manage the portfolio. As a natural practice, information reduction and simplification come into play to reduce the informational complexity. This truncates the information. The investors of this generation of securitization rely on the strategies of information reduction – de-contextualization, encapsulation and detachment (Scott, 2010). Reductionism and simplification as processes stop when the components look justified and appropriate to the user. In the information system literature, authors have called this a principle of **limited reduction.** They have emphasized this analytical behaviour as a method of reducing complexity, though simultaneously it introduces new sources of uncertainty and creates an inherent system flaw. Hence,

| Information Enabler

there is a trade-off between making a point succinctly and over-simplifying the information (Chapman, 2004).

The financial stability oversight council (FSOC) is an outcome of the Dodd-Frank reform act. Its key responsibility is to create a classification of Systemically Important Financial Institutions (SIFI) to monitor with a systemic view of the market. This is an approach in the right direction. It will be interesting to know the basis of classification and the measure of 'systemic importance'.

THE GLOBAL FINANCIAL CRISIS IS NOT FINANCIAL

Chapter 8
Quality of Information (QoI)

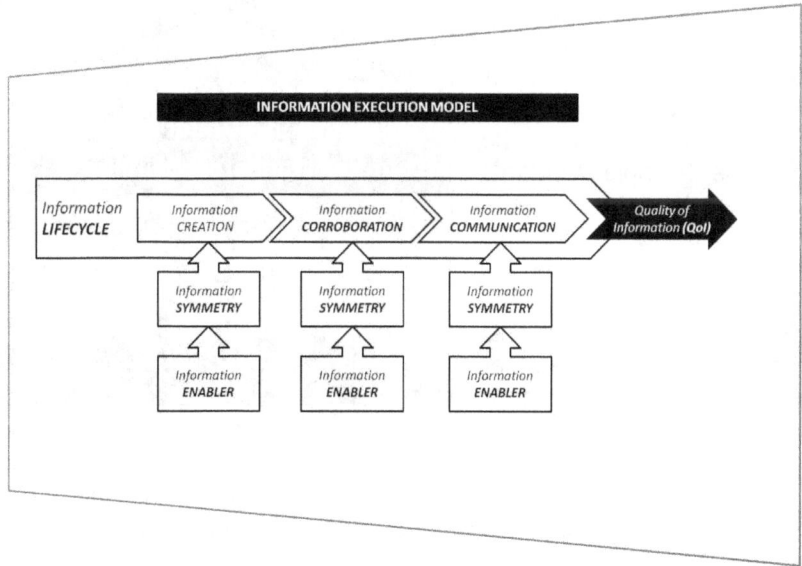

| Quality of Information (QoI)

Unification

In the entire financial system, there are few areas where debates and discussions are in place for having universal standards. Accounting standards in the information creation stage, auditing standards in the information corroboration stage and reporting in the information communication stage are the places to review and redefine the system with respect to standards. From the information execution model point of view, there is a challenge of standardization affecting the entire information life cycle in the financial system.

There is a perspective on having a universal standard in order to have the advantage of convenience of review and understanding by all the players across the landscape. Multiple standards have multiple outlooks on the same object; therefore though standardization brings efficiency to the system, the analyst looking for critical review may miss out on other outlooks. Information that is not part of the standard format will not be part of the system with a conviction that it is insignificant. Though standardization is an outcome of a process of rigorous discussion by experts in the domain, the fear is paramount, as history has shown that this crisis had emanated from the industry sector where the per capita expertise is the highest.

> "If anyone doubts the disparate effects that different accounting practices can have, consider the case of Daimler-Benz. Under German accounting standards, Daimler reported a profit of 168 million Deutschmarks in 1993. Under U.S. GAAP, the company reported a loss of almost a billion Deutschmarks for the same period" (Levitt. 1999).

There are arguments both for and against the standardization of accounting principles. To have a standard that is binding to all countries leaves a risk of flawed accounting for everyone, as it happened in the case of OBSEs in the US, UK and European markets. On the other side of the argument, as in the case of multiple standards, the judgement of fair value will rest on an individual and therefore, can have different outcomes for the same business scenario. Specifically, the collateral valuation rules for counterparties have to move away from judgement to a more observable and standardized framework and that is expected to reduce the vulnerabilities (IMF, Containing Systemic Risks and Restoring Financial Soundness, April 2008).

THE GLOBAL FINANCIAL CRISIS IS NOT FINANCIAL

The standards are much more than the unified and fixed set of methodologies and processes. It is a unification and integration of participants, too. Today, although the business transactions may be termed as global, in a true sense they have a long way to go. The entrepreneurial spirit of the stakeholders is still not global and unified. The risk taking and entrepreneurial outlook of the stakeholders is different in different corners of the world. This is too simplistic an outlook, but let's discuss this argument some more.

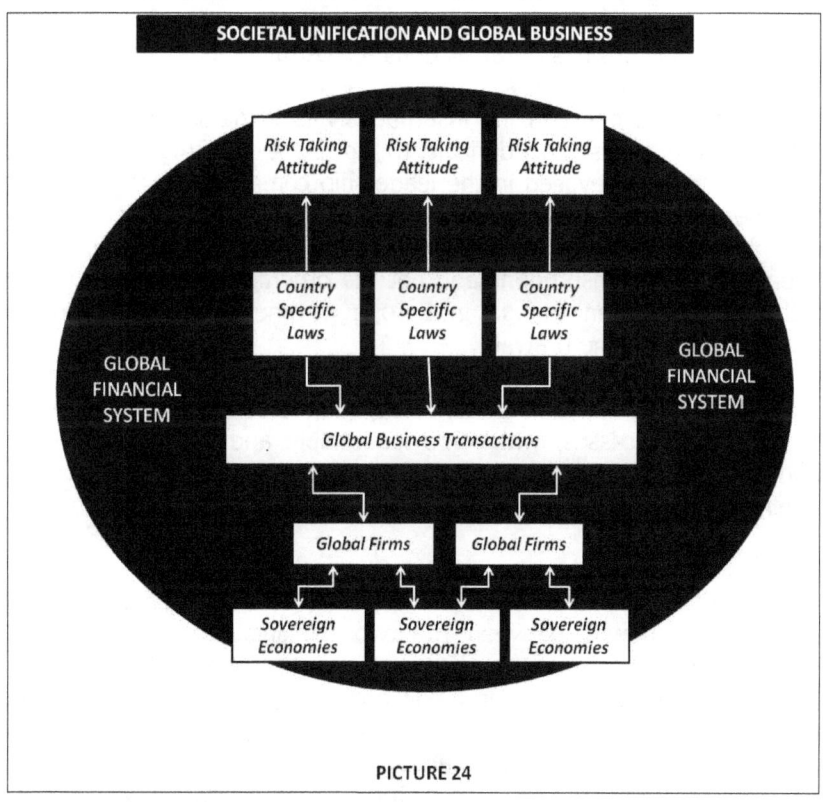

PICTURE 24

The financial crisis draws its origin from the US, where the entrepreneurial spirit and risk taking are considered much higher than in any country in the world. Business failure and bankruptcy are part of the usual business life cycle here, while risk taking and considerations of bankruptcy are perceived very differently in other countries. In the case of the UK, they are regarded as a disgrace, while that is not the case in the US where a failed business is related to entrepreneurial risk. While the US has Chapter 11 proceedings and the entity is salvaged while the

Quality of Information (QoI)

existing administration remains at the helm of the corporate affairs, UK law has provisions for sanctions against the directors of the company and may be personally liable for the debt, with the company being run by a court-appointed administrator (Pullen S & Coles I, 2003). These two approaches to risk taking are vastly different, and without debating the merits of the two approaches, it is important to understand the heterogeneity that exists in globalization.

The fundamental of societal unification will always be a challenge and needs to be considered as a function of global business. Thus globalization of business transactions is certainly not the same as globalization of risk taking. Referring to the financial crisis, the 'too-big-to-fail' banks and non-banking institutions had leadership based in the US. Therefore, it is not difficult to correlate the high risk-taking environment that prevailed in the leadership community, different from the other parts of the world, even though the business transactions were global. This is the author's reasoning in pursuit of answering why US-based financial institutions and not the others, were the first to fail in the domino, even though in Europe commercial and investment banking never had the firewall.

When the regulations refer to standards, they refer to a tangible part of the business processes, which are identifiable and measurable. Risk-taking is an individual attitude and cannot be quantified, as it is influenced by cognitive and cumulative sensibility to the environment.

US banks had recognized about 60% of the write-downs while UK banks had recognized about 40%. Therefore, there is a difference between rates of write-downs between the two banking sectors across the financial poles. The reason for the slower write-down in the European banks is because of the lack in credit cycle, proportion of securitization in US banks, data collection and publication by regulatory authorities and, most importantly, the difference in accounting principles between IFRS and the US GAAP. Of these factors, the credit cycle is a factor of local economy and social behaviour. The proportion of securitization in US banks is again a reflection of regional business processes. The other two factors, that is, data collection and publication by the regulatory authorities along with the accounting variation between IFRS in a globalized market, are not dependent on market behaviour and regional economies but on the structural and policy set-up in that specific country.

THE GLOBAL FINANCIAL CRISIS IS <u>NOT</u> FINANCIAL

There is a connection between globalization and standardization because at the macro-economic level, it is the interaction between two economies which is a super set of regional financial system, laws and attitudes. For a global financial system to bring standardization to its operations, the process of standardization needs to factor these heterogeneous blocks that compose the string of one global business transaction.

This leads us back to the argument that even though there are areas that can be considered as standardized in globalization, for creation and validation of information, there is heterogeneity (IMF, October 2009).

What is the difference between the unification and standardization of the global financial system?

Standardization brings an element of safety to the environment regarding the information created being more authentic rather than information generated by a bespoke process. Somehow, the general convention about a bespoke process is that it may be erroneous or insufficient. Also, since standardization brings a stamp of being an official process, it is assumed to be comprehensive, containing all the vital information that is required by the players in the system. On the critical side, both these advantages of being authentic and comprehensive are based on assumptions by the players in the market and that brings complacency to the system. According to the author, there is always scope for a second opinion and therefore, the system must have space for at least two standards, in order to cover the lost information, however small or insignificant that may be considered.

Standardization certainly brings efficiency to the system, and there is a definitive cost benefit compared to the bespoke processes. But if the custodian of the system assumes that standardization encompasses all the information required and is therefore effective, then there is a risk of creating information asymmetry.

There is always scope for exploratory information that is critical. Unification on the other hand, brings together the standard and bespoke information processes, under one information system. With unification, there comes a perspective of the business that may be different from that displayed by the standard process. In order to create a diversified set of information, unification can be considered as a superset of standardized information set.

| Quality of Information (QoI)

Transparency

When the word 'transparency' is used, those who use it typically assume that it means better quality information (Elliott, 2001). As discussed in previous sections, the financial crisis has emerged from a practice where approximately a trillion dollars were posted in OBSEs. These funds were invisible to both the regulators and auditors and hence were unregulated, which proved disastrous for the entire financial system. The IMF recommends stricter rules for use of Off-Balance Sheet Entities by banks, and improved disclosure so that investors can assess the sponsor's risk to the entity (IMF, Containing Systemic Risks and Restoring Financial Soundness, April 2008). Also, the Dodd-Frank Wall Street Reform and Consumer Protection Act of 2010 aims to regulate standards for credit rating agencies by increasing transparency and improving standards of governance. Moreover, transparency using disclosure methods allows market players to exercise market discipline and reduce vulnerabilities because of appropriate corporate credit risks (IMF, 2005).

Transparency is a general term applied to the condition in the system where the information sought is available without distortion. This also means that the exchange of information resulted in information symmetry in the system. In other words, lack of transparency results in information asymmetry which has its own consequences. Transparency is a process of bringing into the system, a condition of required visibility of information to the players. It may be mistakenly taken for exposure or exceeding data confidentiality and privacy. Transparency as a process needs to bring a striking balance between information that must be visible in ordinary conditions of business-as-usual and under extraordinary conditions of investigations and internal management reporting.

There are two lines of consideration for transparency in the system. As a deliberate effort to bring more information into the system, such as disclosure of the test results of European banks, makes it stable and less prone to uncertainty. This was simpler because information existed in the system and all it required, was to bring it into the public domain. Since the information was macroscopic in nature, it was easier for the players to divulge. In other considerations, the micro-level details of the transactions, where the information is owned by a single entity, it becomes very difficult to introduce transparency there. This is because it is advantageous to withhold the information in cases like the OTC transactions and hedge funds.

There is evidence that legislations have been enacted in the past to enhance transparency in the system and this is supported by regulation. On the regulation side, in order to improve transparency, the US SEC had made a bifurcation in regulations based on the objectives of prudential regulation and securities regulation (Kroeker, 2010). Prudential regulation aims at bringing more transparency into the system in order to provide information that is helpful in decision-making. Despite these regulations, backed by legislations, the severest of the financial crises did happen. The system on its own was unable to check and measure the deteriorating levels of transparency. Therefore, the author argues for an approach that is different from yesteryear; one that is based on a symmetric information system.

How much visibility is transparent? That is the key question that is judged by the players with fear and skepticism. Too much information may over-expose the players with their flaws which in normal circumstances are considered as acceptable deviations. Also, the competitive market may lose out to an element of surprise if much is known about the competitors. The market will find it difficult to have product differentiation, if everything is known. On the other hand, too little information creates blind spots for the regulators and law enforcing authorities, as we have seen in the current crisis.

Trust

Today, the financial system is confused about the confidence level in the market and the trust it exhibits to the players. To invest, the first step is to have trust in the system, which is followed by confidence level. Without trust in the system, the players would never venture into the markets, even if they were confident of high yields. Therefore, the primary criterion for any system to be successful is the environment of 'trust'.

In the period from 1930 till 1933, nearly 9,000 banks had closed down due to panic and bank run. After the formation of the FDIC in 1934, the number of banks that closed in the next seven decades was 2250, with an average of not more than 30 per year. Does this mean that regulation with the FDIC had plugged the problem of bank run by securing the deposits of retail investors? It would also mean that

Quality of Information (QoI)

generally the problem still exists because banks are closing at a rate of at least two per month on a statistical average, but it is only because of the trust posed by deposit insurance that there are fewer bank runs.

Comparing the aviation industry in developed countries with the banking industry, for the bankers, there is something to learn here. If the same statistics were to be used, imagine having an average of two flight disasters per month. The consequence would mean that there would be no passengers flying anymore. So is the safety record of the banks at its best?

The high volume of trading across the globe takes into account the trust in the market system. Trust in the system assumes robust accounting standards, dependable technology, checks on moral hazard, financial security and information symmetry. Any deviation that results in uncertainty leaves individuals and institutions prone to information effect and panic (Summer, 2003). A global economy demands that investors have trust in financial numbers on a global basis (Levitt, 1999). As reported by the IMF (Containing Systemic Risks and Restoring Financial Soundness, April 2008), during the last decade, investors were living under a false sense of security and trust. This was because of the benign performance of the credit market in the last eight years. The trust was sustained, as argued by Chapman (2004), that people would not like to change until the going was good and they would not experience failure.

One reasons out that the false trust was due to information asymmetry, as little was known of the process of risk layering, credit rating and financial reporting. Although the market was seemingly confident, the crisis was looming because of the misinformation. Stated in 'Goodhart Law', whereby it was assumed that markets would never enter recession, substantiates the false sense of security. This sense was being fed into the system by way of risk modelling and statistical methods. Even though the loan quality deteriorated over a period of time, there was no slow down, as the trust posed on the information (asymmetric) was absolute.

Trust in financial institutions can be enhanced, either through supervisory oversight that examines more broadly the risks banks are taking, with closer coordination among supervisors (IMF, Containing Systemic Risks and Restoring Financial Soundness, April 2008), or by providing the information that the investor needs to assess for himself the market condition. This means that investors and regulators have the same information to have an independent perspective on the market.

The quantity of information is not a factor of trust. Of course, there is a threshold of information availability. The information needs to be useful for making decisions and therefore has to be processed to create valuable information. If the information available to the player creates a sense of flexibility in decision-making and the decision taken is validated by the subsequent event, then even if the decision was wrong, it still builds trust in the information system. It is cyclic and interdependent on the information, decision-making and outcome.

Trust in an information system is a measure of QoI because there lays the ability of the players, to participate in the business process. If the players are not confident with the information provided, it brings pessimism and uncertainty into the system and then either the investments collapse or players tend to take riskier options.

The important factors in the building of trust are correctness, consistency and conciseness.

Let's take an example of stock price as seen on a trading terminal to elaborate the characteristics of correctness, consistency and conciseness. The stock price of company X has to be correct at any point in time when it is watched (Correctness). This means that every time the price changes it has to be correctly updated. A time lag to update or a wrong display will lead to wrongful decision-making. The price needs to be available for review whenever the player wants it, and therefore, the availability of the price needs to be consistent so that it satisfies the dependability (Consistency). The price should make sense to the player in order to make a decision. In case the price is available up to four decimal places or changes five times every second, it is not going to help build the trust (Conciseness).

The stress test that the banks conduct does provide a sense of trust; rather the tests have one of the objectives to restore trust of the players in the banking system. The banks, after conducting the tests, have to make public the report of the findings, and that will continue to sustain the trust in the system. The more the information is made public about the test results, the greater will be the symmetry or equality of information between the players, and the higher will be the trust in the

Quality of Information (QoI)

system. Higher trust will not necessarily mean higher investments, but would mean a true reflection of the sentiments in the market.

Together trust is a composition of these factors. The crisis has taught many a lesson of slipping trust. Credit ratings were not correct information. Subsequent to the crisis, investors are going to double-check the ratings before taking a decision. Recheck is only done because there is a drop in trust in the information that is created by the credit rating alphanumeric characters. It will take time before trust is rebuilt into the system.

If one has to prioritize the factors for trust building in the system, correctness of information is mandatory and number one priority. The others are only about logistical and user-friendliness. Correctness is the hygiene factor for any information system. There is only one measure of the correctness of information and that is being 100%. **There is no middle path about the correctness.**

THE GLOBAL FINANCIAL CRISIS IS <u>NOT</u> FINANCIAL

Chapter 9
Global financial Architecture

> **4R Principle**
>
> Right Information at
>
> Right Time with
>
> Right View for
>
> Right Player

4R High Definition (HD) Infoweaver – Global Financial System Architecture

The last decade has seen a rise in increased exploitation of information and communication technology in the financial sector along with intensified financial innovation. There are a few facts that need to be considered before making any arguments regarding the global financial architecture. First, technology and the financial markets have a profound effect on the global economy and represent the core of any sovereign nation. It is imperative that these two core elements are taken together in determining the future of globalization as a process and the functioning of individual countries. Second, on its own the financial market is very intense in information. In a few seconds, there are terabytes of information that change hands containing financial, political, economic and business information,

> **The model of perfect market requires perfect information and all agents have the same information on prices, technology, credit etc. (Pelaez 2009).**

which is either processed or requires processing. The challenge is to get the information that is most desired, something which can be trusted upon and that can provide some sense of foresight. In earlier chapters, the author had argued for a high quality of information (QoI), as the overarching component of the global financial architecture.

In short, if one has to learn from the past, it is the symmetric information life cycle among various financial system players that would have prevented the current financial crisis.

There have been debates about the size of regulation in the market and the impact it will have on the free-flowing nature of business. The arguments being debated are backed by philosophies of 'less government' and others, which have shown results in the past few decades. Countries have grown richer and trade has expanded to dizzy heights. But all that has not come without turbulences and crises. There have been frauds, scandals and other instances of moral hazard. So the debate is about how much regulation is optimum. The model that this book is suggesting is about a combination of both a regulatory and deregulatory approach while **_defining maximum granularity to each unit of information in the system._**

THE GLOBAL FINANCIAL CRISIS IS NOT FINANCIAL

This is a new age of representing information, where a large quantum of information is a way of constructing the present. High Definition (HD) screens of electronic devices compact the density of picture elements (pixels) to provide clearer images that are closer to natural images. The colours and sharpness of the images are so close to reality that sometimes features which are missed by natural eyes get highlighted. It is the power of providing high definition to the smallest part of the available information. Hence, the prefix HD to Infoweaver seems apt to the vision of global financial architecture that exploits the granularity of the smallest unit of information. Architecture has derived the concept of high definition (HD) from this piece of media technology. In principle, HD technology captures, recreates and projects the granularity of information for better appreciation of the reality. Similarly, the proposed global financial architecture will capture the granularity of the financial environment and make it available to the players. The objectives of information communication will be in accordance with the principle of 4R, as discussed later.

The management of risk is based on how accurately the risk is monitored and measured in the system (Crockett, 2001). There is no denial, that risk calculation and monitoring is a function of symmetric information content. The risk in discussion is not the risk due to betting but the entrepreneurial risk which should be based on the financial system's ethos. Attempts to measure the risk in a casino bet is pointless and therefore, any reference to a financial business process that mirrors risk-taking as in a casino, is not for discussion. The best the regulators could do is to apply circuit breakers if they find casino-like tendencies in the system.

Measuring the risk initially, and then monitoring as reality on the ground, is a logical sequence. This is on the prevention side. On the curative side, the financial system, as being developed in the BASEL framework, needs to have a reserve cushion to make the entities resilient. It is a complicated task to continuously assign the right size of cushion for the heterogeneous components in the financial system. Again the right size is a guideline that is dependent on the right information of the asset class and exposure, whose accuracy will define to the overall risk. The right size of cushion for the system will also be determined by the stress test results which the banks have started to conduct on an annual basis. In the earlier chapter on the systemic view, the incompleteness of this stress test has been discussed.

Global financial Architecture

There is both philosophical and practical realization that a sound and stable financial system is required for a peaceful existence of the world because of its supra-systemic nature, culminating in political and social unrest. The supporting financial architecture must be resilient to all phases of the financial cycles, such as volatile credit cycles, business booms and bubbles. As they say: be prepared for the rainy day. There are various techniques suggested by the experts, such as the BASEL framework, for capital adequacy, stress testing and loan-to-value ratios at different times etc. To apply all these techniques and methods, a robust information execution model is a necessity to govern the global financial architecture. As introduced in the chapter about the 'current crisis', the finance and economics is about doing the 'right things', but systems and architecture are about doing those things 'right'. Clearly, this demarcation is not understood well with the experts handling the current crisis. **All those financial remedial strategies, such as bailouts, austerity, interest rates and others, are failing because both the sensing and delivery system of those 'right things' are not effective.**

As seen from the chapter on systemic view, it is understood that there is no single authority responsible and accountable for the regulations across international borders. While in some countries, there is a split in the supervision and the regulation, there is also unification as well as fragmentation of regulators functions (securities, commodities, banking, insurance, and others) in the financial market. All these combinations may not be the source of the real problem. The real problem lies when these supervisors and regulators across the boundaries are responsible for those very large, complex matrix firms, having a common operating structure, across international borders. It is a situation of regulating the complexity in a heterogeneous environment. Though the argument is tending against the concept of globalization and points towards the hazards of globalization, it would be wrong not to accept those hazards as part of the globalized financial market. As a step forward, it will be appropriate to find methods to respect the reality and benefits of a globalized system to minimize the hazards.

If there exist, an objective global view of the financial market and the regulatory system on which the global financial regulation operates, the current crisis has proved that there is a mismatch. On the market side there are unified international and national players while on the regulatory side, there are only national players, ignoring BASEL as an authority. To rephrase this problem: there is no single authority that is responsible, accountable and in control of the entire financial system, when seen from a holistic view. To find one, it then becomes a political reconstruction of the solution between participating governments. It would mean to carve out a global regulatory authority for a unified global financial system, which would also unify the fiscal authorities, that is, the governments. This is probably, not the solution yet (Crockett, 2001).

With the proposed architecture, it is possible to have a single regulating authority by way of making the information available to all regulatory authorities in a standardized (unified) and consistent set-up. The challenge is not about the absence of regulation, but the inability of the regulators to have visibility into the nooks and crannies of the financial system to mitigate the brewing risk. Sheila Bair also shared this opinion in an interview with Reuters, in the June of 2012. So far, as seen in the crisis, the players on all sides, seller, buyer and regulators, seemed powerless because the most important resource, the information, was in deficit supply to make (pursue) a 'perfect informed decision'.

So, what is 4R-HD Infoweaver?

It is the right moment to construct the principle-based information system that will run the global financial architecture for the resilience and stability that was missing, before the crisis and during the crisis. It will be inappropriate to say, after the crisis because the global financial crisis still continues. 4R Infoweaver is a term that is evolved based on our discussion in all previous chapters.

The 4Rs stand for:

- **Right Information at**
- **Right Time with**
- **Right View for**
- **Right Player.**

This architecture is for generating high quality of information (QoI) that will prevail for all those who are in the market as well as for those who intend to be part of the market. The architecture is to address the problems faced in the information life cycle, be it in information

Global financial Architecture

creation, corroboration or communication. The new architecture is to consolidate the components of the financial system, and its hierarchy, upon the information architecture to meet these objectives of 4R. Again, the architecture is to be able do those (financial and economic) things 'right'.

If the state of information asymmetry is to overcome, the information needs to be executed in symmetric units, in whichever part of the information life cycle, they execute the financial system. The author considers the 4R principle as a gold standard for a symmetric information execution which can provide guidance to operate any robust information system.

For an investor, to gather information about transnational markets, the information is expensive and cumbersome to acquire and analyze. These investors then tend to follow the signs and behaviour of others, who are already considered to be informed. **As a result the 'uninformed' follows the 'informed'.** As the dependence on those few 'informed' increases, they become a single point of failure for risk analysis, risk allocation and hence, investment decisions. Thus, it becomes important to bring information parity between all classes of investors if the financial system is to be resilient to 'herd' behaviour. Also,

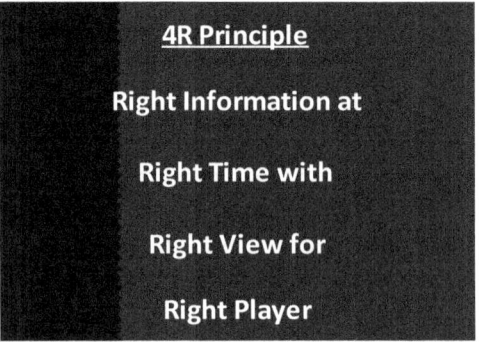

investors want to take advantage of market behaviour as an indicator to their decision-making. The rationality of the decision-making comes from assuming that the market is moving in the direction that is most suitable to the investors. This may not be true, as every investor is following every other.

Currently, the financial market has been working as an extension of the nineteenth and twentieth century marketplace. Transactions are recorded with enhanced computational technologies, ironically, with a risk of informational emptiness due to 'big data' flooding the system. This needs to be changed to intelligent and integrated systems of the twenty-first century, where the information is **woven** through all the corners of the market integrating small and big players, national and

THE GLOBAL FINANCIAL CRISIS IS NOT FINANCIAL

international firms, local and national regulators with national and globalized economies. Hence, the word 'Infoweaver' signifies the objective of symmetric information in global financial architecture.

With this architecture, we are avoiding the situations where large institutions get riskier to the point of becoming too-big-to-fail. By making the interconnectedness, making the systemic view more visible to the entire landscape of players, national and international, in a holistic way, the national and global financial system will be self-governed. The architecture will propagate better governance, as the system will be more transparent and hence, accountable. International coordination of regulators will be easier and there will be an automatic shared responsibility prevailing in the system, since all the regulators will be able to watch their systemic risk entities.

In the cases, where liquidity shortage becomes a potential market shock, it becomes a major blind spot in the financial market, especially when the liquidity risk due to financial and non-financial events, changes the global capital flows. Removing this asymmetric information about the liquidity risk becomes the objective of improvement to the global financial architecture (IMF, Global Financial Stability Report, 2005). In a way, it is about democratization of the financial markets, including the role of government in the participation of the market. This is a complicated assortment of the financial market as a process, and individuals (both as retail and institutional) who participate as a practice where money matters most. The combination then becomes a sentiment of national and international importance. Hence, to bring transparency using information-symmetric architecture, will lead to enhanced trust in the role of the market players. With democratization, the author does not necessarily mean the voting system, but points out to running the system while keeping all the players equally informed, in accordance with the principle of democracy. It is financial information, by the people, of the people and for the people. Any deviation from this democratic principle would amount to ills of information asymmetry, such as fraud, moral hazard and systemic failures.

Of course, in a way, symmetric information is a key to a shareholder's decision-making, which will strengthen their bargaining power. While there is a strong correlation between the activities of different players in the market, there has been negative impact due to the globalized economy. The global info-weaver architecture will convert the threat of

Global financial Architecture

interconnectedness to an opportunity of managing systemic risk, effectively.

Based on the learning, it will be wise to start constructing global financial architecture with a symmetric information system that will make information cheaper, accessible, standard and accurate, where hindsight works as foresight, before future becomes a reality, supported by few assumptions, helping the players make independent decisions. No doubt this is tending towards a utopian system, but if the architecture reduces the impact of catastrophes like the current one, it is worth taking the step. It's an aim for crisis-proof financial architecture to start with; hence there is no reason, not to dare it.

So far, it is seen that the global financial system is dotted with challenges, such as lack of transparency, real-time information, common view, unified accounting standards, moral guidance and holistic controls. Can the regulators make up for these challenges?

What if there exists a system which will provide the investors, irrespective of their size and nationality, with access to a global database of the financial system, where the information is viewed in symmetry along with the bankers, intermediaries, government and regulators. While the investors and market players have access to this symmetric information, they would also have assurance that the information created is from a consistent accounting standard across the globe. It is the author's conviction, that higher visibility brings greater trust and confidence, and with this system not only will the investor recover the trust deficit in the financial system but also they will be more than willing to reinvest with a greater entrepreneurial risk appetite.

One common factor in the market crash of the 1930s and 2008 is the fundamental structure of the market with respect to investment and depository banking. The difference between the two is the availability of information technology to efficiently discipline the market. Making information available to all players will automatically regulate the market. This means that there would exist no information asymmetry using global information system architecture, in which the information criss-crosses the layers of the market and components.

The impeding financial crisis and subsequently, the economic crisis are a result of market dynamics that need to be tracked with a structured

THE GLOBAL FINANCIAL CRISIS IS NOT FINANCIAL

methodology. Expert economists and supervisory institutions had suggested a critical review of the transmission mechanism for analysis of the crisis. Again, this may be the right thing to do in order to negotiate the crisis, but the currently no architecture exist to effectively operate the transmission mechanism.

The potential of a live information system, as in 4R-HD Infoweaver, to operate the transmission mechanism, would satisfy all the gaps that we have encountered in the book so far. It is not just the challenge of running an effective transmission mechanism but it also rests on the effectiveness of the underlying information life cycle. The issues with accounting standards, dependability of auditing standards, conflict of interest of credit rating and blind spots of regulators are some of the key issues that have to be resolved as part of this global financial architecture. These have to be the starting point to implement a sustainable and effective global transmission mechanism. Basically, it is about a sophisticated, real-time monitoring of a transmission mechanism and its systemic interconnectedness. The process of aggregation of economic units, such as sovereign economies, regional economies as European Union, Asian Tigers and APAC, with that of financial units such as institutional investors and retail investors, makes key observation posts for transmission mechanism.

History has demonstrated that credit bubbles precede most severe crises (Walter, 2010). So why is this trend not visible and contained? If the global financial and economic community is blindfolded, then in all probability their mechanism was not effective and is currently not effective either.

This is a new age challenge where the financial innovation, like all other innovations, had brought information asymmetry to the system. Innovation itself has changed direction. This is a feature of this century. Earlier, all innovations, including non-financial innovations, were well understood by the users. They could breakdown the details of the product and its workings to its most comprehensible parts. Today, innovations have brought an era of 'black box' and combinations of black boxes, working for a complex system. Only the experts or those financial engineers know what is going on in that black box. The reduced information available to end-users is only with reference to output from this black box, as a limited resource. The end-users could be a retail investor, a financial intermediary, government or even the regulators.

| Global financial Architecture

In the past, people themselves used to fix their house appliances and automobiles at home, itself. There were guides available to help. Over the period, this ability disappeared because the users were not able to keep up with the complexity of the engineering and innovations. Similarly, the financial innovations have moved the products away from mass comprehensibility to a few experts. No one would doubt, before the crisis, the working knowledge of CDOs remained with fewer than a hundred people across the world, while the entire financial crisis pivoted on the information asymmetry because of those CDOs. So it will be apt to term this age as the age of information 'black box'. The complexity is further added to, when the rating agencies grade the financial products. Again it is no less than as a black box. The investor in this case is left with no choice but to rely on the available information. The proposed information architecture would breakdown the black box to more comprehensible knowledge for the average investors.

An argument for creating an info-weaver for the financial system is related to business in the non-financial sector. How does it happen that Too-Big-to-Fail firms, along with those global banks have a mismatch that pushes them to bankruptcy? It rarely happens that two interconnected manufacturing businesses have a situation where the inventory or delivery of goods between the two entities is mismatched by a few billion dollars. It happens that way because at every stage of transaction, whichever method is used, there are checks and balances. So why is it that in banking and on the financial market, trillions of dollars of OBSEs had been created without being balanced out in the global balance sheet or ducked the radar of auditors or regulators? One finds the answer in the nature of the information system that is used by the manufacturing sector. It is an integrated system that carries information from one corner of the firm to another on a real-time basis with the necessary balances, interlocks and traceability. The integrated system is able to match each penny in the inventory, while simultaneously making the system open for audit and regulations, as required.

As an example, let us take the sequential and generic business process of a typical manufacturing firm, in a cycle from sales order to balance sheet, also called 'quote to cash' cycle. Every business process, right from booking a sale order and making a purchase to match the order, is accounted for, in the books of account. The material from a vendor at the factory gate becomes an inventory as soon as the goods receipt transaction is executed. The purchase order is matched with the goods receipt in order to make the rightful payments. Meanwhile, the goods move to the inventory locations and into the production line after clearing the quality check. In the case of goods being returned because the material failed a quality check, the account is updated with a decrease in the inventory and adjustments to the vendor account balances. If the balance sheet of the firm were to be drawn at this instance, the system would clearly show the assets with the inventory and the liabilities with net amount payable to the vendor. The argument here is the degree of information symmetry that holds the manufacturing line together. Any information asymmetry at any stage of quote to cash cycle will either create cash or material out of sync with the profitability. It is a no-brainer to understand that irrespective of the size of the manufacturing firm, the management is symmetric with the information in the books of account. This happens in 'real-time' as the underlying information system is integrated. The information system in discussion weaves through the business processes of goods receipt, purchase, invoicing, sales, production planning, bank reconciliation and others. The advantage of this information weaving is the accounting of cash and material at every stage of the business processes. Similarly, the global financial system needs to be integrated and woven through the various processes, financial products, trading transactions, banks, financial institutions and national economies.

In retrospection, the 3 Cs (create, corroborate and communicate) of the information life cycle for the global financial system is found to be not executed with the woven information system.

If non-financial firms can keep their financial and manufacturing information symmetric in real-time with their management layers and the stakeholders, then what is stopping the global financial firms from operating with 'perfect' information symmetry? This brings us back to the author's earlier argument in Chapter 1, that money in the financial sector is a virtual product, unlike other sectors where money has a face to physically quantify either in the form of a product, a service or a customer. This distinction has brought challenges that are not addressed, yet.

The Global Financial Architecture

THE GLOBAL FINANCIAL CRISIS IS NOT FINANCIAL

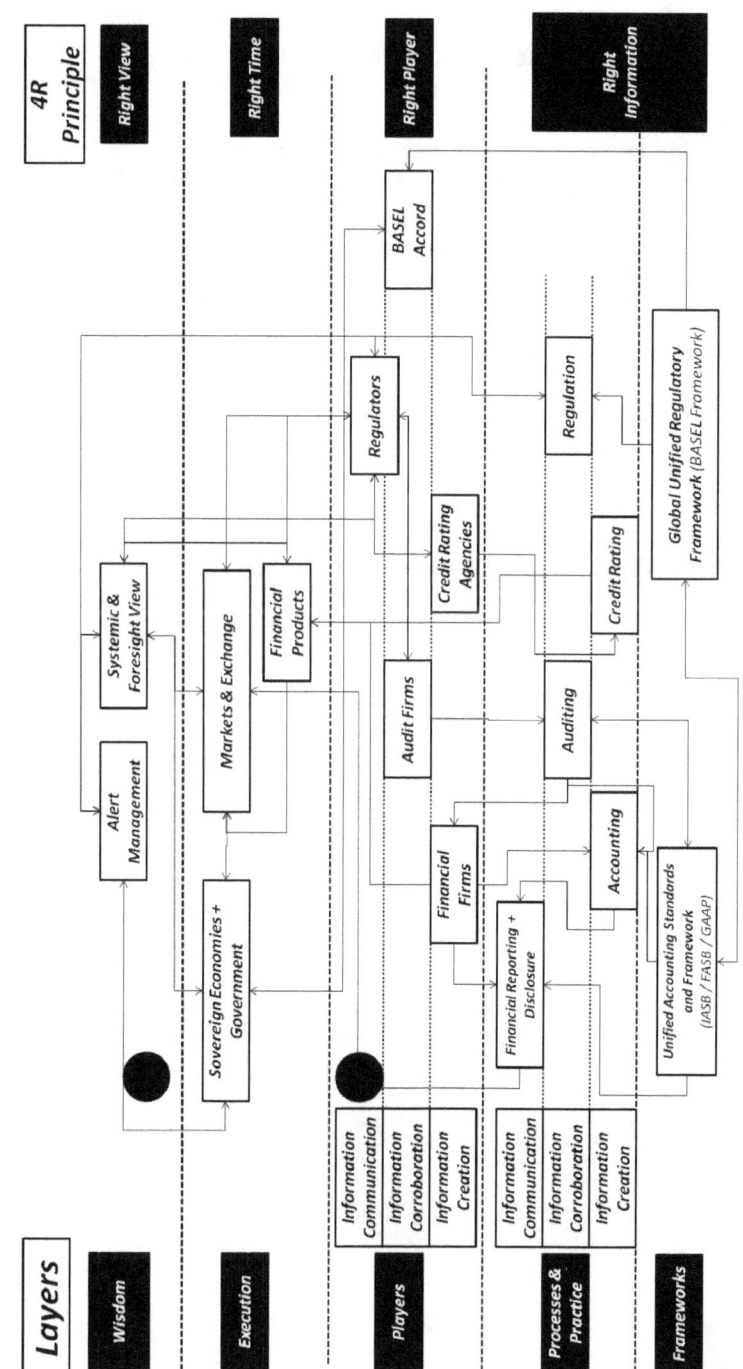

'Quality of Information' in Question

Global financial Architecture

The objective of reconstructing the Infoweaver-based global financial architecture is to create an ecosystem of high quality of information (QoI) by bringing perfect information symmetry to the execution of the financial information life cycle. This would mean that at every stage of information creation, corroboration and communication, the information is symmetric with every player. In order to achieve this objective, the architecture is envisaged in layers. Each layer has processes, practices and entities serving a principle-based objective. The architecture has the following layers:

- Universal Frameworks *(Unification of Diverse Standards)*

- Process and Practice Layer *(Information Creation, Corroboration and Communication)*

- Player Layer *(Players)*

- Execution Layer *(Products and Markets)*

- Wisdom Layer *(Proactive, Predictive and Preventive)*

Each layer addresses the shortcomings discussed in the various sections.

THE GLOBAL FINANCIAL CRISIS IS NOT FINANCIAL

Standards and Framework: Unify the Diversity

Global financial Architecture

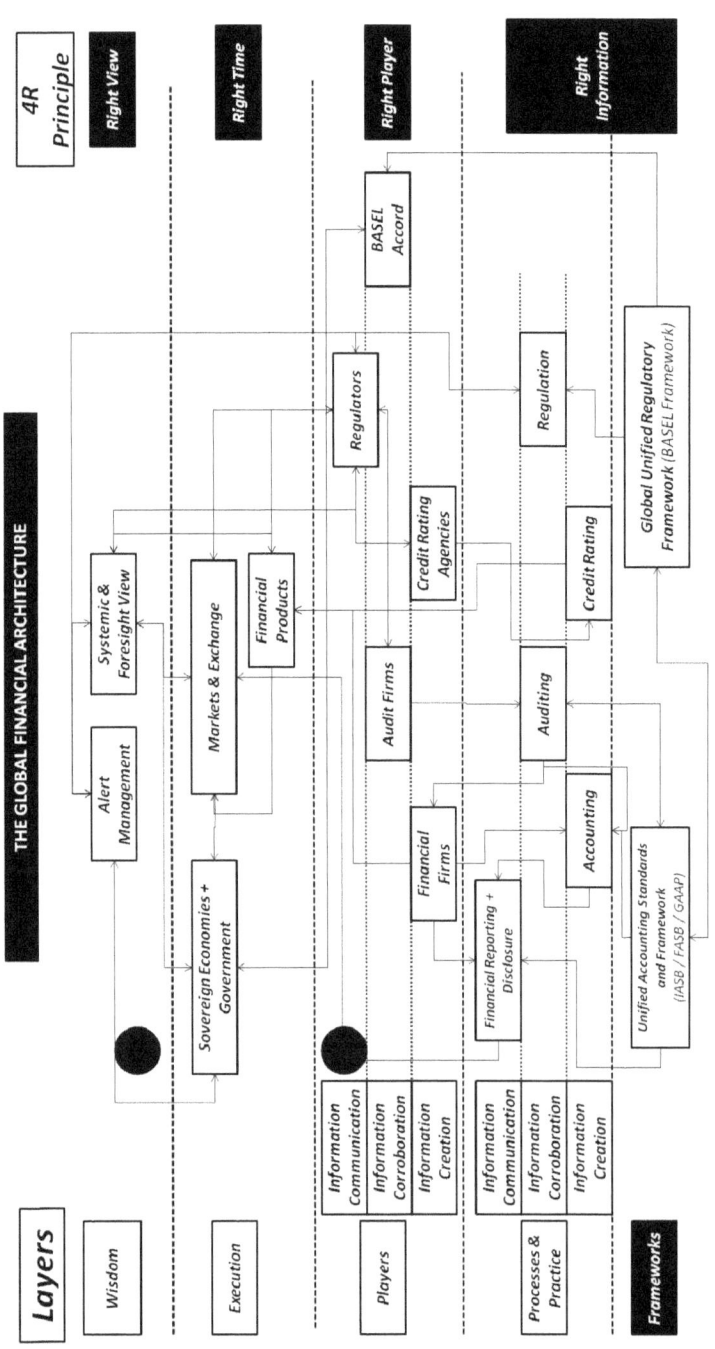

242

THE GLOBAL FINANCIAL CRISIS IS NOT FINANCIAL

This is a layer of standards for accounting, reporting, auditing, disclosures, warning and disclaimers. There are different standards followed across the global financial system and each of them has an advantage. It may be an ideal situation to have universal standards across the board, but that reality seems unlikely for reasons discussed in previous chapters. Therefore, the architecture proposes the use of all the standards together, in parallel, to create a unified framework of diverse standards.

Similarly, the regulatory authorities across the global system work in a mesh of complex networks. They have varied operating guidelines which are in tandem with the national laws. Also, these regulatory authorities have a common minimum principle agreed within the BASEL framework. The pitfall in this arrangement is the non-imposing nature of the BASEL framework. It makes the global regulatory architecture headless or not strong enough to weather the storm.

True Value: Right Information in the system

The players are confused with the information revealed by various accounting and reporting standards. The principle of **true value** in the architecture will match the figures in the statement of accounts with those on the ground. This would mean perpetual feedback using perspectives from different standards from process of accounting, reporting and auditing. In light of that context, the architecture will capture the financial information from different standards and also convert these processes to other standards while placing them in a unified window. The idea is to capture the financial information in its diversity and unify the information made available from various standards. This would mean capturing the transactions and then building the schemas.

What does a schema do?

Schemas would encapsulate information in the form of the given standards, even though till now, the transactions have been reported by a different standard. The US GAAP, reporting schemas for all other standards of balance sheets, is one example that is being followed sparingly. The advantage of schemas for accounting and reporting standards will be the ability to bring multiple standards to a single platform and reconstruct the information as desired by the players.

Another advantage of the schemas would be in terms of exploiting the advantage of one method to overcome the shortfall of another.

Accounting starts with postings in the chart of accounts for a going concern. The chart of accounts, across any accounting landscape is the same. These charts of accounts follow principles of accounting for posting each transaction. Let them be posted as they are and use the idea of schemas to do a shadow posting according to other accounting standards, by way of maintaining parallel ledger for each accounting standard. When the final accounts needs to be published, the right player would have a choice to see all the variations in the account as per different standards.

There is nothing as one value, which is the 'true value'. It is the principle of information symmetry applied to a number of values, derived from various standards that signify 'true value' in the financial system.

Learning from the current crisis is about the inability of the capital adequacy of banks to sustain the pressures of the downward economic curve. As discussed, the primary factor rests on the assessment of assets in the bank's portfolio. In short, the individuality of the assets, which attracts different weighted risk values, was missing in the risk modelling and the calculations of capital adequacy. The missing individuality of the assets had brought the information asymmetry into the system and the faulty capital adequacy ratio. This practice still continues, when the BASEL framework suggests the value of capital adequacy across the members. In the architecture the capital adequacy is tracked based on individual assets rather than a value for an entity.

The current crisis is also an eye-opener for the standards as they treat the individual, main street (high street) and Wall Street account statements in a similar way. The disadvantage was the incompatibility of the three, their inability in providing the realistic picture of their constituents and holistically their role in quantifying the entire financial system. The architecture in its pursuit of 'true value' will segregate these layers with reference to socio-accounting standards. Individual balance sheets, commercial balance sheets and Wall Street balance sheets are meant for diverse purposes, and therefore any standard that attempts to unify the accounting procedure, is incorporating information asymmetry in the process and practice of accounting.

THE GLOBAL FINANCIAL CRISIS IS <u>NOT</u> FINANCIAL

The fallout of the misrepresentation of the account statements in these layers has been the wrong assessment of 'true risk appetite' of the home loan borrowers. As individual risk appetite consolidates to retail risk appetite, which when consolidated appears as accumulated risk in the national and global balance sheets. This is how the current crisis has emerged.

True risk appetite is a function of true value and a stabilizing factor for the entire financial system. Hence, the importance of the principle of 'true value' in the financial system makes this layer the starting point for global financial architecture.

Global financial Architecture

Process and Practice

THE GLOBAL FINANCIAL CRISIS IS NOT FINANCIAL

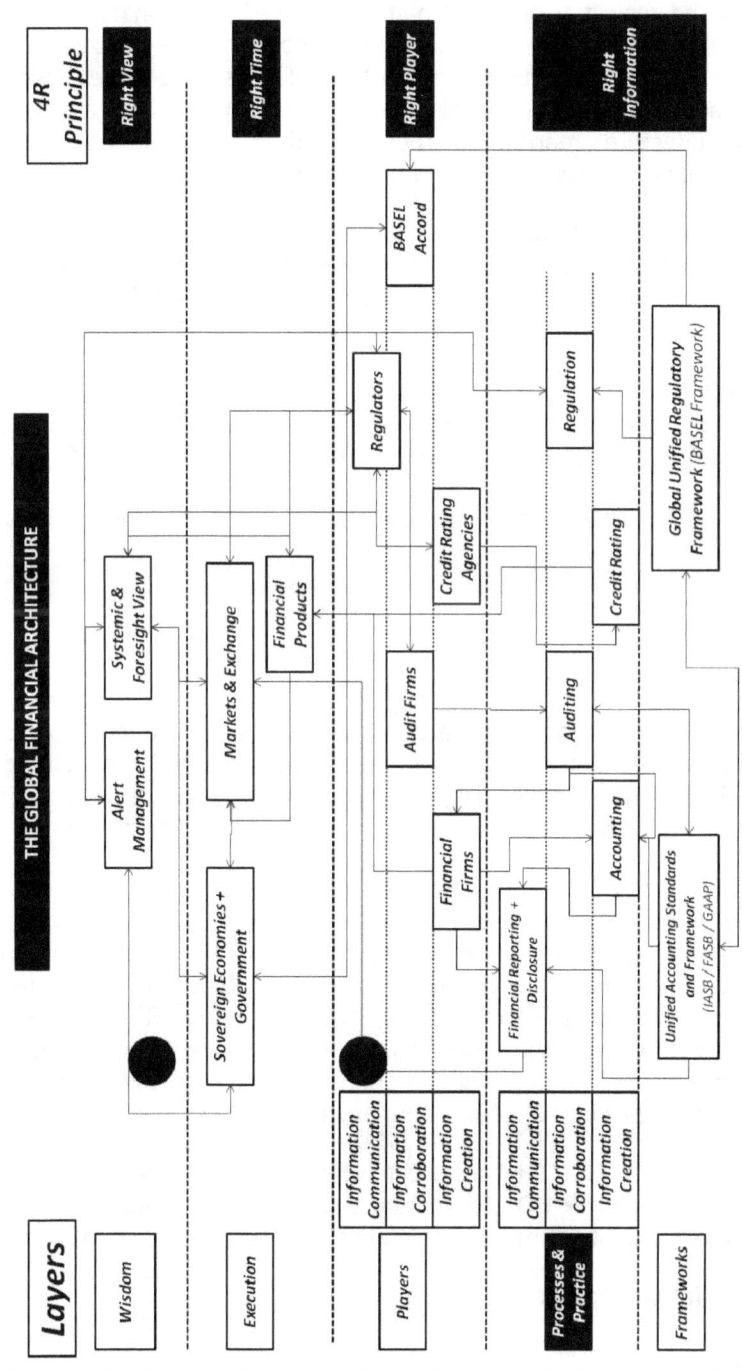

'Quality of Information' in Question   247

Global financial Architecture

This is the mainstay of the dynamism of the global financial system. National and global firms are bound together with these processes and practices to run their businesses. Instead of classifying these processes and practices according to their function in the financial system, the 4R HD architecture rearranged them to their function of creating, corroborating and communicating financial information.

The players, which form the next layer, are the owners of these processes and practices which are guided by the set of standards. In the interconnectedness of the components of the financial system and other systems, these processes and practices play an important part in a typical day. The challenges in business-as-usual, are usually dealt with within their local authorities, but when the impact is beyond a particular firm and is affecting the national, regional and global boundaries, it has to be strategically addressed in the architecture.

The major challenges, as discussed in the previous chapters, are listed here:

Information Creation

Credit rating – The periodicity and accuracy of credit rating had been pointed out as misleading the players, in misjudging the environment. In the 4R HD architecture, the credit rating process is enabled in real-time, so that the products are rated with changing market conditions. This will bring accuracy to the ratings, as the products would be rated more often than in the current practice.

The current crisis had also highlighted the missing regulatory oversight of the credit rating methodology. In fact, the regulators themselves were misled by the ratings. According to the author, it is considered the source of information asymmetry and hence, failure of credit rating processes. In 4R HD architecture, there is a definitive connection established between the processes of regulation and credit rating. The black box of methodology will be opened up for regulation to increase the transparency in the credit rating process.

Accounting – A lot had been redefined in the previous section of frameworks. The 4R HD architecture will redefine accounting principles to create the right information using the concept of 'true value'.

Information Corroboration

THE GLOBAL FINANCIAL CRISIS IS NOT FINANCIAL

Regulation – The process of regulation is one of the most complex processes in the architecture. It weaves through the length and breadth of the financial system and has a significant role to play in all areas. The current crisis had revealed many grey areas which the regulatory process has to redefine. They include embedding into the processes such as credit rating and auditing. The 4R HD architecture facilitates that inclusion. One of the major challenges faced is the lack of timeliness in fire-fighting the issues. The current crisis had found the regulation lagging behind the event curve. The 4R HD architecture provides for a real-time systemic view and alert management, as part of regulatory process and that should resolve not only the issue of timeliness in fire-fighting but also facilitate them in being proactive.

Auditing – The current crisis has shown a missing link between the process of auditing and the feedback to the standards board. The auditors continued to audit the accounts without referring any ambiguous interpretation back to the board. If the link between the auditing process and boards was active, after every audit, the firms would have given a response to the standards board about the key flaws in the process of accounting.

The 4R HD architecture provides for continuous feedback from the auditing firms back to the drawing board to strengthen the process of accounting as well as auditing. At least in scenario of the controversial (misuse) use of Repo 105 transaction, it would have been prevented by the Too-Big-to-Fail firms.

Information Communication

Financial Reporting and Disclosures – The insufficiency of information provided in the standard boilerplate brings informational risk to the system. Also, the timeliness of the reporting is too slow, in today's world of high-frequency trading. Currently, the standard for accounting, auditing, reporting and regulation is a framework that guides the market players in their routines. Since the architecture creates the platform on which the player transacts, the platform will act as the automatic guide to the system by not allowing the players to deviate from the laid down rules of the market. The architecture will provide a common platform for conducting the business across the boundaries and therefore, will leave no scope for process leakages and deviations.

Global financial Architecture

Players

THE GLOBAL FINANCIAL CRISIS IS <u>NOT</u> FINANCIAL

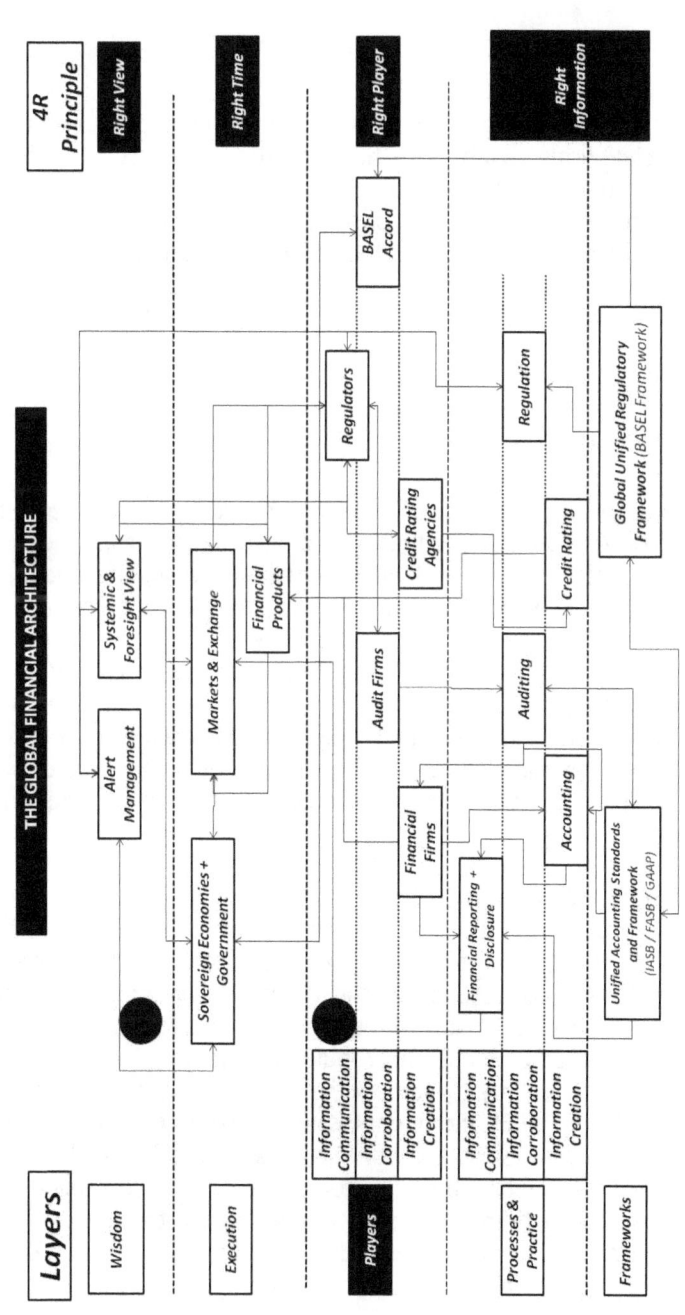

Information Creation

Credit Rating Agencies – They have a conflict of interest with the financial firms, who are floating the products. In the new architecture these agencies are independent and derive their fees directly from the market. The basis of the fees could be based on volumes transacted by that financial product or the total value of the product in the market at a given time. This could be worked out to eliminate the conflict of interest in the process of credit rating. Also, the consulting-based credit rating would be prevented, leading to further independence of the financial product and its ratings.

Information Corroboration

Auditors – Conflict of interest, similar to the credit rating agencies, does exist between the audit firms and the financial firms. The previous chapters have dealt with various ways, the auditors and their firms influence the audit process. In the 4R HD architecture, the audit firms are considered to be independent of those financial firms who hire them directly. In this case, they would be randomly allocated for the purpose of the audit for not more than one financial year. Moreover, the audit firms are to be paid not by the fee from the hiring firm but in proportion to the turnover audited. This would prevent conflict of interest while keeping intact, the shine of the auditing profession.

The BASEL Accord – The current position of the BASEL accord is considered to be a soft and non-binding accord. The time frame for the adoption of BASEL guidelines is flexible, and therefore, there are challenges to the consistency of the global regulation. In the 4R HD architecture, the BASEL accord had been upgraded as 'regulator of regulators' in order to make the regulatory landscape hierarchical and consistent in all markets across the global financial system. The advantage of the BASEL framework is in its ability, to unify the diverse regulatory practices across the borders. Again, as seen in the layers of frameworks, the architecture is consolidating the diversity of the regulatory best practices and redistributing it back to all the sovereign financial systems. The BASEL accord is playing a role of protagonist in the global regulatory framework, as an authority.

THE GLOBAL FINANCIAL CRISIS IS <u>NOT</u> FINANCIAL

Regulators – They have a typical position in the current scenario where they mind the financial space for compliance. From the information life cycle point of view, the regulators are purely corroborators of the information in the system. The only change in the new architecture is the connection of the regulators with the credit rating agencies and auditors. In the current scenario, the regulators have no say over the methodology used by the credit rating agencies. In the new architecture, this position has changed where the regulators have a role of corroboration over the methodology used by the credit rating agencies. Also, in the current scenario, the auditors have no connection with the regulators. They are more attached to the accounting standards boards. In the 4R HD architecture the regulators have a role to play in regulating the behaviour of the audit firms with respect to conflict of interest.

Information Communication

This is a black spot in the global financial system which has caused the widespread information asymmetry and is the primary cause of the current crisis. **There is no single player who is responsible for the distribution of financial information across the system.** It is up to individual players to communicate the information created within their scope. The information could be symmetric or asymmetric and there is no regulatory authority to address this challenge.

The 4R HD architecture upgrades the role of regulators from being a corroborator of information to also ensure the communication of the information to the right player. In a way, the role of the regulators is to ensure information symmetry in the system, as a function of high QoI.

This is an important find from this research.

Execution

THE GLOBAL FINANCIAL CRISIS IS NOT FINANCIAL

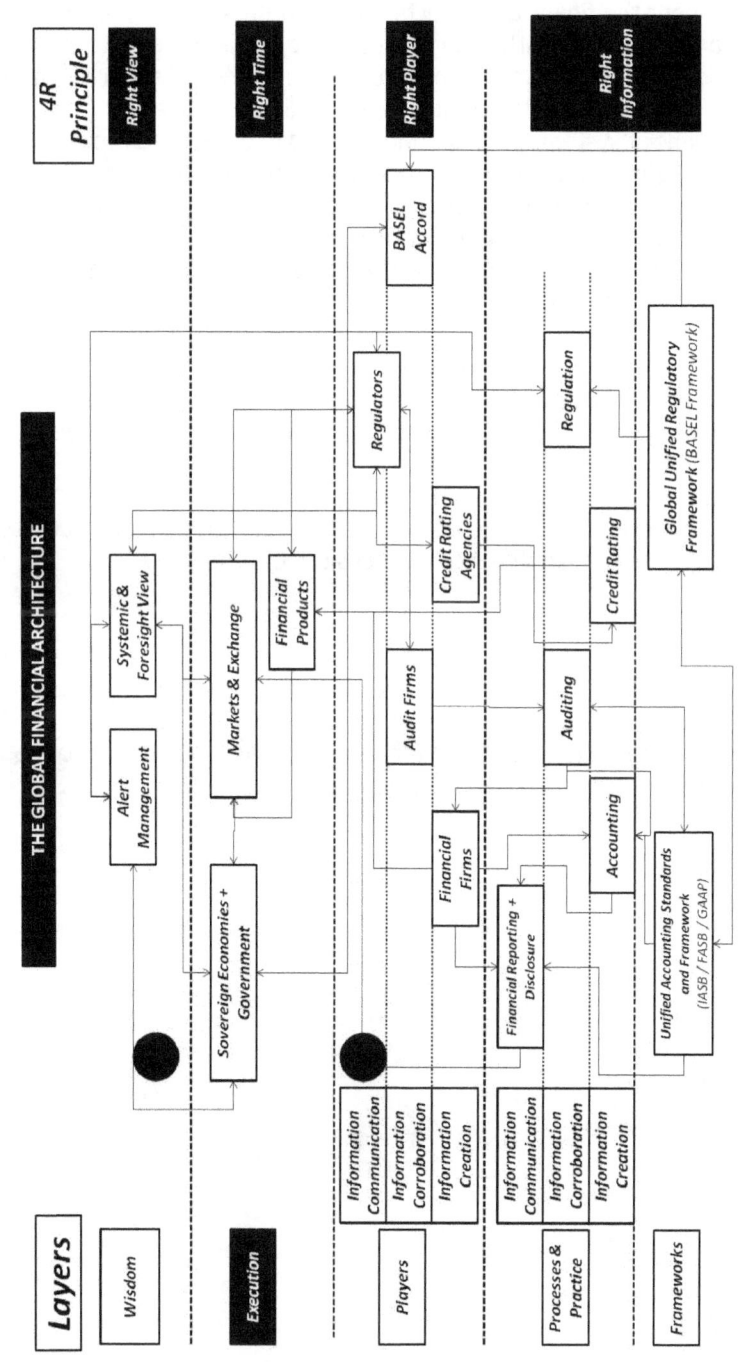

'Quality of Information' in Question

| Global financial Architecture

It is all about the financial products making a presence in the market, to make a profit. The participating economic system benefits from the innovations in the financial market, which is reflected in its annual growth. It is a vast playing field with millions of players across the global financial system, participating on a daily basis. The rapidity of the trading is growing by the day and so is the reach of the financial products into the remote corners of the economy. Conceptually, to put the entire system on a single platform is unimaginable, yet by the very nature of the interconnectedness, the global financial system is no less than a single platform.

The 4R HD architecture has the execution layer that consists of the product and places for the real activity. The timeliness of the information enables the execution of the financial activities. The governments play an important part in the execution as they are the custodians of the health of the economy. The monetary and fiscal policies interplay with the financial markets and their successful response depends on the comprehension of the 'true value' on the ground.

The execution layer in the architecture rests on an efficient and effective information system, where the timeliness is of high essence. There is no significant change in this layer when compared to the current configuration, except for the impetus on the information symmetry as a function of the 'right time'.

THE GLOBAL FINANCIAL CRISIS IS <u>NOT</u> FINANCIAL

Wisdom

Global financial Architecture

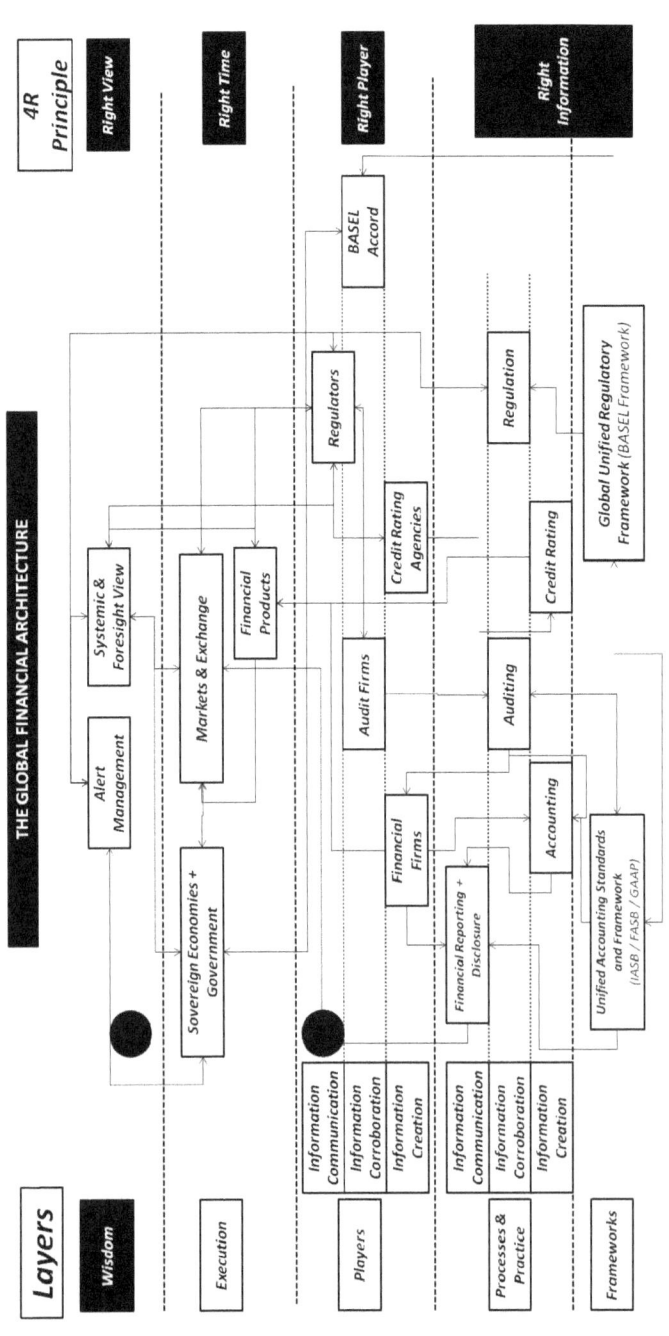

THE GLOBAL FINANCIAL CRISIS IS <u>NOT</u> FINANCIAL

The crisis was inconvincibly predictable because the players were not able to have a systemic view of the market and a holistic outlook was missing. Even though hindsight makes things look simpler than they actually were, it is ridiculously surprising that the making of the current crisis, was not seen.

With learning from the current crisis, this layer becomes an indispensable part of the 4R HD architecture. It has an important function to play, similar to the five senses of the human body. The strength of the financial system is as strong as this layer. For a system to be proactive, predictive and preventive to any destabilizing factor must make this a robust layer of 'wisdom'.

This layer will highlight the risk in **exposure and measure vulnerabilities** from evolving trends. Since the architecture is based on a learning curve of each financial product, individual assets, economic and business cycles and their combinations, it will be easier to fingerprint the pattern and create predictive analysis. The foresight view will be a natural outcome of this holistic methodology.

It will be easier to create an alert for an abnormality in an individual financial product and underlying collaterals.

There were predictions about the looming global financial crisis due to the housing bubble as early as mid-2005. There could be many reasons why the financial system did not take heed of those alerts. One important reason highlighted from the logical construction of the 4R HD architecture is the missing alert management system like the tsunami warning system. Currently, alerts are never made as routine and are not a function in the core financial system. This is another black hole in the global financial system. None of the players, including the public at large, have visibility of an alert to press the panic button.

In the 4R HD Infoweaver, the analytics will help simulate the conditions in the market with different permutations and combinations, making the odd balls curve, to provide variations in situations. More importantly, in pursuit of information symmetry and high QoI, these simulations will be visible to all the market players. The players will be able to drill-down to the micro-linkages of collaterals in the financial products. In the simulation, the architecture will provide visibility as multiple outcomes to

Global financial Architecture

the consequences of the known risks. Over a period of time, the architecture, using its historic information, will be able to build more risk models as derivatives of the existing risks in the system. The architecture, being predictive, will help the market players to proactively safeguard their positions and prevent a crisis.

The foresight layer will extract information from the markets and players across the globe and provide numerous views, slicing and dicing the information by sectors, regions, economies, markets and so on. It will provide a cockpit to the market so that the right view is available to facilitate 'wisdom' in the system. As an example, if the regulators require knowing the fund flow between the markets or products, they will be able to drill-down to the underlying assets across the countries, in real-time. Thus the boundaries of segmented or silo regulation will be diminished and the market will operate as a single platform for all the regulators, globally. For those activities which are systemic in nature, the regulators can intensify their monitoring, using a systemic view to manage the systemic risk.

The development of an architecture based on information symmetry as comprehensive and diverse as the 4R HD Infoweaver, would make the players, big and small, analyze for themselves the intrinsic value of their investments and reduce the phenomenon of 'the uninformed following the informed'.

This could not be too early to mention, hence the sooner the better. Global architecture is the new age way of doing things. It will soon be an essential requirement, when a global view of all these important aspects of the financial market, economic activities, energy maps, environmental movements, industrial production and other activities are redefined into global architecture, similar to the architecture we are discussing in this book. Perhaps I will pick up the topic of 'global architecture' in my next book to provide more thoughts and arguments about what the future holds for global architecture, as a concept.

To conclude, it will be apt to quote Mahatma Gandhi **"There is more to life, than increasing its speed".** In defining the principles for a safer, confident, transparent and trusted financial market, the underlying architecture needs to address the spirit in the quote. The quality of the market need not be measured by the volume of business per day or number of transactions but the trust posed in the market that is devoid of adverse selection and moral hazard. The route to

THE GLOBAL FINANCIAL CRISIS IS NOT FINANCIAL

achieve that spirit treads only through symmetric information in pursuit of high Quality of Information (QoI). Let the Martians find the concept of 'money' the most remarkable innovation, something they will not reject but would like to replicated in their planet.

Chapter 10
QoI Checklist for C(X)Os

THE GLOBAL FINANCIAL CRISIS IS NOT FINANCIAL

No.	26 Point Checklist for High Quality of Information (QoI)	☑
1	What are the top 3 information that must be known by top 3 executives of my organization at any given point in time?	
2	What is the set of information which assures that crisis is 'Prevented'?	
3	What is the set of information based on which 'Predictions' are made in my organization?	
4	What part of my organization can be termed as 'information black box'?	
5	Where are the touch points for assuring high Quality of Information in my organization?	
6	What are the sources of Information Creation, Corroboration and Communication in my organization?	
7	What are the single-point-of-failures for information flow in my organization?	
8	Who regulates the information in my organization and who regulates the regulators?	
9	Which department in my organization is assessing informational risk?	
10	In which element of information cycle, information is processed with a judgment call?	
11	What are the top 3 worst case scenarios in my information system? How are they 'Proactively' addressed?	
12	Has there been a review of my information system for categorizing information as 'Desired', 'Relevant', 'Nice to Have' and 'Redundant'? Is it governed by a natural progression and behavior of the players and users? This is over and above the information authorization code.	
13	Has there been a review of instances where 'actual' information was different from 'known' information?	
14	What is the quantum of information that is sourced from 3rd party which forms the information cycle of my organization?	
15	Do I have a 'Rich Picture' for the information system in my organization, connecting the information players like sources, recipients, processors and users?	
16	Do the players in my organization able to assess the 'Quality of Information'?	
17	Do the employees have control over validity of information created by algorithms?	
18	Which department is specifically responsible for the high quality of information in the system? Does the correct information mean high quality of information?	

QoI Checklist for C(X)Os

No.	26 Point Checklist for High Quality of Information (QoI)	☑
19	Is the quality assurance of information assumed to a natural progression of correctness or fitness to purpose?	
20	Do I have a systemic view of my organization with influencing and influenced entities?	
21	How much of the information in my organization is real-time? Do I need it real-time? What is it that I must know in real-time?	
22	Do the accounts statements of my organization represent the 'reality'? What numbers in the account statement are a misrepresentation of the 'realities'?	
23	Does my organization have a chief audit officer?	
24	Does my information system create alerts at various levels in my organization?	
25	Is my organization's information strategy, in principle aligning with information lifecycle and execution model?	
26	Is my organization equipped enough to make changes in the information system to quench the house fire?	

References

Altman, Edward I, and Anthony Saunders. "Credit Risk Measurement: Development Over Last 20 Years." *Journal of Banking and Finance* 21 (1998): 1721-1742.

Anderlini, Jamil. *China broadens stress tests for banks.* April 22, 2011. http://www.ft.com/cms/s/0/81b4ae7a-6ced-11e0-83fe-00144feab49a.html#axzz1KNRSxIwn.

Angell, I, and D Demetis. *Science's First Mistake: Delusions in Pursuit of Theory.* London: Bloomsbury Academic, 2010.

Armstrong, M.,Sappington,D.E.M. "Recent Developments in the Theory of Regulation." In *Handbook of Industrial Organization (Vol. III)*, by M.,Porter,R., Armstrong, 1566-1575. North-Holland, 1995.

Bair, Sheila C. "Financial Reform: The Road Ahead." *20th Annual Hyman P. Minsky Conference.* New York, NY: FDIC, 2011.

Barth, James R, Daniel E Nolle, Triphon Phumiwasana, and Glenn Yago. "A Cross-Country Analysis of the Bank Supervisory Framework and Bank Performance." *Financial Markets, Institutions & Instruments*, May 2003.

Barth, Mary E, Wayne R Landsman, and Mark H Lang. "International Accouting Standards and Accounting Quality." *Journal of Accounting Research* 46, no. 3 (2008).

Berkshire Hathaway. *Berkshire Hathaway annual report.* Berkshire Hathaway Inc, 2002.

Board of Governors of the Federal Reserve System. "Mission." *About the Federal Reserve Board.* November 6, 2009.

References

—. "Monetary Policy Releases." *Press Release.* November 25, 2008.

Borrus, Amy, Mike McNamee, and Heather Timmons. "The Credit-Raters: How they work and how they might work better." *Business Week*, April 8, 2002: 38-40.

Bowe, Michael, and Maximilian J B Hall. "A Comparison of Capital Standards and Proprietary Surveillance." *International Journal of Finance and Economics*, 1998: 313-319.

Brigagliano, J.A.,Co-Acting Director, Division of Trading and Markets,U.S. Securities and Exchange Commission, interview by The Senate Banking Subcommittee on Securities Insurance and Investment. *Testimony Concerning Dark Pools, Flash Orders, High Frequency Trading, and Other Market Structure Issues* (October 28, 2009).

British Bankers Association. "BBA code for Financial Reporting Disclosure." *bba.* 2010. http://www.bba.org.uk/ (accessed 2012).

British Broadcasting Corporation. *BBC Full Financial Statements 2010/11.* Annual Report, Secretary of State for Culture, Olympics, Media and Sport, London: British Broadcasting Corporation, 2010.

Canedo, J.M.D, and S.M Jaramillo. "A Network of Systemic Risk: Stress Testing the Banking System." *Intelligent Systems in Accounting, Finance and Management* 16 (2009): 87-110.

Casey, K.L.,Commissioner,U.S. Securities and Exchange Commission, interview by The United States Senate Banking Subcommittee on Security and International Trade and Finance. *Testimony Concerning Continuing Oversight on International Cooperation to Modernize Financial Regulation* (July 20, 2010).

Casey, K.L.Commissioner, U.S. Securities and Exchange Commission, interview by The United States Senate Banking Subcommittee on Security and International Trade and Finance. *Testimony Concerning International Cooperation to Modernize Financial Regulation* (September 30, 2009).

Casey, K.L.Commissioner,U.S. Securities and Exchange Commission, interview by The United States Senate Banking Subcommittee on Security and International Trade and Finance. *Testimony Concerning Continuing Oversight on International Cooperation to Modernize Financial Regulation* (July 20, 2010).

Cassa di Risparmio della Repubblica di San Marino SpA v Barclays Bank Ltd. [2011] EWHC 484 (Comm). (Queen's Bench Division, Commercial Court, March 9, 2011).

Chapman, J. *System Failure - Why Government must learn to think differently.* London: Demos, 2004.

Council of Economic Advisors. *Economic Report of the President of United States of America.* Washington: United States Government Printing Office, 2010.

Cox, Christopher, interview by Housing and Urban Affairs U.S. Senate Committee on Banking. *Testimony Concerning Oversight of Nationally Recognized Statistical Rating Organizations* (April 22, 2008).

Crockett, Andrew. "Banking Supervision and Regulation: International Trends." *64th Banking Convention of the Mexican Bankers' Association.* Acapulco: Bank of International Settlements, 2001.

Crotty, James, and Epstein Gerald. "A Financial Precautionary Principle: New Rules for Financial Product Safety." *Wall Street Watch*, July 2009, Working Paper No 1 ed.

References

Damman, Thomas E. "Audit: A Built-in Conflict of Interest." *Corporate Board*, Jan/Feb 2003: 16.

Davenport, T.H. "Putting the Enterprise Into the Enterprise System." *Harvard Business Review*, 1998: 121-31.

DeAngelo, L. "Auditor Size and Audit Quality." *Journal of Accounting and Economics*, 1981: 183-199.

Dodd, C.,Berney,F.,. "Dodd-Frank Wall Street Reform and Consumer Protection Act." Washington.D.C: The Senate and House of Representatives of the United States of America in Congress, January 5, 2010.

Dubberly, P.,Associate Director, Division of Corporation Finance U.S. Securities and Exchange Commission, interview by Subcommittee on Capital Markets Insurance and Government Sponsored Enterprises of the United States House of Representatives Committee on Financial Services. *Testimony Concerning "Recent Innovations in Securtizations"* (September 24, 2009).

Elliott, R.K. *Promotion of International Capital Flow through Accounting Standards.* Oral Testimony, Washington.D.C: House Committe on Financial Services, 2001.

Epstein, G, and J Crotty. November 26, 2009. http://www.ideaswebsite.org/featart/jan2010/Gerald_Epstein.pdf (accessed February 28, 2012).

Faiola, Anthony. Februrary 10, 2010. http://www.washingtonpost.com/wp-dyn/content/story/2010/02/09/ST2010020904032.html?hpid=topnews.

Financial Ombudsman Services. *Annual Review of the customer complaints about Insurance, Credit, Banking, Savings, Investment.* Financial Ombudsman Service Ltd, May 2010.

Financial Stability Board. *Shadow Banking: Scoping the Issues.* A Background Note of the Financial Stability Board, Basel,Switzerland: Financial Stability Board, 2011.

Francis, J.R, and B Ke. "Disclosure of fees paid to auditors and the market valuation of earnings surprises." *Review of Accounting Studies* 11, no. 4 (2006): 495-523.

Gallagher, D.M., Co-Acting Director, Division of Trading and Markets, U.S. Securities and Exchange Commission, interview by Subcommittee on Capital Markets Insurance and Government-Sponsored Enterprises of the United States House of Representatives Committee on Financial Services. *Testimony Concerning "Reforming Credit Rating Agencies"* (September 30, 2009).

Ghosh, Aloke, Sanjay Kallapur, and Doocheol Moon. "Audit and non-audit fees and capital market perceptions of auditor independence." *Journal of Accounting and Public Policy* 28 (2009): 369-385.

Glass, C.,Steagall,H.B. "The Banking Act of 1933." Washington.D.C.: The Senate and House of Representatives of the United States of America in Congress, June 16, 1933.

Gramm, Phil. "Deregulation and the Financial Panic - Loose money and politicized mortgages are the real villains." *http://online.wsj.com.* February 20, 2009. http://online.wsj.com/article/SB123509667125829243.html (accessed September 21, 2011).

Group of Ten. "Report on Consolidation in the Financial Sector." 2001.

Herz, Robert.H. "Accounting Standards and Bank Regulation." (International Journal of Disclosure and Governance) 7 (2010): 97-107.

References

Hu, H.T.C, Director of the Division of Risk, Strategy, and Financial Innovation, U.S. Securities and Exchange Commission, interview by The House Committee on Financial Services. *Testimony Concerning the Over-the-Counter Derivatives Markets Act of 2009* (October 7, 2009).

Huang, X, H Zhou, and H Zhu. "A framework for assessing the systemic risk of major financial institutions." *Journal of Banking & Finance* 33 (2009): 2036-2049.

Huigang Liang, Nilesh Saraf, Qing Hu, Yajiong Xue. "Assimilation of Enterprise Systems: The Effect of Institutional Pressures and the Mediating Role of Top Management." (MIS Quarterly) Vol 31, no. 1 (2007).

IMF. *Global Financial Stability Report.* Washington, D.C: International Monetary Fund, 2005.

IMF, Global Financial Stability Report - Oct. *Sovereign, Funding and Systemic Liquidity.* Washington D.C: International Monetary Fund, 2010.

IMF, Global Financial Stability Report. *Containing Systemic Risks and Restoring Financial Soundness.* Washington.D.C.: Internation Monetary Fund, April, 2008.

IMF, Global Financial Stability Report. *Financial Market Turbulence - Causes, Consequences, and Policies.* Washington.D.C: International Monetary Fund, October, 2007.

IMF, Global Financial Stability Report. *Financial Stress and Deleveraging - Macrofinancial Implications and Policy.* Washington D.C.: International Monetary Fund, October, 2008.

IMF, Global Financial Stability Report. *Global Financial Stability Report.* Washington D.C: International Monetary Fund, 2005.

THE GLOBAL FINANCIAL CRISIS IS <u>NOT</u> FINANCIAL

IMF, Global Financial Stability Report. *Market Developments and Issues.* Washington.D.C.: International Monetary Fund, April,2007.

IMF, Global Financial Stability Report. *Meeting New Challenges to Stability and Building a Safer System.* Washington.D.C.: International Monetary Fund, April,2010.

IMF, Global Financial Stability Report. *Navigating the Financial Challenges Ahead.* Washington.D.C.: International Monetary Fund, October,2009.

IMF, Global Financial Stability Report. *Responding to the Financial Crisis and Measuring Systemic Risks.* Washington.D.C.: International Monetary Fund, April,2009.

International Swaps and Derivatives Association. *ISDA Market Survey.* Survey, International Swaps and Derivatives Association, Inc., 2010.

Johnson., Norman. "Speech by SEC Commissioner:Current Regulatory and Enforcement Developments Affecting the Accounting Profession." *U.S. Securities & Exchange Commission* . January 20, 1999. http://sec.gov/news/speech/speecharchive/1999/spch248.htm.

Jones, B.D. "Bounded Rationality." *Annual Review of Political Science*, 1999: 297–321.

Khuzami, R., Director, Division of Enforcement, U.S. Securities and Exchange Commission, interview by The United States Senate Committee on the Judiciary. *Testimony Concerning Mortgage Fraud, Securities Fraud,and the Financial Meltdown: Prosecuting Those Responsible* (December 9, 2009).

Khuzami, R.,Director, Division of Enforcement,U.S. Securities and Exchange Commission, interview by The House Oversight and Government Reform Committee and Domestic Policy

References

Subcommittee. *Testimony Concerning Events Surrounding Bank of America's Acquisition of Merrill Lynch* (December 11, 2009).

King, Sir Mervyn. "Bank of England." *Bank of England, Quarterly Inflation Report Q&A.* August 8th, 2012.

Krishnan, J, H Sami, and Y Zhang. "Does the provision of nonaudit services affect investor perceptions of auditor independence?" *Auditing: A Journal of Practice and Theory* 24, no. 2 (2005): 111-135.

Kroeker, J.L., Chief Accountant,U.S. Securities and Exchange Commission, interview by The Subcommittee on Capital Markets Insurance and Government Sponsored Enterprises of the House Committee on Financial Services. *Testimony Concerning Accounting and Auditing Standards: Pending Proposals and Emerging Issues* (May 21, 2010).

Kumar, Manish. "Nonlinear Prediction of the S& P 500 and the HSI under a Dynamic Increasing Sample." *Asian Academy of Management Journal of Accounting and Finance* , 2009: 101-118.

Kurzwei, R. *Singularity is Near.* Viking Press, 2005.

Levitt., Arthur. "Speech by SEC Chairman:Quality Information:The Lifeblood of Our Markets." *U.S. Securities & Exchange Commission.* October 18, 1999. http://sec.gov/news/speech/speecharchive/1999/spch304.htm.

Levitt.A. "SEC Speech: Quality Information: The Lifeblood of Our Markets." *http://sec.gov.* 1999. http://sec.gov/news/speech/speecharchive/1999/spch304.htm.

Lindberg, Deborah L, and Deborah L Seifert. "A New Paradigm of Reporting on the Horizon." *Journal of Insurance*

Regulation (National Association of Insurance Commissioners), 2010: 230-252.

Minsky, Hyman P. "The Financial Instability Hypothesis." In *Handbook of Radical Political Economy.* The Jerome Levy Economics Institute of Bard College, 1992.

Na'im, Ainun. "Special Purpose Vehicle Institutions: Their Business Nature and Accounting Implications." *Gadjah Mada International Journal of Business* 8, no. 1 (April 2006): 1-19.

Nijsken, Rob, and Wolf Wagner. "Credit risk transfer activities and systemic risk: How banks became less risky individually but posed greater risks to the financial system at the same time." *Journal of Banking & Finance*, 2010.

Ohlson, J A. "A Framework for Financial Reporting Standards: Issues and a suggested Model." *Accounting Horizons* 24, no. 3 (2010): 471-485.

Pelaez, C.M.,Pelaez,A.P. *Regulation of Banks and Finance .* Palgrave Macmillan, 2009.

Pullen,S; Coles,I. "Key Differences Between the U.S. Bankruptcy Code and the U.K. Insolvency Act 1986." *Mayer Brown*, August 2003.

Sailing Directions - Nova Scotia and Bay of Fundy Pilot. 6th. London: Admiralty - Hydrographic Office, 1911.

Sanio, Jochen. "Managing the crisis: Introductory Remarks." *Munich Economic Summit.* Munich, 2010.

SAP. *SAP Annual Report 2008.* SAP, 2008.

Schapiro, M.L.,Chairman, U.S. Securities and Exchange Commission, interview by The Financial Crisis Inquiry Commission. *Testimony Concerning the State of the Financial Crisis* (January 14, 2010).

References

Schapiro, M.L.,Chairman, U.S. Securities and Exchange Commission, interview by Subcommittee on Capital Markets Insurance and Government-Sponsored Entreprise, The United States House of Representatives Committee on Financial Services. *Testimony: Oversight of the U.S. Securities and Exchange Commission: Evaluating Present Reforms and Future Challenges* (20 July 2010).

Schapiro, M.L.,Chairman,U.S. Securities and Exchange Commission, interview by The House Financial Services Committee. *Testimony Concerning the Lehman Brothers Examiner's Report* (April 20, 2010).

Schwakopf, T.S. "Gramm-Leach-Bliley Act: A New Frontier in Financial Services." *Federal Reserve Bank of San Francisco.* 1999. http://www.frbsf.org/publications/banking/gramm/grammpg1.html.

Securities and Exchange Commission, Plaintiff, Vs Goldman Sachs & Co and Fabrice Tourre, Defendants. 10 CV 3229 (United States District Court, Southern District of New York, April 16, 2010).

Select Committee on Economic Affairs. *Auditors: Market concentration and their role .* 2nd Report of Session 2010–11, Authority of the House of Lords, 2011.

Senate of the United States. *Restoring American Financial Stability Act of 2010.* Washington.D.C: Senate Committee on Banking, 2010.

Shelby, Richard C. *Credit Rating Agency Reform Act of 2006.* US Senate Bill to accompany S.3850, Washington.D.C.: Committee on Banking, Housing, and Urban Affairs, 2006.

Standard & Poor's,. "Understanding Standard & Poor's Rating Definitions." *Global Credit Portal: Ratings Direct.* New York, US: Standard & Poor's Financial Services LLC, June 3, 2009.

Strassmann, Paul A. "Information Economics Metrics." *IEEE Lecture*. George Mason University,: IEEE, 2007.

Summer, M.,. "Banking Regulation and Systematic Risk." *Open Economies Reviews*, 2003: 43-70.

Tett, G. *Repo needs a backstop to avoid future crises.* September 23, 2010. http://www.ft.com/cms/s/0/692d4184-c72d-11df-aeb1-00144feab49a.html.

The Economist. "Measuring the measurers." May 31, 2007.

Tucker, J. "Financial Crisis: A Culture of Complacency." *Journal of Organisational Transformation and Social Change* 7, no. 1 (2010).

Turner, L.E. "Speech by Chief Accountant: Opportunities for Improving Quality." *U.S. Securities & Exchange Commission.* December 15, 2000. http://www.sec.gov/news/speech/spch451.htm.

United States Courts. *Bankruptcy Statistics.* 2011. http://www.uscourts.gov/Statistics/BankruptcyStatistics.aspx (accessed September 21, 2011).

Walter, E.B.,Commissioner,U.S. Securities and Exchange Commission, interview by The Committee on Agriculture United States House of Representatives. *Testimony Concerning the Discussion Draft of The Financial Stability Improvement Act of 2009* (November 17, 2009).

Walter, Stefan. "Basel III and Financial Stability." *5th Biennial Conference on Risk Management and Supervision.* Basel, Switzerland: Financial Stability Institute, Bank for International Settlements, 2010.

Whalen, Charles J. "Stabilizing the Unstable Economy: More on the Minsky-Simons Connection." *Journal of Economic Issues*, 1991: 742-745.

References

Wolfson, Martin H. *Financial Crises: Understanding the postwar US experience.* M.E.Sharpe, Inc., 1994.

Wray, L. Randall. "Minsky Crisis." *Levy Economics Institute of Bard College.* Annandale-on-Hudson, NY, 2011.

Written Testimony, The United States Securities and Exchange Commission, interview by The United States Senate Committee on Banking Housing and Urban Affairs. *Testimony Concerning SEC Oversight of Credit Rating Agencies* (August 5, 2009).

www.ingramcontent.com/pod-product-compliance
Lightning Source LLC
Chambersburg PA
CBHW061503180526
45171CB00001B/26